DIVERSITY ACROSS THE ARABIAN PENINSULA

Diversity across the Arabian Peninsula

Language, Culture, Nature

Edited by Fabio Gasparini, Kamala Russell and
Janet C. E. Watson

https://www.openbookpublishers.com

©2024 Fabio Gasparini, Kamala Russell and Janet C. E. Watson. Copyright of individual chapters are maintained by the chapter author(s).

This work is licensed under an Attribution-NonCommercial 4.0 International (CC BY-NC 4.0). This license allows you to share, copy, distribute, and transmit the text; to adapt the text for non-commercial purposes of the text providing attribution is made to the authors (but not in any way that suggests that they endorse you or your use of the work). Attribution should include the following information:

Fabio Gasparini, Kamala Russell and Janet C. E. Watson, *Diversity across the Arabian Peninsula: Language, Culture, Nature*. Cambridge, UK: Open Book Publishers, 2024, https://doi.org/10.11647/OBP.0411

Further details about CC BY-NC licenses are available at http://creativecommons.org/licenses/by-nc/4.0/

All external links were active at the time of publication unless otherwise stated and have been archived via the Internet Archive Wayback Machine at https://archive.org/web

Any digital material and resources associated with this volume will be available at https://doi.org/10.11647/OBP.0411#resources

Semitic Languages and Cultures 28

ISSN (print): 2632-6906
ISSN (digital): 2632-6914

ISBN Paperback: 978-1-80511-337-9
ISBN Hardback: 978-1-80511-338-6
ISBN Digital (PDF): 978-1-80511-339-3

DOI: 10.11647/OBP.0411

Cover image: Photo by Rabah Al Shammary, titled 'Wild Acacia tree, Ha'il, Arabian Peninsula', July 26, 2021; https://unsplash.com/photos/green-tree-on-brown-sand-under-blue-sky-during-daytime-e-UPgjjEwCM?utm_content=creditCopyText&utm_medium=referral&utm_source=unsplash.
Cover design: Jeevanjot Kaur Nagpal

The main fonts used in this volume are Charis SIL and Scheherazade New.

CONTENTS

Contributors.. vii

Preface... xv

Mark Shockley
    The Dhaid Oasis: Onomastic Investigations in
    Northern Emirati Villages 1

Emily Jane O'Dell
    An Ecolinguistic Approach to Kumzari:
    Ecocultural Assemblages of Language and
    Landscape in Kumzar 27

Janet C. E. Watson, Andrea Boom, Amer al-Kathiri, and Miranda J. Morris
    Three Shehret Texts: Building with Flora.............. 107

Stuart Davis, Wafi Alshammari, Musa Alahmari, and Mamdouh Alhuwaykim
    Aspects of the Phonology and Morphology of
    Saudi Varieties of Arabic... 137

Abdullah Alfaifi
    Distal and Proximal Relative Pronouns in
    Central Faifi Arabic 173

Anton Kungl
    Verbal Noun Formation in Mehri 197

Hongwei Zhang
    Technological Support for Endangered/Minority Languages: Creating Cross-Platform Keyboard Layouts for Modern South Arabian Languages......241

CONTRIBUTORS

Editors

Fabio Gasparini, Freie Universität Berlin

https://orcid.org/0000-0002-9196-8695

Fabio Gasparini received his PhD in African, Asian, and Mediterranean Studies from the University of Naples "L'Orientale." He currently holds a postdoc position at the Free University of Berlin. Together with Miranda J. Morris, he is author of the first descriptive grammar of Bəṭaḥrēt. His research focuses on the Modern South Arabian languages and Semitic in general from a comparative and typological perspective and on the relationship between language, identity and landscape.

Email: fabio.gasparini@fu-berlin.de

Kamala Russell, University of Chicago

https://orcid.org/0000-0002-0907-1580

Kamala Russell is an Assistant Professor of Anthropology at the University of Chicago. She received her PhD in Anthropology from the University of California, Berkeley, in 2021. Her research investigates the relationships between everyday interaction, space and infrastructure, and Islamic ethics through fieldwork projects with speakers of Shehret Modern South Arabian.

Email: kamala@uchicago.edu

Janet C. E. Watson, Sultan Qaboos University, Muscat, and University of St Andrews

https://orcid.org/0000-0002-2922-2964

Janet Watson studied at the University of Exeter and at SOAS, London. She has worked at the Universities of Edinburgh, Durham, and Salford and has held visiting posts at the Universities of Heidelberg (2003–2004) and Oslo (2004–2005). She took up the Leadership Chair for Language at Leeds at the University of Leeds in 2013, and was elected Fellow of the British Academy in 2013. Since 2019, she has directed the Centre for Endangered Languages, Cultures and Ecosystems (CELCE). She is currently an Honorary Professor at the University of St Andrews and a Visiting Professor at Sultan Qaboos University. Her current research areas are on Modern South Arabian and the language–nature relationship.

Email: jcew@st-andrews.ac.uk

Authors

Mark Shockley, Leiden University

Mark Shockley is a doctoral candidate in Descriptive Linguistics at Leiden University Centre for Linguistics. His dissertation focuses on describing and comparing Arabic varieties from the Oman-Emirates border northward into the transnational Ruʾūs al-Jibāl region. He is a recent recipient of the Doctoral Research Grant from the Sheikh Saud bin Saqr Al Qasimi Foundation for Policy Research in Ras Al Khaimah, UAE, in support of his work documenting Emirati Arabic varieties. He also has forthcoming

journal articles in the *Journal of Semitic Studies* and the *Bulletin of the School of Oriental and African Studies*.
Email: markdshockley@gmail.com

Emily Jane O'Dell, Parami University

Dr Emily Jane O'Dell is a Professor at Parami University (Bard College) in Myanmar. In America, she has taught at Columbia, Brown, and Harvard Universities, where she received a teaching award in the Department of Near Eastern Languages and Civilizations. She has also served as the Whittlesey Chair of History and Archaeology at the American University of Beirut, held professorships in Oman and China, and been a Research Fellow in Islamic Law at Yale Law School. She is the author of *The Gift of Rumi: Experiencing the Wisdom of the Sufi Master* (St. Martin's Press), and her research can be found in *Iranian Studies*, the *Journal of Global Slavery*, *Arab Studies Journal*, the *International Journal of Persian Literature*, the *Journal of Literary and Cultural Disability Studies*, the *Journal of Africana Religions*, *Disability & Society*, and Harvard Law School's *SHARIASource*.
Email: emilyjodell27@gmail.com

Andrea Boom, University of Leeds

https://orcid.org/0000-0002-5007-3035

Andrea Boom is a Commonwealth Scholar and PhD candidate at the University of Leeds studying the link between endangered languages, cultures, and ecosystems in southern Arabia. She works mostly with the Mahra tribe of Oman, Yemen, and Saudi Arabia, exploring language and traditions to build resilience in

the languages, cultures, and ecosystems. This research is particularly important today as people become disconnected from their immediate dependence on the natural world and knowledge of the symbiotic relationship between humans and their environment is disappearing.
Email: andrea.j.boom@gmail.com

Amir Azad Adli Al-Kathiri, University of Technology and Applied Sciences, Salalah

https://orcid.org/0009-0004-4071-2077

Amir Azad Adli Al-Kathiri holds an MA in the phonetics of Shehret and a PhD in Omani Arabic dialects from Sultan Qaboos University, Muscat. His research interests lie in the Shehret and Mehri languages of southern Arabia and in Omani Arabic dialects. He is currently Assistant Professor of Arabic at the University of Technology and Applied Sciences in Salalah, having worked as Assistant Professor at the Department of Arabic Language, Dhofar University. He has published a book on the phonetics of Shehret, contributed to *A Comparative Glossary of Modern South Arabian*, and published academic articles on the verb in Shehret, the snake-bite treatment tradition of *raʿbūt* in Dhofar, and on the Kathiri dialect of Arabic.
Email: amir.alkathiri@utas.edu.om

Miranda J. Morris, independent researcher

https://orcid.org/0009-0002-8231-9957

Miranda J. Morris is an independent researcher who has published widely on the languages and cultures of the MSAL-speaking communities of southern Arabia. Her most recent publica-

tions include *The Oral Art of Soqotra: A Collection of Island Voices* (2021), three volumes in Soqoṭri, Arabic, and English, with Ṭānuf Sālim Di-Kišin, and *Ethnographic Texts in the Baṭḥari Language of Oman* (2024); with Fabio Gasparini, she is author of the first descriptive grammar of Bəṭaḥrēt, currently in preparation.
Email: miranda@mirandamorris.com

Stuart Davis, Indiana University

Stuart Davis is a Professor of Linguistics at Indiana University. He earned his PhD at the University of Arizona. His research and teaching interests include phonological theory, morphology, and sociolinguistics, with a major focus on English and Arabic. He has published numerous articles on these topics in a wide variety of journals and edited volumes.
Email: davis@indiana.edu

Wafi Alshammari, University of Ha'il

https://orcid.org/0000-0002-6849-7995

Wafi Alshammari is an Associate Professor of Linguistics in the Department of English, University of Ha'il, Saudi Arabia. He earned his PhD in Linguistics from Indiana University-Bloomington, USA. His research interests include sociolinguistics, Arabic dialectology, Arabic-based pidgins and creoles, and Arabic morphology.
Email: wf.alshammari@uoh.edu.sa

Musa Alahmari, King Khalid University

Musa Alahmari is an Associate Professor of Linguistics in the Department of English, Faculty of Languages and Translation, King

Khalid University, Saudi Arabia. He earned his PhD in Linguistics from Indiana University-Bloomington, USA. His research interests lie primarily in the fields of phonology, phonetics, and morphology. He lectures and offers graduate and undergraduate courses in general linguistics, sociolinguistics, language acquisition, morphology, phonetics, and phonology.
Email: alahmari@kku.edu.sa

Mamdouh Alhuwaykim, Jouf University

Mamdouh Alhuwaykim is an Assistant Professor of Linguistics in the Department of English, College of Arts, Jouf University, Saudi Arabia. He has earned his PhD degree in Linguistics from Indiana University-Bloomington, USA. His research interests lie primarily in the fields of phonology, phonetics, and morphology. He teaches graduate and undergraduate courses in general linguistics, language acquisition, language variation, phonetics, and phonology.
Email: m.alhuwaykim@ju.edu.sa

Abdullah Alfaifi, University of Bisha

Dr Abdullah Alfaifi is an Assistant Professor at the University of Bisha, Saudi Arabia. His primary areas of research are Arabic dialectology and dialect documentation. Within these fields, he is particularly interested in the phonological characteristics present in Arabic dialects. Furthermore, he has an interest in investigating Arabic sounds from an articulatory perspective, utilising speech imaging technology.
Email: ahalfifi@ub.edu.sa

Anton Kungl, Nantes Université

Anton Kungl is an associate member of LLING - UMR6310 (Nantes Université), after having completed a thesis in 2023 on the nominal morphophonology of the Modern South Arabian Languages, particularly Mehri.

Email: anton.kungl@univ-nantes.fr

Hongwei Zhang, Shanghai International Studies University

https://orcid.org/0000-0002-6371-0398

Hongwei Zhang (PhD, The University of Chicago, 2021) is an Assistant Researcher of Historical Linguistics and Semitic Languages at the Institute for the Global History of Civilizations at Shanghai International Studies University. He works on the Semitic languages, with attention to related Afroasiatic languages and unrelated contact languages, mainly from the perspectives of historical and contact linguistics. He is also interested in writing systems and keyboard designs.

Email: hongwei.zhang.aa@shisu.edu.cn

PREFACE

Southern Arabia is a site of considerable linguistic, ecological, and cultural diversity. Yet, it remains relatively understudied as a region in comparison to other areas of the Arabian Peninsula and the wider MENA region—this notwithstanding the endangered status of its cultures and environment. Furthermore, research in the Humanities is generally characterised by a lack of collaboration between peers, especially across narrowly defined disciplines. This sense of isolation was aggravated by the COVID pandemic. To reverse this trend, a growing community of researchers, professionals, native speakers, and students interested in this particular area have engaged in new and multi-lateral forms of collective discussion and collaboration. This volume is the result of our first efforts in this direction.

The papers in this volume grew out of the 'Language and Nature in South Arabia Workshop' that was held virtually from 2020–2021. Despite its dreadful implications for the lives of many, the COVID-19 pandemic opened up new possibilities for the scholarly community that cut across institutions, geographical locations, and career stages. Prof. Janet Watson (University of Leeds) saw an opportunity, as virtual seminars became routine, to use this format to host talks and discussions that would bring together a wide variety of people interested in Southern Arabia. Starting on 23 March 2020, the day the UK went into lockdown, Prof. Watson initiated this workshop, whose sessions highlighted wide-ranging themes around the environmental, linguistic, and social ecologies of historical and contemporary

Southern Arabia. Since then, the workshop has met more than thirty times, at first weekly, later bi-weekly, and then monthly, as life slowly went back to normal. Prof. Watson was joined by co-organisers Dr Fabio Gasparini and Dr Kamala Russell. The 'Language and Nature in South Arabia Workshop' became a sustainable and regular forum open to all interested in the diverse and at-times precarious linguistic, cultural, and natural resources of Southern Arabia. Although meetings had subsided as of Spring 2021, this workshop succeeded in attracting a multi-lateral audience to research about and from South Arabia. This success is proven through the numerous connections, collaborations, and individual interests that have grown out of the talks and discussions it hosted. The papers in this volume are but a small sample of the wide variety of topics and formats for presentations that this workshop promoted.

The workshop was organised following two fundamental principles, which guaranteed its success. First, we as organisers wanted to provide a platform for sharing ideas and fostering feedback across institutions, communities, and professional backgrounds. Second, we aimed to host multilingual presentations and post-presentation discussions, so as to make the workshop as inclusive as possible. These commitments allowed the workshop to attract and remain accessible to scholars based in different countries and even on different continents as well as to those outside academic research circles.

1.0. Community Engagement

Across empirical fields, there is growing recognition of the importance of conducting research, particularly field research, in ways that include, rather than objectify, research participants. This entails not that researchers seek community permission to carry out their projects, but that research should be a substantively collaborative process, in which the consultants have agency and are encouraged to cooperate with the researcher in order to better define the object of study and shape the research approach itself. This requires rethinking on not only how research questions come about, but also traditional approaches to the dissemination of scholarship in academic and public settings, based on the model of the individual scholar as the exclusive author of their research. Also in need of reassessment are standards observed by academic conferences, workshops, and publications concerning language(s), barriers to admission, and authorship, which are additional factors that result in the exclusion of consultants.

In this vein, the 'Language and Nature in South Arabia Workshop' series aimed to create a space for sharing research in both traditional and non-traditional forms. What this means is that many different presentation formats were allowed, from traditional to informal approaches, and we combined different types of talks and topics within the same online event: for example, we would jump from a classic research presentation in English by a professor in the UK, to a presentation in Arabic by a student from Saudi Arabia, then move to another presentation about frankincense by a farmer connecting remotely from the middle of the plantation in Oman where he cultivates it, followed by a collaborative bilingual presentation from a UK-based graduate student and a native MSAL speaker about terms and practices for female beautification. Our participants joined via Zoom from across continents and time-zones—from Oman, to the UK, to California, to Australia. Trying to make the best out of the pandemic conditions, they joined from home offices, bedrooms, and even from their cars.

As a measure of success, the workshop has fostered and enabled continuing partnerships and interests. By bringing together scholars across fields, this workshop was a platform for exposing historical linguists to the concerns of documentary linguists, of botanists to anthropological methods, and of development workers to the aims of community members. This workshop made several new collaborations possible. Two participants who are native speakers of MSAL have joined with participants from academic institutions to apply for a starter grant to produce a children's book in each of their endangered languages. A children's book in Mehri had already been conceived, shared in the workshop, and since published. Many presentations we hosted were jointly presented.

Quite a bit of this diversity in topic and collaborative form did not make it into the present volume. First and foremost, we found ourselves unable to produce a multilingual volume, which excluded several of our core participants who write in Arabic or in a MSAL (for which an official orthography has not yet been proposed). We also struggled to solicit and include contributions from those outside traditional academic institutions, since they were less used to this kind of medium. Despite such limitations, this volume still represents a diversity of topics, methods, scholars, and institutions. The papers here proposed engage with data from under-researched languages, including the MSAL, Kumzari, and Faifi, about which very little has been published in either Arabic or English. For all these reasons, we believe that this volume is a small but important contribution towards a shift in the way research is performed in the area.

2.0. Why Language, Culture and Nature

Many of the languages and varieties of Southern Arabia are spoken by populations who have undergone huge changes in lifestyle and livelihood quite rapidly at the same time as the region is experiencing climate change. This affects both everyday activities and ways in which languages are used in relation to culture and nature. We believe that languages should be studied by taking into account the social and ecological settings in which they are spoken, with attention paid to the changing social and environmental conditions that affect the everyday speakers' everyday lives. In line with the workshop from which this volume emerged, we complement traditional papers focused on purely linguistic investigations on the languages spoken in Southern Arabia with other works assessing the interconnectedness of the ecological and botanical worlds with language use, change, and structure, and the impact of modernisation and cultural change on traditional knowledge systems.

3.0. Contributions of Individual Papers

Mark Shockley's chapter explores place names of non-Arabic origin in the Eastern Arabian Peninsula (Qatar, UAE, Bahrain) as evidence for historical South Arabian substrate influence. Building on prior work indicating that the Persian, Akkadian, and Aramaic sources for place names reflect historical multilingualism and ecologies of language varieties unexpected from contemporary points of view, Shockley argues that there is a considerable presence in this region of place names and place name elements of ancient South Arabian origin. Here, onomastics serves as a gateway to historical dialectological speculation about past multilingual ecologies.

Emily Jane O'Dell's chapter analyses Kumzari identity as an ecosystem of affiliations that are linguistic, cultural, tribal, and sectarian in nature, and that reflect the biodiversity of the Musandam Peninsula and the Strait of Hormuz. O'Dell presents a panoply of ecological terminology in Kumzari while detailing the threats that both climate change and language loss/shift pose to the rich taxonomical and ecological knowledge embedded in Kumzari speech practices, lexicon, and lifeways.

Janet C. E. Watson, Andrea Boom, Amer al-Kathiri, and **Miranda J. Morris**'s chapter presents the transcriptions and translations of three Śḥerēt audio texts that deal with the use of indigenous flora for the building of houses for people and pens for livestock. Due to the recent process of sedentarisation that accompanied the unification of Oman, MSAL community members have become alienated from once-intimate knowledge of local ecology and of the techniques that their ancestors had developed to adapt to their inhabited landscape. Their work investigates how anthropological and linguistic documentation practices can assist in the maintenance of culture.

Stuart Davis, Wafi Alshammari, Musa Alahmari, and **Mamdouh Alhuwaykim** analyse some unusual and poorly known features of the phonology and morphology of various Saudi varieties of Arabic, widely relying on the intuition of their consultants, and evaluate whether they are archaic features or reflect internal innovation. The features they describe include the augmentative, allomorphy of the 2nd person masculine singular possessive pronoun, and the relationship between degemination and word-final vowel shortening.

Abdullah Al-Faifi's chapter provides novel data about Faifi, an understudied Arabic variety spoken in Southwestern Saudi Arabia that was possibly influenced historically by Ancient South Arabian. Eliciting data from native speakers and drawing parallels with Modern Standard Arabic and other spoken Arabic varieties, Al-Faifi focuses on relative pronouns in Central Faifi Arabic, demonstrating that they possibly denote proximality and distality when an adverb of place is found in the clause.

Anton Kungl provides a thorough linguistic examination of the morphophonology of Mehri verbal nouns, an understudied and still unsatisfactorily described category in MSAL. Kungl seeks to bring order to the sometimes unreliable available documentation, while adding further important contributions on the basis of his own fieldwork data gathered with speakers of the Eastern variety of Mehri. His work also allows for further analysis of the many intricate phonological processes that the language features.

Hongwei Zhang's chapter considers the contribution of digital media to the 'ecological' footprint of a language. Though no official writing system has emerged (from governmental, community, or research channels) for the MSAL or other minority languages of Oman, their speakers currently engage in text-based communication. These improvised writing systems may work on a small scale, but it takes work like Zhang's to create standard orthographic input tools and keyboard layouts to make possible the development of fuller digital access for speakers of these languages.

4.0. Symbols and Abbreviations

The default transcription employed throughout this volume is based on the *Journal of Semitic Studies* transcription system, with additional symbols for the MSAL languages, which present a richer phonology than that usually encountered in Semitic languages. Whenever further abbreviations or other transcription systems are employed (as in Kungl's contribution), these are explained by the relevant author.

5.0. Acknowledgements

We are very grateful to Geoffrey Khan and his team for accepting the volume in the Cambridge Semitic Languages and Cultures series. We thank, in particular, Aaron Hornkohl and Alessandra Tosi for their careful copy-editing. We also thank Adam Gargani, for first suggesting Zoom as a platform for international workshops and all those—too many to cite one by one!—who participated in the workshops.

THE DHAID OASIS: ONOMASTIC INVESTIGATIONS IN NORTHERN EMIRATI VILLAGES

Mark Shockley

1.0. Introduction

The eastern Arabian peninsula had two primary sources of influence in antiquity: Mesopotamia and South Arabia (Holes 2016, 12; Rohmer et al. 2018, 300). This study presents evidence of linguistic contact with both regions from primary and secondary data from the northern United Arab Emirates and the adjoining areas of Oman. This chapter is also a first attempt at elucidating the origins of several unique proper names found in the northern UAE, using an onomastic database comprising more than ninethousand eastern Arabian proper names, including toponyms, family names, and personal names. While most Emirati names are transparently Arabic, a few names have their origins in Akkadian, Aramaic, and Persian. Other names resemble those of Ancient South Arabian onomastics, corroborating traditional accounts that link certain Emirati tribes with southwestern Arabia. In particular, this paper focuses on the name of the oasis town Dhaid (*il-ḏēd*), in Sharjah Emirate, and the Bani Kitab (*banī kitab*) tribe, for whom Dhaid is a historic centre.

1.1. Data Sources

While living in Qatar and the United Arab Emirates, the author compiled a lexical database with over 11,000 stems in Arabian dialects, from primary and secondary data (Shockley 2020). The author has digitised and coded 6,650 toponyms and 2,557 family names from J. G. Lorimer's (1908) *Gazetteer of the Persian Gulf* (Shockley 2024). Primary data also includes over five-hundred personal names used in the United Arab Emirates. The author is conducting linguistic fieldwork in the northern Emirates and is gathering lexical and onomastic data from public media and local Arabic-language cultural publications, as well as field interviews.

1.2. Linguistic Situation in Ancient Eastern Arabia

Evidence pertaining to the linguistic situation of eastern Arabia in antiquity is not easy to come by (Holes 2016, 10; Al-Jallad 2018, 10). Bilingual inscriptions in Aramaic and Hasaitic scripts have been found in Thāj (eastern Saudi Arabia) and Mleiḥa (Sharjah, UAE), some dating back to the third century BCE, showing that in some areas Aramaic co-existed with another poorly documented Arabian language (Rohmer et al. 2018; Multhoff and Stein 2018).[1] Mleiḥa was inhabited from the third century BCE to the third century CE.

---

[1] Though the Hasaitic script is closely related to monumental Ancient South Arabian script, the language recorded is currently classified as an Ancient North Arabian language. The paucity of data and some peculiarities in the inscriptions have led to several speculations; see Al-Jallad 2018, 30–33 for a helpful summary of the issues.

Recent Syriac studies on the communities of Beth Qaṭraye ('region of the Qataris', corresponding roughly to northeastern Arabia, including Qatar, Bahrain, and parts of the UAE) have enriched our knowledge considerably for the period from the fourth to ninth centuries CE. During this time period, the churches and monasteries of the Gulf region wrote, corresponded, and performed liturgy in Syriac. Persian and Arabic were also certainly in use during this period (Kozah et al. 2021, 9). In a helpful new book, Kozah et al. (2021) give lexical evidence that by the eighth century the spoken language of Beth Qaṭraye (called *Qaṭrāyīth* in Syriac sources) was substantially Arabic in its lexicon. Of fifty Qaṭrāyīth vocabulary words recorded in Syriac sources, forty are found in Arabic, six derive from Syriac, three from Pahlavi, and one from Aramaic.

Contemporary Aramaic borrowings are sufficiently numerous enough to say that it was probably the spoken language of several communities along the Gulf at the time of Arabisation, though scholars disagree somewhat. Stein (2018) argues that Aramaic in the first millennium BCE in the eastern Arabian Peninsula was not a language of wider communication, but was circumscribed to administrative use. Holes (2001) presents evidence from medieval Arabic geographies that ancient Bahrainis were "settled, Aramaic-speaking agriculturalists" (referred to as 'Nabataeans'; see Holes 2001, xxiv). In another study, the same author clarifies that ancient northeastern Arabians were "probably polyglot in language," noting the use of Persian in religious music in Beth Qaṭraye in the fifth century (Holes 2002, 270).

The semantic range of localised Aramaic loanwords does not justify Stein's contention as the ongoing situation (cf. Holes 2016, 14–15). Several Aramaic borrowings were observed in the northern Emirates (primary data) and in the wider Gulf region (secondary data), and there is a notable commonality with Jewish Babylonian Aramaic (JBA).[2]

(1) *ōgiyānūs* 'ocean' (Hasa, Aramco 1958, 270); cf. JBA *ūqiaʾnāws* 'ocean';

(2) *glūla* 'cannonball' (Khorfakkan, UAE); cf. Syriac *glōlā* 'globe, ball',[3] cf. MSA *qulla*;

(3) *čīša* 'small palm-tree' (Holes 2001, 81); cf. JBA *kyšʾ* 'a bunch of vegetables or reeds';

(4) *rāz (i/u)* 'to estimate the weight of s.th.' (Qafisheh 1997, 284); cf. JBA *ryz* 'a rare measure of volume';[4]

(5) *kārūk* 'cradle' (Qafisheh 1997, 484; Khorfakkan, UAE); cf. JBA *kārōk* 'bundle'.

Toponyms also provide evidence of contact with Persian, Aramaic, and Ancient South Arabian languages. Potts and Blau (1998, 33) note in Ptolemy's *Geography* the presence of Aramaic toponyms, none of them now in use. With modern data, Holes identifies several toponyms of Persian origin and others with

---

[2] The reference used for Jewish Babylonian Aramaic is Sokoloff (2002).

[3] Payne-Smith (1902, 70). This is probably also the origin of Persian *ġalūla* 'ball, pellet' (Steingass 1892, 986).

[4] Holes (2001) gives the origin as Persian *razn* 'balancing anything in the hand to try its weight' (Steingass 1892, 574). Morano (2019, 289) gives *rēze rēze* 'gradually, particularly' in northern Oman. Apparently, *rēze* was a measure and the verb was derived from this measure.

Persian elements (Holes 2002, 273; Holes 2016, 12, n. 29). He also identifies two village names that he considers Aramaic in origin (*dēr*, cf. Syriac *dēr* 'monastery'; *samāhīǧ*, cf. JBA *mašmāhīǧ* 'a bishopric').

In this review of northern Emirati toponyms and anthroponyms, there are few names with Aramaic or Persian origins. In ancient eastern Arabia, language contact was likely spotty.

1.3. South Arabian Origins in Tradition and Dialectology

The northern Emirates was for centuries on an ancient trade route that transferred goods between South Arabia and Mesopotamia (Sedov 1995; Stein 2017, 119–20; Rohmer et al. 2018, 300). Today, the northern UAE is the meeting point for several Arabic varieties: Gulf Arabic, Omani Arabic (sedentary and Bedouin varieties), and Šiḥḥi Arabic. The ruling families of Bahrain, Qatar, and the UAE are Gulf Arabic speakers with a relatively recent Najdi provenance. The Qāsimī family, which rules Sharjah and Ras al-Khaimah, claims to be descended from ʿAdnān, which would mean they have traditional associations with northern Arabia (Lorimer 1908, 1547).

Omani tradition recorded in the work *Kašf al-Ġumma* states that the Azd tribe emigrated from Sirāt in southwestern Arabia in the first or second century CE (Groom 1994). The Azd tribe is considered the earliest Arab tribe of Oman, with certain later groups coming from northern Arabia (Lorimer 1908, 1389). In past generations, the Šiḥḥi tribe and the Kumzari people were frequently regarded as being of ancient South Arabian

'Himyarite' origin (for references, see van der Wal Anonby 2014; 2015, 12–14).

Holes (2016, 18–32) and Wilmsen (2020) have studied dialectological commonalities within Arabic that specifically link Yemen with the northern Emirates and Bahrain. This study looks at modern names and their possible links with languages other than Arabic, including Aramaic, Persian, and the languages of Ancient South Arabian inscriptions.

1.4. The Dhaid Oasis

Dhaid (Omani Bedouin Arabic, *il-Ḏēd*) is an important oasis town in inland Sharjah emirate (Qafisheh 1997, 247). Heard-Bey writes that Dhaid is the most important village in the interior of the Emirates because of its strategic position and access to water (Heard-Bey 1996, 95). Dhaid is 20 km north of Mleiḥa, an important archaeological site already mentioned. The name *Ḏēd* (*ḏ-y-d*?) does not have any clear Arabic meaning, and fieldwork has not uncovered any folk etymologies.

The etymon *ḏyd* does appear in multiple Hasaitic and Qatabanic inscriptions, but the name has been the subject of dispute. In Beeston's (1962, 13) grammar of Ancient South Arabian, he takes note of a few names where *ḏ* is written where *z* is expected. One of these is *ḏyd*. Beeston here assumes that *ḏyd* is an unattested form and that the plain reading of the name is, therefore, highly unlikely.

Prioletta et al. (2019, 252–53) present an alabaster fragment with the name *ḏydʾl*. According to Prioletta, Hayajneh

(1998, 142–43, as cited by Prioletta) interprets the root *ḏyd* in relation to Arabic *ḏwd*, meaning 'protect'.

In analysing the two Hasaitic instances, Rohmer et al. (2018, 299) propose a "global re-reading" of the Hasaitic glyph that would otherwise be recognisable as *ḏ*. This was based on a lack of attestation: "No such root exists in Semitic and this name is not known in Arabic or any other Semitic language" (Rohmer et al. 2018, 299; cf. Al-Jallad 2018, 32). As has already been shown, this root *ḏyd* is attested in Arabic and Qatabanic, and is included in a Qatabanic onomasticon.

In one Qatabanic inscription, RES 3878, *ḏyd* and *zyd* appear together. Such a close collocation would imply free variation, which is not what is observed in other Qatabanic data. Because both Thāj and Dhaid are on the ancient trade route between South Arabia and Mesopotamia, it is possible, though unproven, that all these instances of the root *ḏ-y-d* relate to a common (South Arabian?) root. With four attestations of *ḏyd* in two Arabian scripts as well as a modern Emirati toponym, the burden of proof now rests on those who want to prove that all four ancient uses of *ḏyd* were in fact intended to be *zyd*.

1.5. Banī Kitab

Banī Kitab (Omani Bedouin Arabic, *Kitab*; singular *Kitbī*) are one of the most prominent and influential tribes in the northern Emirates and Oman. Banī Kitab are found today in an inland corridor stretching from Ras al-Khaimah in the northern UAE, south through al-Ain and Buraimi into the Dhahirah region of Oman (Lorimer 1908, 1559). Their name has several phonetic variants, partly depending on the dialect: Lorimer (1908, 1558) prefers the spellings Qitab and Qatab, probably as back-formations for two phonetic rules (*$q > k$, and short vowel raising in open syllables). In the northern Emirates, the pronunciation *Kitab*, singular *Kitbī*, is most typical; the spelling with *qāf* appears to be more frequent in Oman. Among Gulf Arabic speakers, the old pronunciation was *Banī Čitab*, singular *Ičtibī*.

Though their current area of influence extends through much of the Dhahirah region, local tradition in the northern Emirates states that the Bani Kitab are the remains of the Ancient South Arabian kingdom of Qataban. Ptolemy's *Geography* includes the name 'Cottabani' in southeastern Arabia, which may attest a transition between ancient, southwestern Qataban and modern, northeastern Bani Kitab. 'Cottabani' has long been thought to resemble *Qatabān*, the problem being that Qataban is in southwestern Arabia and the Cottabani were in southeastern Arabia (Sprenger 1874). For chronological reasons, Groom (1994, 206–7) suggests that the Cottabani in southeastern Arabia may have been refugees from Qataban. Hawley (1970, 61, 294) points out the possible connection between Ptolemy's Cottabani and the modern Bani Kitab.

The possibility of continuity from *Bani Kitab* to *Qatabān* is linguistically tenable. (1) The initial vowel is raised from *a* to *i* by a well-known regular sound change found in many Arabian dialects (blocked by the presence of the pharyngeal in *Ka'ab*) (Johnstone 1967, 27–28). (2) The sound alternation $q \sim k$ is found in certain sedentary dialects (Holes 2016, 31) and is attested in several names, such as *Maskat* ~ *Masqaṭ* 'Muscat, the capital of Oman'. (3) In certain Arabic names the suffix -*ān* may be used in one form and not another, i.e., *Qumzān* 'clan name' > *Qamzi* 'member of the *Qumzān* clan'; *Āl Bu Kalbī* 'tribal name' > *Kalbāni* 'member of the *Āl Bu Kalbī* tribe'; etc. The shift from *Qatabān* to *Bani Qatab* has a close parallel in the tribe known as either *Kaʿabān* or *Bani Kaʿab* (singular *Kaʿbī* or *Čaʿbī*), who also inhabit the area around Dhaid.

The sections that follow survey some interesting names of non-Arabic origin and their features.

2.0. Names of Non-Arabic Origin

2.1. Mesopotamian Influence

(i) The term *ṣīr* or *ṣayr* appears in several Emirati toponyms. In Lorimer (1908, 1825–26), *Ṣīr* is a cultivated tract of northern Ras al-Khaimah (south of Rams), with 2,500 inhabitants; but he writes that the name once referred to the entire area of Ras al-Khaimah. Though the origin is obscure, it seems to be related to Old Babylonian *ṣēru* 'hinterland, fields, plain, steppeland' (*CAD* 1962, XVI:138). ʿUbayd (2016, 46) records *iṣ-ṣayr* (?) as referring to a coastal hill in this area, apparently by association. *Ṣīr* is also found in the name of several islands, such as *Ṣīr Banī Yās* in Abu Dhabi emirate. The use of this word as a generic to refer to islands appears to be a semantic innovation.

(ii) Shees (*Šīṣ*) is a verdant, historic village, now a tourist area, equipped with a *falaǧ* irrigation system for cultivation of palm and fruit trees. The word *šīṣ* is recorded by Arabic lexicographers with the meaning 'inferior quality dates', and Holes (2016, 13) has already pointed out that this is most likely a borrowing from Aramaic *šīṣā*, ultimately from Akkadian *šuṣu* (same meaning).

(iii) The same Aramaic borrowing gives its name to a harbour in Musandam, *Šīṣih* (n.b., the vowel of the feminine singular suffix is raised unconditionally in Šiḥḥi Arabic, known as short *imāla*; see Bernabela 2011). These names probably came indirectly through the borrowed lexical item *šīṣ*.

(iv) Dubai (Gulf Arabic, *Dibay*) is today the most populous city in the UAE and one of the seven emirates. Its name has several proposed origins: (a) *Dibay* is possibly a diminutive of the name of the nearby town *Diba*. ʿUbayd even cites a proverb that says "From Diba came Dubai." This suggests it is a secondary or derived toponym (Shockley 2024). (b) The name *Dibay* may also be a diminutive of *diba*, meaning 'locust'. According to ʿUbayd (2016, 69), thirteenth-century geographer Yāqūt al-Ḥamawī notes the presence of locust there, but this is perhaps only a folk etymology. (c) Thirdly, *Dubayyī* also appears as a location on the Tigris (Lorimer 1908, 1893). For this reason, Sheikh Sultan bin Muhammad Al-Qasimi, Ruler of Sharjah, concludes that *Dibay*, along with several other important Emirati names, has its origin in Mesopotamia (Al-Qasimi 2014).

(v) Ras al-Khaimah (Gulf Arabic, *Rās il-Ḫēmah*; var., *Rās Ḫīmah* or *Rās Ḫīmih*) is a town as well as the name of the northernmost emirate in the UAE. There are various folk etymologies in Emirati culture, usually stating that the name means 'head of the tent'; *rās*, as used in place names, means 'cape' or 'headland'. Another possibility is Sheikh Sultan bin Muhammad Al-Qasimi's

(2014) proposal that this name is related to *al-Ḥaymah*, the name of a settlement near Baghdad (Lorimer 1908, 100).

(vi) Sharjah (Modern Standard Arabic, *al-Šāriqah*) is the third most populous city in the UAE and one of the seven emirates. Al-Qasimi (2014) also links *il-Šarǧih*—this is his pronunciation, and he specifies that the vowels are short—to a quarter (*ḥārah*) in Baghdad by that name, thus linking the names of three emirates to the Baghdad area. Indeed, Al-Qasimi himself claims north Arabian roots. The name of the quarter in Baghdad is today spelled Shorja; it is adjacent to the eastern gate of the city (*il-Bāb il-Šarqī*) which is likely the origin of the name, by affrication (*$q > g > ǧ$).

2.3. Persian Influence

(i) Limah (*Līmih*) is the name of a village with a harbour in Musandam, as well as an island opposite (Lorimer 1908, 1609). The words *lūmī* and *līm* are apparently doublets, both derived from Persian or Urdu *līmū*, all meaning 'lime' (Holes 2016, 122). The pattern *CīCū* is quite uncommon in Arabic and is resisted in borrowings: in *līm*, by elision of the final vowel, and in *lūmī*, by non-adjacent metathesis. Leem (*Līm*) is also the name of a park in Hatta.

(ii) Khor Fakkan (*Ḫōrfakkān* or *Ḫōrfukkān*) is a significant coastal town on the Gulf of Oman in the northern UAE. In both English and Arabic, the name is frequently spelled as one word. Though the typical English spelling is Khorfakkan or Khor Fakkan, ʿUbayd (2016, 38) records this word as *Ḫōrfukkān*. The vowel change *$a > u$ is possibly caused by the adjacent labial *f*, but this usually occurs in open syllables (Johnstone 1967, 28). The folk etymology given is that this name derives from Classical Arabic *Ḥawr Fakkān* 'the bay of two jaws', which, ʿUbayd points out, is not even the expected use of the oblique dual suffix (it would be *Fakkayn*, not *Fakkān*). Lorimer (1908, 516) notes a significant presence of "Arabicised Persians" there.

The endings *-akān* and *-akkān* appear in numerous toponyms in Bahrain and Persia, most of them coastal locations, e.g., *Karzakkān* 'hamlet in Bahrain', *Dastakān* 'the southwestern point of Qishm island, Iran', *Rās Rākān* 'northernmost point in Qatar', *Gīsakān* 'mountain near Bushehr', among others. This suffix is likely related to the Persian adjectival suffix *-gān*, but it is unclear why devoicing has occurred in all examples, unless *-akkān* is composed of the diminutive suffix *-ak*, with the adjectival suffix *-gān*, with voicing assimilation.

(iii) Zirku (*Zar-koh* in Steingass 1892, 615; *Zirko* in Lorimer 1908, 1945) is the name of an island belonging to Abu Dhabi; *koh* is a Persian word for 'mountain'. Lorimer (1908, 1652) lists two other islands in the Strait of Hormuz with the same suffix: *Šanaku* and *Fanaku*, called in Kumzari *Mūmar* and *Dīdāmar*, respectively.

2.4. South Arabian Influence

(i) *Banī Ḥaḍram* (singular *Ḥaḍarmi*) appears in Lorimer (1908, 887) as a section of the Banī Jābir tribe, historically the rivals of the Banī Kitab tribe. Today, members of the Banī Jābir are met frequently in the northern Emirates.

(ii) *Banī Ḥaḍram* is also the name of a separate tribe in Oman (Lorimer 1908, 1393). As recorded by Lorimer, both these tribes (Banī Ḥaḍram and Banī Jābir) are Ghafiri politically and Ibadhi Muslims.

(iii) *Ḥaẓrūm* and *Ḥuẓayrim* are male personal names found in inland Sharjah. Both names are diminutives from the root *ḥ-ḍ-r-m*, which transparently refers to Ḥaḍramawt. It is uncommon for Arabic personal names to be derived from toponyms, except for the names of a few places with religious significance (*Yaṯrib, Zamzam*). These names are possibly derived from the tribal name *Ḥaḍram*, which itself more likely came from the toponym *Ḥaḍramawt*.

(iv) *Maġāyil Ḥaẓrūm* is the name of a well in Abu Dhabi emirate (south of the study area), as recorded by Lorimer (1908, 1032). The well likely received its name by transonymisation from the personal name *Ḥaẓrūm*. Several wells and other manmade structures in the database are named after men; otherwise, personal names do not usually appear as toponyms in the Gulf region.

(v) *Maġāyil Balqahais* is the name of a well near *Maġāyil Ḥaẓrūm* (Lorimer 1908, 1032). The anthroponymic prefix *ba(l)-* is characteristic of South Arabia and is not found anywhere else in the data.

(vi) *Āl Bū Muhair* (singular, *Muhayrī*) is a numerous and widespread tribe in the Emirates, associated with the Banī Yās. Older sources disagree whether they are part of the Banī Yās; however, today, they are clearly adopted as part of the confederation. Lorimer (1908, 1121) records local tradition: "they are said to be of Mahra origin and to have come originally from Hadhramaut."

A South Arabian origin for this tribe is not implausible. Diminutivisation is extremely common during transonymisation in Arabian names (Shockley 2024), and so the form *Muhayr* may signify that this group separated from a group with a name from the root *m-h-r*.

2.5. Names of Likely Arabic Origin

(i) *Diba* (var. *Dibaʿ*) is the name of a historic town straddling the Musandam border.[5] The noun *diba* means 'locust' in certain Gulf dialects (Qafisheh 1997, 210; see Holes 2001, 169, for references), and Arabic toponyms frequently arise from names for fauna and, especially, flora. However, during fieldwork, Omani Arabic speakers (Bedouins) pronounced this name *Dibaʿ*.[6] It is not clear whether this was an innovation (*ʿanʿana*), as occasionally occurs in words with no emphatic or pharyngeal consonants. Alternatively, *Dibaʿ* may be the older pronunciation, and *Diba* the innovation; in Šiḥḥi Arabic, a word-final pharyngeal may be realised as a glottal stop or as compensatory lengthening on a vowel (Bernabela 2011, 95).

(ii) Qidfa (*Gidfaʿ*, var. *Ǧidfaʿ*) is a coastal settlement in Fujairah emirate. Lorimer (1908, 1697) records the variant *Ǧidfaʿ*.

---

[5] Miles (1919, 5) records that the name was given by the "Dibba, or Lizard tribe" of Najd. Not only does this involve poor transcription (conflating *diba* with *ḍabba* 'lizard'), but no other reference available to me mentions this tradition or this Najdi tribe.

[6] The name *dbʿ* is a lineage name in Sabaic (Avanzini et al. 2022).

The name may be from Arabic *quḏfah* 'summit' since it is an area with a dramatic hilltop; or it could be from the root *ǧ-d-f* with meanings related to rowing. In any case, the final pharyngeal is likely an innovation.

(iii) Al-Rams (*il-Rams*) is a village in northern Ras al-Khaimah emirate. (a) The plainest understanding of this word in Gulf Arabic would be that it refers to 'conversation', as a noun related to the characteristically Emirati word *rimas* 'speak' (cf. Omani *ramis* 'evening conversation', Morano 2019, 288). It is not clear why this word would be used as a toponym. In addition, the verbal noun for *rimas* locally is *ramsih*, not *rams*. (b) Since *rams* also means 'gravesite' in Classical Arabic, ʿUbayd (2016, 54–55) muses that the name may have referred to some monument now lost, or the area may have been known for its gravesites. However, this meaning has not been recorded in local dialects, and there is no clear evidence that it is or was known as a place of burial. (c) ʿUbayd also points out that *al-ramṣ* is recorded in classical sources, and states that Old Arabic *ṣ* has as its reflex *s* in certain Emirati dialects, but I have not encountered this sound change. (d) The name *rms¹* is attested as a lineage name in Sabaic (Avanzini et al. 2022), so the name may be a survival from an Arabian (non-Arabic) substrate.

2.6. Names of Obscure Origin

(i) Wadi Bayh or Bih (*Bayḥ* or *Bīh*) is a canyon between Ras al-Khaimah emirate (UAE) and Musandam (Oman), with a road that was in the past a significant border crossing. Bayh has several variant spellings and pronunciations. In Šiḥḥi Arabic, Old Arabic *ay is raised to *ī* in this position, and *ḥ* may be realised as [ħ], [h], or [ɦ] (see Bernabela 2011, 23, 35). This toponym closely resembles the name of Wādi Bayḥān, the centre of the kingdom of Qataban.

(ii) Shaʾam (Gulf Arabic, *Šaʿam*; Šiḥḥi Arabic, *Šaʾam*) is a historic fishing village in northern Ras al-Khaimah, on the Musandam border. The root s^2-ʿ-*m* is rare in Arabic. A type of fish is called *šiʿim* in Qatar, but typically settlements named after fauna include the inalienable possession marker *bū* (e.g., *Bū Ẓabī* 'having gazelles'). Onomastic entries based on the root s^2-ʿ-*m* are found in several ancient Arabian inscriptions and *Šaʿam* may be a survival from a non-Arabic substrate. In Safaitic, $s^{2ʿ}m$ appears as a personal name, and in Qatabanic, $s^{2ʿ}m(m)$ is attested as a toponym.

(iii) Shindagha (*Šindaġah*, var. *Šandaġah*) is the name of a neighbourhood of historic importance in Dubai. The name was also applied to a small area in Buraimi, Oman (Lorimer 1908, 264). The only possible cognate discovered is Shandaq (*Bayt Šandaq*), a village near Sanaʾa, Yemen (*ġ* ~ *q* in certain Arabian dialects; cf. Shockley 2020, 89).

(iv) *Taryam* is a male personal name recorded in Sharjah. It may bear some relation to the word *tirǧimān* 'interpreter', with the Gulf Arabic sound change *ǧ* > *y*, but *Tarǧam* is not attested as a personal name.

(v) *Al Dhait* (*il-Ẓayt* or *il-Ẓēt*) is an area in Ras al-Khaimah. The name has no obvious root or cognates. The -*t* ending here may be the feminine singular ending, which appears in Arabic only in the construct form, but is retained in Modern South

Arabian languages. The word ẓyt is also recorded in Sabaic, where it is translated 'pure' (Avanzini et al. 2022).

ʿUbayd (2016, 56) relates Ẓayt to medieval Ḍawt (a toponym recorded by Ibn Durayd), but Ibn Durayd is very vague, the vowel alternation ē/ay ~ ō/aw is quite rare (cf. for instance, zēbag ~ zōbag 'mercury', Qafisheh 1997, 300).

(vi) *Yibir* is the name of a mountain in Ras al-Khaimah emirate. This name may be from Arabic ǧabr 'power' or may be related to the Banī Jābir tribe. The sound change ǧ > y is probably not typical of this area of the UAE. *Ybr* is both a toponym and a tribe name in Sabaic.

(vii) Shakhbout (*Šaḫbūṭ*) is a male personal name found in the Emirati royal family. There is a Gulf Arabic verb with the same root, *šaḫbaṭ* 'to scribble'. Because uvulars cause emphasis spread in Gulf Arabic, *Šaḫbūṭ* may come from *šaḫbūt*. The suffix -ūt sometimes appears in Arabic loanwords from Syriac (i.e., *malakūt, ǧabarūt*); it is also possible that the suffix -ūt here is a vestige of a Modern South Arabian borrowing, since -ūt is a common feminine ending. In this study, I did not uncover compelling evidence of Modern South Arabian influence on Emirati toponyms, and this is an open question for future research.

3.0. Characteristic Morphology

3.1. Non-Arabic Morphology

Despite strong evidence of language contact, very little evidence of non-Arabic morphology appears in Emirati names. In the examples above, three unusual morphemes have been mentioned that appear in northern Emirati toponyms:

(1) The South Arabian prefix *Ba-* or *Bā-*, used in family names, attested only in the toponym *Maġāyil Balqahais;*
(2) The Aramaic suffix *-ūt*, possibly obscured by emphasis spread in the male personal name *Šaḫbūṭ;*
(3) The Persian suffix *-(ak)kān* (< **gān*?), found in coastal settlements throughout the Gulf region.

The first two are unique attestations in data from the Gulf region. The third is attested only three times in the Gulf region, including once in the northern Emirates. It is possible that it was productive in Gulf Arabic in some past period, but it is now only found in frozen forms. The suffix *-(ak)kān* is therefore better considered an idiosyncratic vestige of past Persian speakers, rather than a truly borrowed morpheme.

3.2. Diminutives

The morphology of Emirati personal names exhibits unique characteristics among Arabic varieties. Several Omani Bedouin Arabic personal names in the study area are found primarily or exclusively in the diminutive *CCēC* pattern:

(1) *Hwēšil* (M) < *hāšil* 'wanderer, vagrant'(?)
(2) *Ḫlēs* (M) < *ḥalis* 'brave'(?)
(3) *Hwēdin* (M) < *hādin* 'one who makes truces'

Of these, only the first is attested as a name in a non-diminutive form (*Hāšil*). The diminutive pattern *CCēC* may serve to identify an onymic here (cf. Shockley 2024). Interestingly, both *hayšalah* and *hawdanah* are recorded by Ibn Manẓūr as epithets of the camel. It is possible that both *Hwēšil* and *Hwēdin* have some connection to Bedouin life, since these names are found in a Bedouin area in inland Sharjah.

Other morphologically diminutive male personal names without any non-diminutive form include *Šaḫbūṭ* and *Ṭaḥnūn*, both names found in the Emirati royal family.

3.3. Form IX

A number of common female personal names are of the ninth form:

(1) *Mayṯa* (F) (< Arabic *Mayṯāʾ*, for which no origin or meaning is given; *myṯ* is attested as a name of unknown gender in Qatabanic, Avanzini et al. 2004)
(2) *Šamma* < Arabic *šammāʾ* 'most honourable'
(3) *Šayma* < Arabic *šaymāʾ* 'having a mole'

3.4. Reduplication

Saqamqam (*Saqamqam*, var. *Sakamkam*) is a wadi in Fujairah emirate. This morphological form, with reduplication of the second and third consonants, is uncommon in Arabic and Gulf Arabic, but is more productive in other Semitic languages, including Ethiopic languages. This is the only such occurrence in the entire dataset of east Arabian toponyms.

3.5. Quadriliteral Roots

Two male personal names appear to derive from quadriliteral roots beginning with *y-*, e.g., *Yaʿrūf* (< *uǧrūf 'carpenter ant'?), *Yaʿrūb* (probably from *Yaʿrub* 'name of a famed South Arabian king; also applied to an Omani tribe'). The same phenomenon is seen in three toponyms in inland Sharjah emirate: *Yaʿakal* 'an inland village' (Lorimer 1908, 1478); *Yaḥfar Muṣayfī* 'a single well', and *Yaḥfar il-Fāyiḥ* 'a single well' (Lorimer 1908, 1442–43; cf. *ǧaʿfar* 'creek'). *Yanqul* in northern Oman and *Yaṯrib* (= Medina) are two similar examples outside the study area.

4.0. Conclusion

The vast majority of place names, family names, and personal names along the eastern littoral of the Arabian Peninsula are of Arabic origin (cf. Kozah 2021), but there are certain areas that betray the presence of substrates (Aramaic, Persian, and perhaps others). Documentary and archaeological evidence corroborates the presence of Aramaic, Persian, and the poorly known Arabian language known by its Hasaitic script. Non-Arabic names are concentrated in areas with agriculture or influential ports, e.g., Khor Fakkan, Ras al-Khaimah, and Bahrain.

As Holes (2001; 2002) has pointed out, there are traces of Akkadian influence in Gulf Arabic. Loanwords may have been taken directly from Akkadian, or by way of Aramaic. A few Aramaic loanwords relate strongly to local sedentary culture (types of palms, weighing items for trade, ornamental cradles). Shared vocabulary with Jewish Babylonian Aramaic may strengthen a previous proposal that a southeastern variety of Aramaic was used as a vernacular in the Gulf (Contini 2003). Mesopotamian influence is noticeable in areas linked to palm cultivation and agriculture (*Šīṣ*, *Ṣīr*).

Though Persian loanwords are abundant in the Gulf Arabic lexicon, Persian forms in the onomasticon are rather uncommon, localised to the names of islands and coastal settlements. The toponymic suffix *-(ak)kān* may be derived from Persian *-gān*. It is not surprising that several islands under Emirati control retain Persian names.

This paper has explored some evidence of South Arabian names in the northern Emirates. As already noted, Arabic dialectology has established links between Yemen and sedentary Gulf societies (i.e., Bahrain and the northern Emirates; see Holes 2016; Wilmsen 2020). These dialects skirt the coast of the Arabian Peninsula, supporting the hypothesis of an ancient pattern of northward migration that had already been suggested by local traditions. This pattern may extend to both Arabic-speaking and non-Arabic-speaking South Arabian groups. Hasaitic inscriptions already attest to a poorly known Arabian language. The modern toponym Dhaid (*il-Ḏēd*) has no Arabic cognates, but the root *ḏyd* is attested in Hasaitic (East Arabian) and Qatabanic (South Arabian) inscriptions. Local names from the root *ḥ-ḍ-r-m* are found repeatedly in the inland Emirates. A few Emirati toponyms and anthroponyms, though lacking compelling Arabic etymologiea, correspond well to Sabaic and Qatabanic names (*Šaʿam, il-Ẓēt, Yibir*). This may be evidence of an Arabian substrate, related to both Ancient North Arabian and Ancient South Arabian languages, and which naturally shared numerous onomastic features with these languages.

Data is sorely lacking on Šiḥḥi Arabic, and there are still many toponyms of unclear origin in northern Ras al-Khaimah and Musandam. The confluence of three dialects obscures root identification through an abundance of segmental processes (*ğ > g, ǧ, y; *q > g, ǧ, y; etc.). There is much more work to be done, but I hope that this paper has advanced our understanding of the linguistic situation of ancient Arabia through the names of its modern people and places.

References

Al-Jallad, Ahmad. 2018. 'What is Ancient North Arabian?' In *Reengaging Comparative Semitic and Arabic Studies*, 1–44. Edited by Daniel Birnstiel and Na'ama Pat-El. Wiesbaden: Harrassowitz.

Al-Qasimi, Sheikh Sultan bin Muhammad. 2014. 'Under the Banner of Occupation, Part 2'. Sharjah Radio interview. [Arabic]

Arabian American Oil Company (ARAMCO). 1958. *English-Arabic Word List*. Monterey, CA: Defence Language Institute.

Avanzini, Alessandra, Alessia Prioletta, and Irene Rossi. 2022. *Corpus of South Arabian Inscriptions*. Pisa: University of Pisa.

Beeston, Alfred F. L. 1962. *A Descriptive Grammar of Epigraphic South Arabian*. London: Luzac.

Bernabela, Roy S. 2011. 'A Phonology and Morphology Sketch of the Šiḥḥi Arabic dialect of əlǦēdih (Oman)'. MA thesis, Leiden University.

Contini, Riccardo. 2003. 'La lingua del Bēt Qaṭrāyē'. In *Mélanges David Cohen*, edited by Jérôme Lentin and Antoine Lonnet, 173–81. Paris: Maisonneuve & Larose.

Groom, Nigel. 1994. 'Oman and the Emirates in Ptolemy's Map'. *Arabian Archaeology and Epigraphy* 5: 198–214.

Hawley, Donald. 1970. *The Trucial States*. Wilby: Michael Russell.

Heard-Bey, Frauke. 1996. *From Trucial States to United Arab Emirates*. New edition. London: Longman.

Holes, Clive. 2001. *Dialect, Culture, and Society in Eastern Arabia. Volume One: Glossary*. Leiden: Brill.

———. 2002. 'Non-Arabic Semitic Elements in the Arabic Dialects of Eastern Arabia'. In *Sprich doch mit Deinen Knechten Aramäisch, Wir Verstehen Es!: 60 Beiträge zur Semitistik—Festschrift für Otto Jastrow zum 60. Geburtstag*, edited by Werner Arnold and Hartmut Bobzin, 269–80. Wiesbaden: Harassowitz.

———. 2016. *Dialect, Culture, and Society in Eastern Arabia. Volume Three: Phonology, Morphology, Syntax, Style*. Leiden: Brill.

Johnstone, Thomas M. 1967. *Eastern Arabian Dialect Studies*. London: Oxford University Press.

Kozah, Mario, George Kiraz, Abdulrahim AbuHusayn, Saif AlMurikhi, and Haya Al Thani. 2021. *Beth Qaṭraye: A Lexical and Toponymical Survey*. Piscataway: Gorgias Press.

Lorimer, John G. 1908. *Gazetteer of the Persian Gulf, 'Omān and Central Arabia*. Calcutta: Superintendent Government Printing.

Miles, Samuel B. 1919. *The Countries and Tribes of the Persian Gulf*. London: Harrison & Sons.

Morano, Roberta. 2019. 'The Arabic Dialect Spoken in the alʿAwābī District, Northern Oman'. PhD dissertation, University of Leeds.

Potts, Daniel T., and Soren Blau. 1998. 'Identities in the East Arabian Region'. *Mediterranean Archaeology* 11: 27–38.

Prioletta, Alessia, Kerry Hull, and Lincoln H. Blumell. 2019. 'The Ancient South Arabian collection at Tokai University (Japan) and a Miscellaneous Item'. *Semitica et Classica* 12: 245–58.

Qafisheh, Hamdi. 1997. *NTC's Gulf Arabic-English Dictionary*. Chicago: NTC/Contemporary.

Rohmer, Jérôme, Ahmad Al-Jallad, Mahmud al-Hajiri, Rozan Alkhatib Alkontar, Tara Beuzen-Waller, Paul Calou, Damien Gazagne, and Kosmas Pavlopoulos. 2018. 'The Thāj Archaeological Project: Results of the First Field Season'. *Proceedings of the Seminar for Arabian Studies* 48: 287–302.

Sedov, Alexander V. 1995. 'Two South Arabian Coins from Mleiha'. *Arabian Archaeology and Epigraphy* 6: 61–64.

Shockley, Mark. 2020. 'The Vowels of Urban Qatari Arabic'. MA thesis, University of North Dakota.

———. 2024. 'Diminutive Names in Peninsular Arabic'. *Bulletin of the School of Oriental and African Studies*. Preprint, viewed 18 March 2024.

Sokoloff, Michael. 2002. *A Dictionary of Jewish Babylonian Aramaic of the Talmudic and Geonic Periods*. Baltimore: JHU Press.

Sprenger, Aloys. 1874. *Die alte Geographie Arabiens als Grundlage der Entwicklungsgeschichte des Semitismus*. Bern: Huber.

Stein, Peter. 2017. 'South Arabian Zabūr script in the Gulf: Some Recent Discoveries from Mleiha (Sharjah, UAE)'. *Arabian Archaeology and Epigraphy* 28/1: 110–24.

———. 2018. 'The Role of Aramaic on the Arabian Peninsula in the Second Half of the First Millennium B.C.' *Proceedings of the Seminar for Arabian Studies* 48: 39–53.

Steingass, Francis Joseph. 1892. A Comprehensive Persian-English dictionary, including the Arabic words and phrases to be met with in Persian literature. London: Routledge & K. Paul.

ʿUbayd, Aḥmad Muḥammad. 2005. The Historical Origins of Place Names in the United Arab Emirates. Sharjah: Sharjah Institute for Heritage. [Arabic]

van der Wal Anonby, Christina. 2014. 'Traces of Arabian in Kumzari'. *Supplement to the Proceedings of the Seminar for Arabian Studies* 44: 137–46.

———. 2015. 'A Grammar of Kumzari: A Mixed Perso-Arabian Language of Oman'. PhD dissertation, Leiden University.

Wilmsen, David. 2020. 'Emirati Dialects' Singular Features: The 'Sharjah Museums Authority Recordings' as a Data Source'. Invited conference talk at Sorbonne University, Abu Dhabi – CEFAS Diwan, 10 December 2020.

AN ECOLINGUISTIC APPROACH TO KUMZARI: ECOCULTURAL ASSEMBLAGES OF LANGUAGE AND LANDSCAPE IN KUMZAR[*]

Emily Jane O'Dell

1.0. Introduction

Due to the symbiotic relationship between the indigenous language of Kumzar and the marine ecology of Kumzar's natural environment, Kumzari language, identity, and culture are deeply ecocentric in nature. The diversity of environmental terminology in Kumzari reflects the biodiversity of the Musandam Peninsula and the Strait of Hormuz, along with the cultural adaptation of Kumzari speakers to the region's ecosystems. Daily life in the fishing village of Kumzar is intimately connected to the sea, as illustrated through the numerous Kumzari words and phrases related to fishing, ethnozoological knowledge, tides, and coastal watching. The marine ecosystem and aqua-culture of Kumzar are embedded in the Kumzari language and the sea-related stories of

---

[*] Special thanks to Ahlam Al-Kumzari for her helpful insights into Kumzari language and culture and to Cathy Birdsong Dutchak and Jacques Van Dinteren for permission to reproduce their photographs of Kumzar.

several Kumzari oral traditions. The endangerment of Kumzari threatens not just the language's longevity, but also the traditional bio-ecological awareness and ecological labour knowledge related to sardine fishing, goat husbandry, and palm harvesting contained and expressed within it. Centring the ecological dimensions and assemblages of Kumzari identity, language, and labour is essential for considering how a sustainable future for the people of Kumzar and the endangered Kumzari language itself might be imagined and cultivated.

Kumzari is spoken primarily in the fishing village of Kumzar, located on the tip of the Musandam Peninsula on the Strait of Hormuz in the far north of the Sultanate of Oman. It is also spoken in nearby cities in Oman, like Dibba (*Dāba*) and Khasab (*Xāṣab*), a few coastal cities of the United Arab Emirates, and Larak Island (*Rārik*) in the Islamic Republic of Iran. Speakers of the language on Larak Island call their language variety *Rārikī*. Thus, there are two main groups of Kumzari speakers on both sides of the Strait of Hormuz—the Kumzari inhabiting the Musandam Peninsula and the Laraki, who reside primarily on Larak Island in Iran. This chapter focuses on the larger group of speakers, the Kumzari of Musandam, who until relatively recently lived a very traditional lifestyle, as Kumzar did not get electricity (*kahraba*) until 1980.

Situated in an isolated cove between the mountains and the sea, villagers in Kumzar have traditionally been almost completely dependent on nature, which explains Kumzari's unique ecological lexicon. For instance, several Kumzari words related to the landscape of Kumzar have no equivalent word in English.

These landscape-specific terms capture the unique features of the aqua-ecosystem of Kumzar and exhibit the attentional field and directional orientation of Kumzari in relation to the sea. For instance, the word *pišt* means 'shallows far from land'. Likewise, the Kumzari verb *baraḥa* 'appear under water' has no English equivalent, and its existence is clearly connected to the aqua-oriented lifestyle of Kumzar. Terms like *barḥ* 'appearance under water' and *ma'daf* 'seamount' illustrate the orientation and awareness of Kumzari speakers towards what is beneath the surface of the water, as the underwater landscape and the species who inhabit it are essential components of the daily labour and livelihood of Kumzari fishermen.

Kumzari is an endangered language due to its small population of speakers, unwritten status, and ubiquitous use of Arabic in the education system and other sectors of daily life in Kumzar. Over the past several years, a growing number of Kumzari families have begun speaking Arabic instead of Kumzari to their children in the home, due to the "internationalization of outsiders' negative attitudes toward the Kumzari language" (Anonby 2011, 39). Thus, "[t]hrough the official educational apparatus, mainly, with its vast social and symbolic impact," the official language of Arabic "enjoys dissemination at the optimal age of language acquisition in the case of children" alongside a "discourse that denigrates and stigmatizes" Kumzari, which is presented as a language "without any fixed and written standard but purely as oral, dialectal and secondary"—and thus vulnerable to disuse (Bastardas-Boada 2017, 8). As a result of these factors, UNESCO has classified Kumzari as severely endangered. Today, Kumzari is spoken by only around four-thousand speakers, around 1,500 of them residing primarily in Kumzar, with summer migration to nearby Khasab.

With only a few thousand speakers of Kumzari, the language is teetering on the brink of extinction, though there are increasing efforts among academics and speakers to preserve the language. Languages in general around the world are currently in crisis, as "intergenerational transmission of half the world's languages is collapsing" (Roche 2022). This "Gramscian crisis of linguistic justice" (Roche 2022) and language oppression worldwide, ignited by the forces of nationalism, colonialism, racism, and capitalism, has prompted linguists to start considering "positive interventions in the global system towards a future of greater linguistic justice" (Roche 2022). Within academia, Kumzari had been almost completely ignored in scholarship until recently (Anonby 2008; 2010; 2011; Al-Jahdhami 2013; al Kumzari 2009; van der Wal Anonby 2015). As a result, a written Kumzari alphabet (Anonby 2010), grammar (van der Wal Anonby 2015), and dictionary (Anonby and van der Wal Anonby 2011) have been produced.[1] Thus, Kumzari has not yet fully undergone a standardisation process.

Kumzari has thrived for centuries as an orally transmitted language, but the powerful forces of modernisation, globalisa-

---

[1] This chapter uses the Kumzari writing system as developed by Anonby (2010) and vocabulary from van der Wal Anonby's grammar (2015) and dictionary (Anonby and van der Wal Anonby, 2011), in addition to findings from the author's own field-research in Kumzar (2017) and from Kumzari informants from Kumzar.

tion, and nationalism have brought new threats to its survival through the hegemony of Arabic and changes to the coastal environment and species inhabiting it. Modernisation processes have "wrought important ecosystemic changes that frequently have an impact at the level of language" (Bastardas-Boada 2017, 7). Kumzari's status as an 'unwritten' language does not necessarily doom it to extinction (as it has thrived until the present day in oral form only), but the rapid pace of modernisation poses a distinct new threat.

As local languages continue to be replaced by hegemonic languages, like English, under the powerful and accelerating forces of globalisation, it is not just language that is being lost, but also the sustainable local cultures and traditional ecological knowledge embedded in endangered languages. In Abram's (1996) book, *The Spell of the Sensuous: Perception and Language in a More-than-Human World*, he argues that nature, or the environment at-large 'the more than human world', shapes language in oral cultures, thereby empowering its speakers to become more attuned to their environment and live sustainably within it. Accordingly, living in 'literate' cultures divorces people from nature and related ecological awareness. Due to the dependence of Kumzari villagers on their environment for survival, the hegemony of Arabic and English threaten not just the language of Kumzari, but also the indigenous environmental knowledge embedded within it and the community's collective awareness of local nature.

Kumzari identity itself is an ecosystem of affiliations that are linguistic, cultural, tribal, and sectarian in nature. The

Kumzari of Musandam are divided into three clans (*jēluman*): the Aql, Ǧušban, and Bōʿin. While Kumzari in Musandam identify ethnically with their language community, they also view themselves as a sub-group of the Šiḥuḥ (Thomas 1929, 75), the dominant Arab population of the Musandam Peninsula (al-Kumzari 2006), and they consider themselves members of the Šatair (*štērī*) confederation. The Kumzari of Musandam and Laraki are Sunni Muslims, which distinguishes them from the dominant sects of Islam in their countries, as Oman is predominantly Ibadi and Iran Shiʾa.

2.0. *Khoren* as Refuge and Weapon: Ecosystems of Maritime Violence, Imperialism, and Slavery

Today, the isolated village of Kumzar can be reached by only sailing from Khasab on a *dhow* (*lanj*) for around two hours, or by taking a one-hour motorboat ride. Located on the tip of the peninsula *(xarṭum)* of Musandam, Kumzar is in geographic proximity to *Jēẓurtō* (Goat Island), *Quṣm* (Qeshm Island), *Rārik* (Larak Island), *Gumrō* (Bandar Abbas), *Qdōrō* (Qadr), *Qēdē* (Qada), *Pxa* (Bukha), and *Msandam* (Musandam Island). While the town is often described today as 'isolated' in western discourse, in the past Kumzar served as a important geographic location between the trading centres of Zanzibar, Muscat, Basra, Persia, and India, because of the ubiquity of sea travel in the days before road and air travel. In fact, Kumzar played an essential role in providing fresh water for passing ships, as did Khark Island in the northern Persian Gulf.

Kumzar's geographic location in the Strait of Hormuz has been entangled in ecosystems of maritime violence, slavery, and imperialism over the past few centuries. There is a long and complex history of 'pirates' in Musandam along the 'Pirate Coast', stretching from modern-day Oman to the Qatar Peninsula. Edward Balfour (1885, 225) mentions in his writing that the Persian Gulf coast from "Kasab [Oman] to the island of Bahrain" bore "the designation of the Pirate Coast"—a designation employed from the seventeenth to the nineteenth century. The coastal landscape of Musandam has long been a contested space of sovereignty, commercialism, and imperialism.

The Musandam Peninsula's most recognisable natural feature is its 'fjords', which are used today in advertising campaigns to market the region for tourist consumption. In Kumzari, the word for the peninsula's cliffs jutting from the water is *khor* (PL *khoren*). In the past, the *khoren* of the Musandam Peninsula served as convenient spaces of refuge for those conducting raids on passing vessels. The inhabitants of the 'Pirate Coast' had the advantage of being familiar with the geomorphological features of the *khoren*, along with the region's wind patterns, currents, and coves, in conducting raids against large British vessels, which were not as familiar with the topography and inlets of the region. British and Indian merchant ships were plundered for goods, while Arab merchant ships and *ḥajj* vessels were attacked for merchandise and slaves.

Long before the British sought to dominate trade in the Persian Gulf, maritime violence was used by coastal sheikhs and communities to further local expansionist political projects and assert sea power over trade routes and coastal waters. In the wake of the expulsion of the Portuguese from Oman, Omani naval fleets began to dominate trade in the Persian Gulf in the eighteenth century. As Balfour (1885, 224) explains: "In recent times, the Muscat Arabs, during the period of their ascendency, from 1694 to 1736, were highly predatory; but it was not until 1787 that the Bombay records made mention of the systematic continuance of piracy." Muscat eventually became the prime portal through which naval traffic flowed into the Persian Gulf. By the end of the eighteenth century, it is "estimated that about five eighths, ad valorem, of the whole trade for the Persian Gulf passed through Muscat" (Fukuda 1992). According to Biddulph (1907, 73), "[t]here were no more determined pirates than the Arabs of Muscat". Thus, 'piracy' in the Persian Gulf was enacted by not only local inhabitants of the 'Pirate Coast', but Muscat Arabs, too.

Despite the ubiquity of maritime violence in the Persian Gulf and the Gulf of Oman, there were geographical, physical, and cultural distinctions drawn between those enacting such violence from the 'Pirate Coast' and those from other locales like Muscat. As Balfour (1885, 225) notes:

> The inhabitants of the Pirate Coast consider themselves to be far superior to either the Bedouin or town Arab. The latter, especially those from Oman, they hold in such contempt, that a Muscatti and an arrant coward are by them held to be nearly synonymous. They are taller, fairer, and in general more muscular than either of the above classes, until they attain the age of 30 or 40 years, when they acquire a similar patriarchal appearance.

These Arab 'pirates' and coastal imaginaries found their way into British literature as well. For instance, the book *Captain Antifer* by Jules Verne (1895, 122) mentions "pirates, who are rather plentiful in the Straits of Ormuz." Even the characteristic eyepatch of a 'pirate' was inspired by the Qāsimī 'pirate' Raḥmah bin Jābir al-Jalhamī (Aboelezz 2022). In nineteenth-century British-centric narratives, both bureaucratic and literary, Muslim Arab 'pirates' of the 'Pirate Coast' were inherently violent and wicked, and thus British guidance, laws, and dictates were branded as necessary to 'keep the peace', enforce morality, and secure the trading routes for vessels of the East India Company, which held a monopoly over trade in the Indian Ocean.

The British branded 'pirates' from the Al Qasimi tribal confederation, based on the western coast of the Musandam Peninsula, as the main perpetrators of maritime violence in the Persian Gulf. The designation of the Qawāsim as 'pirates' followed the refusal of the British to pay tolls that the Qawāsim imposed on all trade in the Strait of Hormuz (Allday 2014). Thus, in the late eighteenth and early nineteenth centuries, British officials attached to the Bombay Government (and its naval arm, the Bombay Marine) who oversaw imperial interests in the Persian Gulf referred to the Qawāsim (SG Qāsim) as "Joasmee" pirates (Davies 1997). Accordingly, British authorities, newspapers, and writers framed the Qawāsim as inherently violent, menacing, dishonest, and immoral. For example, in *Sketches of Persia, From the Journals of a Traveller in the East* (1828), John Malcolm, a British customs official who served in the Persian Gulf from the eighteenth century to the nineteenth century, recounts an Arab servant of his saying about the Qawāsim: "their occupation is piracy, and their delight murder; and to make it worse, they give you the most pious reasons for every villainy they commit" (Malcolm 1828, 27). The landscape of their main port-city of Ras al Khaimah, with its shallow inlet where pirates harboured their fleets, empowered the Qawāsim to launch swift and successful attacks on British vessels of the East India Company, which, in turn, further fuelled the British demonisation of the Qawāsim and inhabitants of the 'Pirate Coast' in general.

The British authorities framed maritime violence along the 'Pirate Coast' as an immoral act resulting from an inherent character flaw in the Arab coastal inhabitants and their rulers. The fierce moral condemnation by the British of the Qawāsim 'pirates' aimed to legitimise British imperialism, delegitimise rulers on the 'Pirate Coast', and condemn Qawāsim-organised attacks on the vessels of the East India Company. It also empowered the British to undermine the political sovereignty of the Qawāsim (Suzuki 2018) and herald themselves as the 'civilised' and 'moral' protector of these prime trade routes. The British designated themselves the guarantors of security in the Persian Gulf, and, as they had done in India, established a protection racket to insulate the region and expand their influence.

Until relatively recently, western scholarship has recycled the British designation of 'pirate' to describe the maritime violence along the 'Pirate Coast'. Over the years, however, scholars and even the ruler of Sharjah, Dr Sheikh Sultan bin Muhammed al Qasimi (Al-Qasimi 2017), have challenged this imperial designation and narrative. In his book, *The Myth of Arab Piracy in the*

Gulf, al-Qasimi argues that the British strategically and unfairly labelled the Al Qawāsim tribe 'pirates' to eliminate Arab trade with India, enable the East India Company to dominate the waterways without interference or competition, and justify violent attacks against the coastal inhabitants at a time when the British Empire was claiming extra-national sovereignty over international waters and trade. Recently, more scholars have critiqued British-centric narratives to consider whether these 'pirates' were instead collectively challenging British imperialism and European commercial interests, exercising autonomy and authority in their own independent lives (Hightower fc.), or, as James Onley (2009) has suggested, merely following the orders of their rulers. Whatever their intentions, so-called 'pirates' around Musandam were not just a local threat to British merchant shipping and trade, but a global threat to the imperial, capitalist economic world order emerging at the time.

To control Persian Gulf trade, the British militarised the coveted waterway. As Edward Balfour (1885, 224) explains: "The British continue to guard against piracy in the Persian Gulf up to the present day, and armed ships of the Indian and British navies, all through the close of the 18th and in all the 19th century, have been employed there in protecting commerce." British infiltration and militarisation of the Persian Gulf was directed more from British India than London (Crouzet 2019), as the British sought to establish a buffer zone in the Persian Gulf around India to protect their trade routes and guard against French penetration.

Musandam's landscape, with its shallow inlets and rocky shoreline, aided the coastal inhabitants in their resistance to British imperial penetration of their commercial waterways and trade routes. Nature was, in effect, their best weapon. Until the British survey of the Persian Gulf began in 1820 off Ras Musandam in Oman, the *khoren* and inlets of the Musandam Peninsula had not been effectively mapped by Europeans, which gave the coastal inhabitants an advantage in using the local landscape and seascapes to their own advantage for hiding and launching raids. Europe's navigational knowledge of the Persian Gulf at the time, including of the Musandam Peninsula and Strait of Hormuz, was very limited, as European maps showed only one basic route[2] with a single line of soundings and no additional details about the coastal topography (Peszko 2014). The coastal topographical information captured in the survey of the 1820s, conducted by Bombay Marine officers, bolstered British political, economic, and commercial interference in the region, as it supplied them with more knowledge on the shorelines, especially uncharted shoals, harbours, and wind and current patterns, in addition to the tribal, cultural, and religious identifications and expressions of the coastal inhabitants on both sides of the Persian Gulf. Foucault once asked of geographers: "What are the relations between knowledge (*savoir*), war and power? What does it mean to call spatial knowledge a science? What do geographers understand by power?" (Crampton 2007, 33). The British employed the

---

[2] See 'Nautical Chart of the Persian Gulf [2r] (1/2)', British Library: Map Collections, IOR/X/414/220, in Qatar Digital Library, https://www.qdl.qa/archive/81055/vdc_100023733662.0x000004.

discipline of geography and the practice of cartography in the service of empire and acquisition of sea power in the Persian Gulf, robbing the coastal inhabitants of their advantage in using the landscape to hide and mount attacks.

Though maritime violence was also waged by European imperial powers in the Persian Gulf and Indian Ocean, this violence was not considered by the British to be 'piracy'. In the sixteenth and seventeenth centuries, the Portuguese waged "piratical" raids for goods and slaves in the Persian Gulf (Pearson 1981, 32). Later, eighteenth-century British privateering (Starkey 1990; 1994) and the economic nationalism of mercantilism in the Atlantic 'New World' gave rise and shape to European piracy in the Indian Ocean (McDonald 2022) and Persian Gulf. After all, the British Empire had been enriched by privateering ventures in the Caribbean. From British custom officials collecting tolls in the 'New World' to East India Company vessel operators attacking communities on the 'Pirate Coast' in raids and the Anglo-Qasimi wars, British enterprises engaged in the same 'piratical' actions for which they vilified inhabitants of the 'Pirate Coast'. The interconnectedness of the Indo-Atlantic world through the prism of 'piracy' is only now beginning to be explored in scholarship on European imperialism.

Pearling ships along the 'Pirate Coast' also participated in maritime violence in the Persian Gulf. Balfour (1885, 225) explains:

> The Beniya tribe inhabit the most northerly district of Oman, called Sir (Seer). The tribe has three branches– Beniya, Manasir, and Owaimir.... [T]he coast dwellers fish in small boats, and dive for pearls. Their pearl fishery is

accounted to produce 10,000 tomans yearly. They seize the small boats that approach their coasts.

Balfour was referring to the Bani Yas tribal confederation of Abu Dhabi in Trucial Oman, composed mostly of the Rumaithāt, Rawashid and Al bu Falasah sections. The reference to Sir (صير) is to Bani Yas Island in today's UAE (جزيرة صير بني ياس). As Edward C. Ross (political resident at the time) noted, pearl diving was "carried on almost entirely by domestic slaves" (Hopper 2015, 143)—a history that has been almost completely neglected in scholarship (Willis 2016). Because enslaved "Africans were essential to the massive Gulf pearling industry" (Hopper 2015, 80), including in Trucial Oman, maritime violence around the Musandam Peninsula included slavery (O'Dell 2020), which was not abolished in Oman until 1970.

Though Kumzari villagers did not have pearling boats in Kumzar, some did participate in the industry. Lorimer (1908, 1040) explains: "The Kumzaris have no pearl-boats of their own, but a few of them go to the banks[3] on Sharjah and Dibai vessels," and during the seasonal migration to "Khasab and Dibah [Dibba]," the women would "go to the date harvest there or elsewhere, the men to the date harvest or pearl fishery, and the 3 or 4 individuals who remain take charge of the flocks of the absentees." It is likely that on the pearling vessels from Sharjah and

---

[3] For a map of the pearl banks around Kumzar, Musandam, and elsewhere in the Persian Gulf, see Shaykh Maniʾ ibn al-Shaykh Rashid Al-Maktum, 'A Map of Pearl Banks in Persian Gulf' [13r] (1/2), British Library: India Office Records and Private Papers, IOR/R/15/1/616, f 13, in Qatar Digital Library. https://www.qdl.qa/archive/81055/vdc_100023403859.0x000019.

Dubai, as well as in Khasab, Kumzari villagers would have encountered enslaved African pearl divers.

Enslaved pearl divers on the Pirate Coast knew how to stealthily navigate through Musandam's waterscapes and some even stealthily climbed onto British ships in hopes of being freed. After a pearl diver named Joah, who had been enslaved in Dubai, climbed aboard the British cruiser *May Frere* in 1873, Major Grant, the resident ranking officer onboard, granted him asylum. This triggered a diplomatic maelstrom back in the United Kingdom, where authorities argued that such actions would bankrupt Arab slave owners, sow distrust, and damage British interests in the Persian Gulf. In the words of Edward C. Ross, if asylum were to be granted to fugitive slaves from the pearling industry: "We should no longer be looked on as the friendly protectors of the maritime Arabs" (Hopper 2015, 143). Further, a commander would be incentivised to steal pearling boats "on account of the head money he would be entitled to for them" (Hopper 2015, 143). As a result, the Admiralty Office issued 'Circular No. 33' (31 July 1875) to order all those aboard Her Majesty's ships and vessels to deny refuge to fugitive slaves. The British government's resistance to abolition in the Persian Gulf in the interest of preserving British economic interests demonstrates that 'abolition' was merely a tool for imperial ends when it suited the crown, not a moral imperative or unwavering policy commitment.

The nineteenth-century landscape of Musandam and the Persian Gulf was captured through warfare and lawfare waged by the British to assert British supremacy over the waterway. After fifty Qawāsim ships raided the coast of Sindh in a series of attacks in 1808, the British Royal Navy ransacked the 'Pirate Coast' in 1809–1810, laying waste to the Qawāsim capital of Ras Al Khaimah, other coastal and island communities (including Qeshm Island, which reverted to the Imam of Muscat), and hundreds of ships. A second, even larger campaign waged by the British (led by Major-General Sir William Grant Keir, with a combined force of the East India Company's Bombay Marine [Indian Navy], British Royal Navy, and Omani Navy under Sayyed Saʿid, the Sultan of Muscat) against the Qawāsim's ports in 1819 forced sheikhs ruling the major ports of the Arabian Peninsula in the Persian Gulf to sign the General Maritime Treaty of 1820 (Sato 2016; Balfour-Paul 1994; Dubuisson 1978). This treaty claimed to establish "a lasting peace between the British Government and the Arab tribes," and forced the region's sheikhs to agree to a "cessation of plunder and piracy," as well as to stop carrying slaves on their vessels.

The Arabic version of this treaty indicates that 'pirate' and 'piracy' were not part of the lexicon or conceptual framework of tribal leaders and inhabitants of the Persian Gulf (Woodbridge et al. 2021). In the 1820 treaty, the word 'piracy' is translated *ghārāt* 'raids'. Though "modern Arabic dictionaries list the terms *qurṣān* 'pirate' and *qarṣanah* 'piracy' under the trilateral root Q-R-Ṣ, giving the impression that this is a true Arabic word derived from this root (which generally means 'to pinch/sting')," the term is "actually a relatively recent addition to the Arabic language, and is a cognate of the English term 'corsair' from the Latin cursarius" (Aboelezz 2022). The foreign origin of *qurṣān* and *qarṣanah*, words which entered the Arabic language through North Africa

(Aboelezz 2022), illustrate that the concept of 'piracy' was imported and imposed on the coastal inhabitants of the Persian Gulf, who were forced into maritime treaties employing this foreign word.[4] Further, according to a Kumzari informant, there is still no word in Kumzari today for 'pirate' or 'piracy', and thus nineteenth-century Arabic- and Kumzari-speaking inhabitants of the Persian Gulf would have likely been unfamiliar with this foreign term and framing.

In 1853, the United Kingdom pressured the sheikhs of the littoral sheikhdoms to sign a new treaty to agree to a "Perpetual Maritime Truce," to designate the 'Pirate Coast' as the "Trucial Coast," and to establish the Trucial States (modern-day United Arab Emirates). These treaties and truces served to protect British trade into and out of the Persian Gulf, assert British political supremacy and dominance in the region, reduce the threat of France extending its reach any further in Oman and India, and upend the entire political structure of the 'Pirate Coast' by replacing the local protector-protegé network that had been "lubricated by tribute and inter-marriage among the local rulers" (Suzuki 2018, 70) with the British-made Trucial System. This Anglo-Indian imperial expansion extended the reach of the western flank, or 'frontier', around the same time that the British were trying to secure Burma in the east.[5]

---

[4] See London, British Library, 'File 2902/1916: Treaties and Engagements between the British Government and the Chiefs of the Arabian Coast of the Persian Gulf.' IOR/L/PS/10/606. Qatar Digital Library.

[5] The First Anglo-Burmese War began in 1824.

Foreign, and specifically 'western', interventions to 'protect' this waterway have a long, complicated, and suspect history. We might consider whether recent calls by western scholars and environmentalists to 'preserve' the languages, marine and terrestrial wildlife, and environment of the Arabian Peninsula are merely a modern incarnation of past attempts to 'protect' this region in the service of capitalism, knowledge production, western 'values', development, and imperialism. We might consider: what makes the cultures, languages, and landscapes in this volume in particular need of 'protecting' and 'preserving'—and could it be related to their geographical importance in a waterway which happens to be the most important strategic centre for oil exportation today?

The legacy of so-called 'piracy' in the Persian Gulf continues today in the fishing boats and motorboats that smuggle goods across the Strait of Hormuz (goats from Iran are traded for electronics in Oman) to evade sanctions. Perhaps these acts of smuggling, like past acts of 'piracy', should instead be considered forms of resistance to western imperialism, nationalism, and capitalism. Because this waterway is harder to surveil and police than roadways, it lends itself to fostering 'illegal' trade.

Today, Kumzar remains inaccessible by road; it is reachable only by boat. To reach Kumzar by boat, one must pass by Telegraph Island, where the notorious nineteenth-century British telegraph station once stood. The station's submarine copper telegraph cables served as the British Empire's vital connection between Great Britain, Iraq, and India. Its foundations remain, as do the station's stone stairs leading down to the water. The island is now a stopping point for tourist *dhow* cruises, the imperial ecosystem of the past replaced by today's ecosystem of global capital and unsustainable tourism.

Telegraph Island (which had been known as *Jazirat al-Maqlab* before the telegraph station was constructed in 1865) was chosen by the British to host the telegraph cables, because it was thought to be safer than the mainland, where it was vulnerable to attack by local tribes. This bare islet, which is tucked inside one of the *khoren*, gave rise to the English phrase "going round the bend," as officials stationed on Telegraph Island apparently experienced very serious mental and emotional distress from the isolated location, extreme heat, and stark landscape, particularly the *khoren*, which obscure the horizon line and full view of the Strait of Hormuz. In 1867, Lieutenant Colonel Patrick Stewart, director-general of the Indo-European Telegraph, wrote that the heat as well as "the high encircling rocks and limited view to seaward must have a depressing effect upon Europeans, especially during the hot season" (Teller 2014). After only three years, the station was closed down, and the cable re-routed through the Iranian island of Hengham. In this case, Musandam's unique coastal landscape resisted British imperial designs and power, as it produced destructive effects on the minds and bodies of the British soldiers who attempted to occupy it.

Today, on nearby Goat Island, the Omani military operates the Musandam Naval Base (with the help of the United States and Great Britain), which operates as a listening post for surveillance on Iran (Middleton 1986). One of the four Omani air bases that the United States has invested large sums of money in is the

Khasab airfield. In fact, over the past few decades, the whole Musandam Peninsula has been undergoing a process of "development" as part of a "U.S.-led operation" carried out by Tetra Tech International, a "company that deals with water and energy resources as well as underwater weapons development" and whose president, James H. Critchfield, "served the CIA as Middle East desk officer and a national intelligence officer for energy until 1974" (Dickey 1986). This same company has overseen Musandam's "agriculture and fisheries, power, water, the post office and telecommunications, information, land affairs, municipalities, youth affairs and public works" (Dickey 1986), as well as a computerised census of the region. The presence of British and American military operations on the Musandam Peninsula today raises questions about the sovereignty of the Sultanate of Oman and the Persian Gulf.

In addition to its imperial pasts and presents, the Musandam Peninsula is also entangled in tribal and national tensions, as it is separated from the rest of the Sultanate of Oman by the United Arab Emirates, which has indicated interest in territorially claiming it, most recently through the issuance of maps that provocatively claim it as UAE territory (Sheline 2020). The UAE and Musandam have long and close historical ties. The Omani government has tried to appease the local population (some of whose tribes favour being incorporated into the UAE) with investment projects and development promises, yet discontent remains and poses an ongoing threat to Omani sovereignty, territorial integrity, and national cohesion. Kumzari villagers began residing in the UAE in the 1960s for work-related reasons, and the UAE has issued many of them passports. The 'Khasab Coastal Road' (*Karnaš*) is connected to the United Arab Emirates via the E11 Highway on the UAE side, which facilitates close connections between this Omani territory and the UAE, particularly Ras al-Khaimah which many Kumzaris frequent.

3.0. Ecolinguistic Approaches to the Anthropocene, Climate Change, and Coastologies in Kumzari

Today, the impressive biodiversity of Kumzar, along with its traditional language, culture, and economy, is threatened by commercial fishing, neoliberal capitalism, and consumerism. The severe droughts of the past six decades have posed serious environmental and economic challenges as well. Ecolinguistics, which explores the role of language in the life-sustaining interactions of humans with the environment and other species, is well-designed to understand the marine ecosystem of Kumzar and indigenous understandings of it. As a trans-discipline (Bang and Trampe 2014; Fill 2001; Finke 2018; Halliday 1990; Stibbe 2021b), ecolinguistics brings together the seemingly disparate disciplines of ecology and linguistics (Alexander and Stibbe 2014; Zhou 2017) and also draws upon regional studies, cultural anthropology, geography studies, environmental studies, and sustainability studies. In addition to being members of societies, embodiments of culture, and speakers of languages, human beings are also embedded components and functions of the larger ecosystems that life depends upon.

The discipline of ecolinguistics provides a foregrounding for approaching the linguistic ecology of Kumzari by taking into consideration Musandam's remarkable biodiversity and unique coastal environment.[6] Though linguists have pondered the ecological contexts and consequences of language since Einar Haugen's 1972 book *The Ecology of Language*, especially within the context of the ubiquitous destruction of ecosystems around the globe and the dawn of the Anthropocene, such attention has not yet been thoroughly given to Kumzari and the aqua-coastographies of Kumzar, an understudied ecosystem which stands to benefit from not just an ecolinguistical approach, but more specifically a coastological approach that centres the primacy of the coast and coastal sustainability practices in the language and lives of Kumzari speakers.

Ecolinguistics employs critical discourse analysis about ecological systems (Stibbe 2014) to uncover and highlight the manifestation and organisation of cognitive and linguistic processes in organism-environment relations (Bang and Trampe 2014, 89). Ecolinguistics "explores the role of language in the life-sustaining interactions of humans, other species and the physical environment" and can be used to "address key ecological issues, from climate change and biodiversity loss to environmental justice" (https://www.ecolinguistics-association.org/). As ecolinguistics emphasises the interrelationships between living beings and their environments, it is a prime prism through which to view how the delicate ecosystems of Kumzar are reproduced in the Kumzari language, and how the indigenous people of Kumzar have successfully navigated in and through this coastal

---

[6] For more on ecological approaches in linguistics, see Cuoto (2014, 2018); Eliasson (2015).

and mountainous landscape by way of their knowledge of local land and sea ecosystems as encoded in Kumzari.

As the world becomes ever more aware of the threats of climate change, the link between the decline in global biological diversity and the decrease in the world's linguistic diversity becomes more obvious and difficult to ignore. In addition, the destructive and irresponsible environmental impacts of 'growthism', the idea that economic growth and development are inherently 'good', have become more apparent and seemingly irreversible. Today, the village of Kumzar is comprised of two mosques, a school for teaching the Qur'an (in which boys and girls study at different times), several small grocery stores, two restaurants, a laundromat, a mobile café, two barbershops, and a tailor for women's clothes. Two-storey houses (designed with entertainment and comfort in mind) have recently been built, as has a supermarket close to the beach.

While many villagers in Kumzar are interested in developing the village for tourism and modern conveniences, there is a lack of available areas for construction due to a lack of space in the village, as the mountains are so close to the shore. Development and modernisation have already greatly impacted Kumzar's marine and home environments: commercial fishing has decreased Kumzar's fish stocks, and television and the internet have enabled Arabic to reduce the influence of Kumzari in the home, resulting in broken chains of language transmission between generations.

Taking an ecolinguistic research approach to Kumzari is essential for discerning, appreciating, and protecting the symbiotic linkages between the biodiversity of Kumzar and Kumzari linguistic and ecocultural identities. As the United Nations Environment Program notes: "Biodiversity also incorporates human cultural diversity, which can be affected by the same drivers as biodiversity, and which has impacts on the diversity of genes, other species, and ecosystems" (UNEP 2017, 160). To protect the ecosystems that Kumzari villagers depend on, it is necessary to explore Kumzari ecological understandings and environmental interdependence.

4.0. Kumzari Assemblages: Mixed Language Ecologies and Linguistic Geographies

Designated by some as a mixed language (van der Wal Anonby 2014; 2015), Kumzari is a product of several different language ecologies and geographies. Linguists and Kumzari speakers alike have argued that Kumzari is a blend of Arabic, Persian, Portuguese, English (take, for example, *nāylō* 'nylon thread'), Hindi, and Balochi, and, of course, uniquely local words. Hence Betram Thomas's reference to Kumzari as "this strange tongue." As the study of Kumzari is still in its infancy, with a thorough grammar produced only recently (van der Wal Anonby 2015), its 'mixed' status is still open to debate.

The phonology, lexicon, and morpho-syntax of Kumzari are rooted in Arabian and Persian. Accordingly, Kumzari could be conceptualised as deriving from two different language ecologies. The first reference to Kumzari is found in an article by Samuel Zwemer, a Protestant missionary, who travelled throughout

Oman in 1900. On his journey, Zwemer heard about the Kumzari people and their language, which he later wrote about:

> There is coffeehouse babble in Eastern Oman concerning a mysterious race of light-complexioned people who live somewhere in the mountains, shun strangers, and speak a language of their own.... At Khasab, near Ras Musandam, live a tribe whose speech is neither Persian, Arabic, nor Baluchi, but resembles the Himyaritic dialect of the Mahras.... This language is used by them in talking to each other, although they speak Arabic with strangers. (Zwemer 1902, 57)

Around the same time, Atmaram Sadashiva Grandin Jayakar (1844–1911), an Indian Medical Service officer based in Muscat, travelled around the Musandam Peninsula with a British political expedition. In his writings, Jayakar mentioned Kumzari grammar and included a lexicon of 158 items within his longer discussion (1902) of the Arabic dialect of the Shihuh tribe. In Bertram Thomas's 1930 study on Kumzari grammar (which includes a lexicon of 553 words), he noted the high prevalence of Persian vocabulary and determined that Kumzari was "largely a compound of Arabic and Persian, but it is distinct from them both [and] as spoken is comprehensible neither to the Arab nor to the Persian visitor of usual illiteracy" (Thomas 1930, 785). While Kumzari's core vocabulary and verbal morphology have led to its categorisation as a Southwestern Iranian language (Skjærvø 1989) and thus its placement within the Indo-European linguistic ecology, more recent research has challenged or at least complicated this classification (van der Wal Anonby 2014). Though recent scholarship has begun to explore and articulate in more depth the common features between Kumzari and MSAL, this proposed connection is not necessarily new.

The ongoing debate about the linguistic ecologies embedded in Kumzari, coupled with the environmental embeddedness of the language, illustrates that Kumzari is a complex ecolinguistic system. Recent scholarship has suggested that instead of Kumzari being a Persian language with loan words from Arabic, it may instead be an Arabian language with borrowed words from Persian, with origins "in Middle Persian, even prior to the changes that took place in Iranian languages due to the seventh-century invasion of Fars by Arabic speakers" (van der Wal Anonby 2014, 139). The morphosyntax, sound-system, and grammatical retentions of Kumzari seem to belong not to the linguistic ecologies of Persian or Arabic, but to South Arabian and Shihhi (*šiḥḥī*).

Clues that Kumzari may belong to an Arabian ecology include Semitic roots in prime vocabulary (van der Wal Anonby 2014), prolific verb derivations, and lexically pervasive emphatic consonants. Contact with Arabic (Bayshak 2002), especially the Shihhi dialect, over the centuries seems to have changed the basic structures of the language (Zwemer 1902; Bayshak 2002; Anonby 2011b; van der Wal Anonby 2015), such as the lexicon, parallel verbal system, and prime elements of the phonological system. Further indicators include verbal nouns of the form *CaCCit* derived from Kumzari Semitic verbs (Holes 2004, 149–50), and the use of the 'feminine' suffix ending even on masculine words (Rubin 2010, 65)—a blurring of linguistic ecologies, as grammatical gender varies between Arabic, Iranian, and South Iranian.[7]

Most significantly, Kumzari has post-constituent and multiply marked negation (van der Wal Anonby 2022), a feature of South Arabian languages, but not Iranian languages. It employs negation after a verb or a negated constituent—negation is doubly marked on arguments following a negated verb. As other Western Iranian languages use pre-verbal negation, Kumzari thus seems to belong to another ecology of negation—primarily, the post-negation ecology of MSAL (van der Wal Anonby 2014; 2015).

Though the linguistic origins of Kumzari remain contested, there is evidence that Kumzari predates the Muslim conquest of the region in the seventh century CE, based on the lack of key phonological innovations of Iranian languages in the New Iranian period (beginning with the Arab takeover of Sassanid Persia in the 640s CE) and the Arabic lexicon of Kumzari. Kumzari speakers in Musandam believe that their ancestors came from Yemen (Jayakar 1902; Dostal 1972). The ancestors of the Kumzari may in fact have come from the Azd tribe, who migrated from Yemen around the third to fifth centuries CE, when Oman was occupied and governed by Sasanians (van der Wal Anonby 2014, 137; 2015, 10).

Though Bertram Thomas disagreed with the possible South Arabian origins of Kumzari and refuted Kumzari claims that they descended from third-century migrations of Azd from Yemen

---

[7] For details on the gemination of the feminine t-element in Musandam Arabic, see Anonby, Bettega and Procházka (2022).

(Thomas 1930, 785), recent scholarship (van der Wal Anonby 2014; 2022) argues that Arabian features or even the foundations of Kumzari may derive from when invasions of north-central Arabians in the seventh century forced many to seek refuge in Oman's northern mountains. For instance, Bayshak (2002) tries to prove this theory by linking Arabic structures in Kumzari with MSAL. While discussions of the linguistic ecologies of Kumzari have become more nuanced, the social and cultural practices of the Kumzari language have gone largely unexplored. Language is, of course, a social practice and cultural artefact inseparable from its environment and embodiment. From linguistic constructions and cultural understandings of subjectivity, relationality, and identity to the use of popular idioms and filler words, there is much more research still needed to explore the interrelations of Kumzari with social practices and the affective dimensions of Kumzari across time, ecosystems, and geographies. For starters, it may be easiest and most useful to consider how the unique aqua-landscape features of Kumzar are expressed in Kumzari, before exploring how aspects of cultural and labour practices like fishing, boating, and date cultivation are expressed in the language today.

5.0. Constructing Coastal Kumzar: Aqua-Landscapes, Climate Patterns, and Beach Spatialities

There are a number of words in Kumzari that describe Kumzar's unique aqua-landscapes. Some Kumzari words used to describe features of the region's marinescape include: *xēlij* 'gulf in the ocean', *ğēlila* 'lagoon, wadi streambed', *wīdī/wīǰī* 'wadi', *xilxil* 'small wadi', *bandar* 'cove', *xōr* 'ocean inlet', *jōbō* 'a water-collecting rock hollow', *ğābana* 'inlet', *ēr* 'an exposed rock in the sea', and *maʾdaf* 'seamount'. The Kumzari word for sea is *dirya* (similar to Persian دریا *daryâ*), but *dirya* can also be used for 'fishing'. Similarly, the Kumzari word for 'seawater', *sōr*, is also used for 'salt fish', 'pickled food', and 'brine'.

The average cover of algae in the Gulf of Oman and Persian Gulf has increased since the 2000s due to an abundance of dead coral skeletons providing the conditions for algae overgrowth. Kumzari words related to algae include: *awkē* 'red algae bloom', *xawẓa* 'a type of slimy green algae', *xall* 'seaweed, string green algae'. More frequent and lethal Harmful Algal Blooms (HABs, or Red Tides) have caused serious mortality of sea life over the past two decades in the Persian Gulf (Samimi-Namin et al. 2010) and the Arabian Sea (Bauman et al. 2010). The coral reefs of northeastern Arabia have suffered over the past two decades from large-scale bleaching events, disease outbreaks, a super-cyclone, large-scale harmful algal blooms (Bauman et al. 2010; Burt et al. 2014), overfishing, coastal development, dive boat anchoring, marine pollution, and climate change. The serious decline in coral cover was exacerbated by "bleaching during the hottest summer on record" in the Persian Gulf in 2017, which resulted in the region losing "40.1% of the living coral cover between 1996 and 2019" (Souter et al. 2021, 62) and the average cover of algae increasing from a "low of 13.0% in 2003 to a peak of 37.3% in 2018" (Souter et al. 2021, 63). Today, over half the coral reefs in Oman are at high to severe risk from a variety of natural and man-made threats and more than 75 percent of the coral reefs in Oman are "projected to be under high threat levels by 2030, and virtually all reefs in Oman under critical threat by 2050" (Burke et al. 2011). The coral reefs in the Persian Gulf have proven less likely to return to pre-disturbance assemblages than those in the Gulf of Oman.

Just as Kumzari has historically been conceptualised as a bridge between two language families (or ecologies), so, too, does the aqua-lifestyle of the Musandam Peninsula straddle two different coral ecosystems—the Persian Gulf and the Gulf of Oman. The coral reefs of Oman are "among the least studied in the region, with just 4% of regional reef-related publications focused on reefs in Oman" (Burt et al. 2016). In fact, the "species richness of hard corals in the Gulf of Oman" (with around 70 species) is "more than the entire Persian Gulf" (Owfi et al. 2015, 21). Coral cover in Oman is highest around the shores of the Musandam Peninsula. The rapid growth and high cover of coral on Musandam's reefs is due to the "high abundances of fast-growing branching corals such as Acropora and Pocillopora," which "cover over 40% of the reef bottom at the surveyed sites in the Musandam" (Burt et al. 2016). The coral reefs of Musandam, however, are vulnerable to high temperatures, whereas the coral reefs on the Gulf of Oman are at risk of cyclone damage. For instance, when a severe bleaching event damaged the coral reefs Musandam in 1990, as a result of temperatures over 30°C for three months, coral reefs in Muscat were not as affected because the "onset of monsoonal upwelling brought cool waters which minimized long-term bleaching and mortality there" (Burt et al.

2016). Conversely, Musandam was not as affected by the 2007 cyclone Gonu as Muscat, since the cyclone turned into a tropical storm and blew out to sea after ravaging Muscat[8] (Coles et al. 2015) in the Gulf of Oman. Thus, the monsoon of southern Oman has a particularly significant effect on coral reefs in the Gulf of Oman.

Traditionally, the sea has been the main source of livelihood, transportation, and recreation for Kumzari villagers. Kumzari has only a few words related to 'swimming' (šnāw). Though the village does not have a swim culture per se, children do play in the water. The main activities associated with the sea are fishing and boating (including cultural activities like wedding processions on dhows). Kumzari *lambiya* 'a swim on one's back' happens to also be the word for 'lullaby'. More general Kumzari words related to seawater include *barm* 'wave' and *ẓābid* 'foam on water'. Seawater may be described as *dawq* 'calm',[9] *šartaǧ* 'choppy', *ḥabasa* 'still', or as having *dīlub* 'a strong, swirling current'. Kumzari also has a number of words that spatially differentiate different sections of the *čāf/sīf/jum* 'beach'. For instance, *čāfčāf* is used for 'the water's edge' or 'right at the shore', while *tēla āwan* is the 'place where the waves wash onto the shore'.

---

[8] I was in Oman in the immediate aftermath of Gonu, staying at Al Bustan Palace by the Ritz-Carlton in Muscat, and the entire beach had been so battered by the cyclone that there was little sand left—just black stones; the hotel had to purchase a large amount of sand to recreate the beach.

[9] The Kumzari noun for a 'calm sea' is *ṣirx*.

These words illustrate the nuanced attention to location and positionality on land in relation to the water.

Weather in Kumzar has traditionally played a central role in the daily lives of Kumzari villagers and fishermen. The Kumzari word for 'weather', as well as for 'climate', is *jaww*. Not surprisingly, there are a number of Kumzari words for describing different kinds of rain, as sailing and navigation require careful attention to different types of rain and weather patterns. Rain in Kumzari can be described in terms of its direction, such as *pxūn* 'approaching rain', and its duration, such as *šdūd* 'ongoing rain showers' and *ḥalaba* 'raining heavily and constantly'. The magnitude of rain can be described nominally as *šōbub* 'pouring rain' or verbally as *ṣalaba* 'driving rain'. A rain that 'sprinkles', *naffa*, produces *nafnaf* 'scattered raindrops'. The word *tūtū* can also be used for 'scattered raindrops'. There are also Kumzari terms for the effects of a rainstorm, such as *čixčax* 'a stream that forms during a heavy rain'. Other natural phenomena related to the effects of a 'storm', *ǧātal*, include *ra'd* 'thunder', *num* 'clouds', and *qanḍaḥa* 'rainbows'. Another obstacle to sea navigation is *daǧbērit* 'thick, dusty haze'. Kumzari also has a word for 'staying out of the cold', *dafya*, which captures the act of avoiding uncomfortable weather conditions.

6.0. Directionality, Temporality, and Magnitude: Motion, Tides, and Wind in Kumzari

Traditionally, Kumzari villagers do not use the cardinal directions for navigation and describing location. Their spatial reference terms correlate instead to topographic variation, similar to the situation in Sulawesi (McKenzie 1997) and Oceania (Palmer 2002). Kumzari villagers tend to refer instead to 'up' and 'down', with the mountains being 'up' and the sea being 'down'. Kumzari does, of course, have words for 'east' and 'west' in *šarqī/mašraq* and *maġrab*, respectively, but their sense of directionality is set to a vertical dimension. Similarly, in the mountains of southern Oman in Salalah, "Mehri *rawrəm* 'sea', Śḥerēt *rɛmnəm*, describe a general southerly direction, and Mehri *nagd* 'Najd', Śḥerēt *fagər* 'stony desert' general north" (Saeed al-Mahri, p.c., cited in al-Ghanim and Watson 2021), while "around the port town of Taqah and to the south of the mountains, Śḥerēt *rɛmnəm* 'sea' indicates general south, and *śḥɛr* 'mountains' general north" (Al-Ghanim and Watson 2021, 65). Kumzaris' rootedness and orientation in space and place is intimately tied to Kumzar's local landscape. Their experience and expression of embodiment, motion, and movement is defined by their bodily relation to local natural features.

Where cardinal directions do come into play in Kumzari is in descriptions of wind. As the daily life of Kumzaris is closely tied to the sea and fishing, wind plays a prime role in everyday affairs. In fact, Kumzaris greet one another with the expression *či kawlā?* 'What kind of wind?' Kumzari has many words for the direction of the *kawl* 'wind', such as *kawl bālīʾī* 'east wind', *kawšī* 'east-southeast wind', *maṭlēʾī* 'strong east wind', *ōfur* 'west, northwest wind', *qāṭarī* 'strong west, northwest wind', *jāẓrī* 'northeast wind', *sālāwī* 'breeze from the east', *naʾšī/nāšī* 'north-northeast wind, nor'easter', *nāšī ārabī* 'north wind', and *nāšī fārsī* 'northeast wind'. Wind in Kumzari is also described temporally in relation to the time of day, such as *gāʾī* 'morning gusts', *škēẓī* 'evening wind', and *qāmarī* 'night wind', as well as descriptively, such as *ḍarbit* 'blustering wind', *jars* 'biting'. The deverbal *qadaḥa* 'blowing hard' is also used to describe a powerful gust of wind. The word *xwār* describes 'a calm sea with a gentle breeze', linking the wind with the waterscape. Whereas directionality on land is oriented on a vertical axis and described in relation to the mountains and sea, sea navigation requires more precise directional, temporal, and descriptive language not tied to land, particularly in the case of wind.

Similarly, in Dhofar and al-Mahrah, winds are described according to the direction from which they blow and their severity. For instance, though Mehri has general terms for winds, e.g., *həzēz* and *rīyēḥ*, it also has terms like "*mdīt* 'sea breeze', *zəfzōf ḏə-mdīt* 'perpetual sea breeze', *xrūb* 'hot desert wind', *xrūb tōrəb* 'blasting hot desert wind', *blēt* 'wind from the north' and *blēt šəmmamyət* 'severe north wind'" (Al-Ghanim and Watson 2021, 66). Despite the processes of modernisation and mechanisation, Kumzari villagers are still heavily dependent on the wind and weather for daily navigation and fishing; thus, these processes affect and shape the eco-focused cognitive processes, environmental literacy, and language production of Kumzari speakers.

As in South Arabian sea-going cultures, the sea-dependent lifestyle of Kumzar is reflected in the language. Kumzari contains a number of words to describe the diversity of tides and tidal motions in Kumzar. Similarly, while English spoken in non-sea-dependent English-speaking communities tends to just use 'ebb' and 'flow', or 'high' and 'low', in sea-dependent English-speaking communities there is a larger and richer vocabulary of tides (Story, Kirwin, and Widdowson 1990). For tidal descriptions, Kumzari has an assortment of single words that describe the magnitude and time of tides (although, of course, Kumzari also has *ōǧar* 'ebbing tide' and *purya* 'flowing tide'). Some Kumzari terms emphasise the magnitude of a tide, such as *gābanō* 'exceptionally high-level tide' and the verb *šaʾata* to describe 'an extremely low tide'.[10] *Gābanō* can also be used in a seasonal sense, to describe what is also called *proxigean* 'a spring tide'. Tides can also be described temporally in Kumzari as part of a cluster at a particular time, such as *kasr* 'a period of very high tides' and *ḥaml* 'the month's highest tides'. Kumzari also has the word *dawm* to demarcate 'the sea between tides', marking the absence, or stasis, of tidal action.

The traditional dependence of Kumzari villagers on the weather and sea for subsistence and navigation made the use of a calendar to track the tides and weather patterns essential. While Kumzari has a general word *taqwim* 'calendar', the people of Kumzar have traditionally used a *dar/dōrō* 'Gulf calendar'. Until recently, this calendar was fundamental to Kumzari subsistence, labour, time management, navigation, migration, and socio-cultural life. As van der Wal Anonby (2015, 54) notes, "In recent years, the presence of water pollution, prolonged drought, and extraordinary algae blooms have necessitated adjustments to the calendar or outright decline in its use." The calendar is composed of ten-day weeks, and these are categorised by predictable

---

[10] *Qaraḥa* is the action of water 'dropping very low', indicating a change in the state of the water.

weather patterns (such as searing heat or rough seas), with their corresponding labour and economic activities, such as fishing under favourable weather and tidal conditions predicted by phases of the moon, wind patterns, and currents.

7.0. Kumzar's Biodiversity: Capturing Terms for Creatures, Animal Groupings, and Ideophones in Kumzari

An ecolinguistics approach implicitly decentres anthropocentrism and speciesism, shedding light on the complexity and diversity of the ecosystems in which humans are embedded and function. As there are hundreds of names for different fish species in Kumzari, listing all of them is beyond the scope of this chapter. The general Kumzari term for fish is *may*. In children's speech in Kumzar, fish are called *baḥḥa*. Some of the most popular species of fish in the Musandam area are: *jaydar* and *wīr* 'tuna fish', *ālaq* 'needlefish', *angiẓ* 'squid/cuttlefish', *fār* 'flying fish', *ēraraǧ* 'bream', *xāǧur* 'type of bream fish', *manṭa* 'marlin', *faql* 'porcupinefish', *mayg* 'shrimp', *ṣābuṭ* 'jellyfish', *ūmat* 'sardine', *gēlō* 'catfish', *xarkuk* 'parrotfish', *rīšō* 'goatfish', *šang* 'butterflyfish', *sikl* 'cobia fish', *sēḥak* 'guitarfish', *tirxēnit* 'milkfish', *xālaq* 'type of grouper fish', *šamšīrī* 'sawfish', *šāwan* 'type of codfish', *bahlul* 'potato grouper', *šangaw* 'type of crab', *čāwuẓ* 'rabbitfish', *ṣnāfē* 'type of rabbitfish', *gewgaw* 'type of rabbitfish', *šayn* 'type of queenfish', *ṣārm* 'type of queenfish', *šāxur* and *šuqqar* 'types of snapper fish'. The *qātal* 'killer' fish is a poisonous and deadly fish. While many of these words are connected to regional fish lexicons, more work is being done to properly associate these fish species with their scientific names (Anonby and Al Kumzari fc.).

Many fish populations in the Persian Gulf, especially species of groupers, have been heavily exploited over the past two decades, prompting local communities to be more vocal in pushing for the maintenance of optimum levels. In Musandam, there is a higher prevalence of fish from the *Lutjanidae* (snappers) and *Chaetodontidae* (butterflyfish) families, as opposed to the *Haemulidae* (sweetlips) and *Scaridae* (parrotfish) families. Types of fish well-defined in Kumzari indigenous knowledge but, to the best of my knowledge, not yet classified by English translators include: *aragumba, lēdam, lāḥafī, lākō, lāẓuq, kanʾad, īfē, jaǧbib, kārarağ, māmadī, qambab, qāṭ, qāpṭ, qarṭabō, qrambiṣ, qunwaḥ, qurfē, rāmišt, ṣāl, sāfin, skindan, tiḥādī, umbē, xrō diryīʾin, xubbaṭ, xubr, mēd, jārid, lašt, kōr, mazāraq, laḥlaḥ, maysānī, šōban, šōbubō, ṣōman, siftik, sanksar, rōbāyō, tarbō, sitrağ, xēnō, sabū, ṣāwawē, laḥlaḥ, ẓbayšō, nagrō, pārawē, kūkū, jurbaḥ, imbē, kanʾad, kōfar, gurgurō, garagumba, lašt, gmō, ẓbēdī.* Additionally, a *būt* is a 'type of small fish'.

Kumzari has several words to refer to a grouping of fish. While a *maḥdaqa* is a 'fish habitat', a *qiš* is a 'deep-water fish habitation'. A mass of fish underwater can be referred to as *rāʾim*, *xūyū*, or *kard* (also used for a 'cluster of dates' or 'flock'). A *čikkit* is a 'string of fish'. Thus, there is attention in Kumzari to different types of fish habitations and fish formations.

The waters of the Musandam Peninsula are known for their large dolphin populations. Many tourists who visit the Musandam region go dolphin watching on *dhows* that depart from

Khasab. Kumzari has words for both the 'white dolphin' in *kārabō* and the 'black dolphin' in *fijmē*. Other words for sea creatures in Kumzari include: *ḥēmis* 'sea turtle', *jāwar* 'large sea turtle', *bām* 'giant sea turtle', *šufrāqō* 'frog', *timsaḥ* 'crocodile', *šawḥaṭ* 'whale', *sēlik* 'moray eel', *sīflindō* 'type of eel', *rubbaṭ* 'type of stingray', *rāmak* 'type of ray', *rubyan* 'prawns', *asp* 'seahorse', and *mṣaww* 'barnacle'. Barnacles in Musandam cover only 5 percent of settlement tiles, as opposed to the Gulf of Oman, where they cover nearly a quarter (22 percent) (Bento et al. 2017). The Kumzari word *qabqab* describes a 'small crab', but it can also be used for a 'quick person'. While the Kumzari word for 'octopus ink' has been documented as *mādad*, other terms related to the effects or productions of sea creatures have yet to be studied in detail.

Today, there are 32 shark species in the Persian Gulf. Fishermen in Kumzar catch a variety of sharks: blacktip, hammerhead, whitetip reef, and some whale sharks (Jabado et al. 2014; Notarbartolo di Sciara and Jabado 2021). While *kūlī* is a general word in Kumzari for 'shark', Kumzari also has a number of words to refer to different types of sharks, from *dībē* 'great white shark' to various types of sharks still undefined in English (*nāwukō, qāẓum, jmēs, jubbē, xiṣwānī, manqab, pēčak, qrādī, rējimī, tirxēnit*). Fisherman from Kumzar lure sharks using a sea trap consisting of a long, weighted rope with live fish that are baited through the cheek and hooked onto the rope. They return a day or two later to see if a shark has been caught by the sea trap. Although shark fishing is a tradition in Kumzar, shark fishing did not become a specific means of livelihood until after the 1970s (Castelier

2020), when the oil boom in the Persian Gulf connected Oman to Asian markets.

Today, the fishermen of Kumzar are embedded in the global shark trade's ecosystems of exploitation. The shark fishing business in Oman (and the Persian Gulf in general) is very lucrative, as it supplies shark fins and meat from a variety of shark species for customers around the world—specifically wealthy customers in Asia (Castelier and Müller 2017). According to the United Nations Food and Agriculture Organization, Oman exported US$2,438,000 worth of shark fin between 2000 and 2011 (Dent and Clarke 2015, 20). Several species of shark are being unsustainably fished in Musandam, trafficked via Khasab to the United Arab Emirates (Jabado et al. 2014; Jabado et al. 2015; Jabado et al. 2018a; Jabado et al. 2018b) and flown to Hong Kong, from where they are sold to markets in China, Taiwan, Malaysia, Singapore, and Indonesia. In Asia, shark fin soup is considered a delicacy, and the preferred species for shark fin soup is the hammerhead shark (all three kinds: Scalloped Hammerhead, Great Hammerhead, and Smooth Hammerhead) (Dent and Clarke, 2015). Due to this demand, hammerhead sharks in eastern and southern Arabia have experienced "the greatest mean perceived decline (80%) of sharks in the region" (Almojil 2021). While shark fishing is not illegal in Oman, there are some stipulations.

In Oman, sharks must be sold whole, as 'finning' (removing the fins for sale without the body) is prohibited. Finning is not a new practice in Kumzar: in 1908, Lorimer wrote: "They [Kumzaris] own 40 or 50 fishing boats and 5 sea-going boats that run to Qishm, Dibai, and Masqat Town with cargoes of salt fish and shark-fins" (1040). In 2008, Oman became a signatory to the Convention on International Trade in Endangered Species of Wild Fauna and Flora (CITES), which stipulates that the great hammerhead shark and the whale shark should be protected from sale and trade. Despite these regulations, however, sharks continue to be overexploited in Oman, where just one hammerhead shark can earn a fisherman close to US$1500.

Oman is ranked seventeenth among countries in terms of quantity of shark fin exportation. According to Dr Rima Jabado, a biologist who studies sharks in the Persian Gulf, overfishing in Oman and the UAE is endangering the shark populations there. In her research she found that "sharks were found to be increasingly targeted owing to their high value in the global fin trade industry" and "the majority of fishermen (80%) confirmed that changes in species composition, abundance and sizes of sharks have been continuing for more than two decades, mainly because of overfishing, raising concerns about the sustainability of this fishery" (Jabado et al. 2014). She found that almost 50 percent of shark species traded in the UAE are at high risk of global extinction. Kumzar's entanglement in the global shark trade is leading to overfishing (Dulvey et al. 2021) in Musandam and contributing to the endangerment of several shark species. Further, due to the violation of international regulations and the involvement of criminal networks involved in shark fishing and finning, shark fishing (like the falcon trade) remains a sensitive subject in Oman and the Arabian Peninsula in general.

Figure 1: Dolphin swimming in Musandam (Photo: Emily Jane O'Dell)

In addition to further work needed on identifying specific fish species in Kumzari, more attention must also be paid to bird terminology and the cultural place of birds in Kumzari culture. The general term in Kumzari for bird is *ṭēr*, and other Kumzari words for birds in the Musandam region include *ḥaqm* 'domestic pigeon', *murwa barrō* 'domestic chicken', *alʾul* 'heron', *būm* 'owl', *murwa kōʾō* 'sandgrouse', *ḥāmamō* 'dove', *šāʾin* 'eagle, hawk, vulture', *xrō* 'rooster', *ṣuqr* 'osprey, falcon', *bībī mattō* 'parrot', *baǧbaǧa* 'parrot', *nābī* 'gull', *bišram bēšir* 'gull', *ǧrāb* 'crow', *ǧuwwē* 'white tern', *ṣufṣuf* 'sparrow', and other types of birds still not yet defined, such as *saqqa* and *ṣufrit*. The 'caw' of a crow is captured in Kumzari by the ideophone *qā*, and the ideophone of a rooster crowing is *qāq*. The Kumzari word for the 'comb' of a rooster and the 'crown' of a hoopoe is *farrūgit*.

Kumzari words for animals outside the direct ecology of the sea include creatures indigenous to the Musandam Peninsula and those far from it. Words that illustrate the diverse animal species existent in Kumzari include: *numr* 'leopard, panther, tiger', *arnab* 'hare', *jāmal* 'camel', *ḥamra* 'hyena', *sābalō* 'monkey', *qambuṣṣō* 'hedgehog', *ḍaby* 'oryx', *ḍabʾ* 'hyena', *ğāẓalē* 'gazelle', *fahd* 'cheetah', *asp* 'horse', *dīb* 'wolf', *aqrab* 'scorpion', *ẓubd* 'type of gecko', *ḍabb* 'type of large lizard', *muğlī* 'type of venomous snake', and *mār* 'snake'. Kumzar and the Musandam Peninsula in general are also home to insect inhabitants and communities. Kumzari words for insects include: *gīrağ* 'ant', *abū šayban* 'spider', *šurṣ* 'cockroach', *gārad* 'locust', *mām abū kō* 'butterfly', *qarraṣ* 'mosquitos', *qmaylō* 'weevil', *ẓirraḥ* 'type of flying insect', *ḍēṣa* 'type of stinging insect', *asp* 'moth', *rišk* 'type of louse', *qāt* 'type of beetle', and *sūrō* 'wasp'. In Kumzari, *dupsī* is a 'plague of insects'. Of course, like humans and other animals, insects construct their own homes and communities, such as *sāban* 'wasp nests'.

Kumzari uses several animals to metaphorically describe the behaviour and physical appearance of human beings. For instance, the Kumzari word for *čēl* 'albatross', a bird whose breeding cycle stretches over two years, is also used to describe a 'slow person'. The Kumzari word for cow, as in Arabic, is *bāqara*, which is also used in Kumzari to describe a 'stupid person'. A *šēw* is a type of snake, and this word is also used for a 'very thin person'. Not only can animal aspects be used to describe human physicality and cognition, but animal names can also be subsumed into Kumzari nicknames and given names.

In Kumzari, a 'nickname' (*lāqab*) is often assumed by those with common names so they can be distinguished from others who share their popular given name. These creative long nicknames can draw upon one's parents' names, physical appearance, tribal affiliation, occupation, an animal totem, or a feature of the landscape. This phenomenon is not, however, restricted to nicknames, as traditional names can also contain pertinent ecological information. For instance, Kumzari who live in the mountains may have traditional names with the ending -kō 'mountain', such as ēlikōʿ (for Ali) and īsakōʿ (for Isa). Two examples given by van der Wal Anonby (2015) of the phenomenon of incorporating animals and landscapes into nicknames include Ēlikō Šōbubō (Alikō + 'fish species') and Ēl-Ḥam-Ōlō (Ali Ḥamed + 'mountain peak'). As van der Wal Anonby (2015, 52) observes, it is common for nouns of culturally familiar items, especially those with "semantic ties to Kumzari identity and subsistence," such as "fish species, date stages, tides and weather, and parts of a boat," to assume the same morphology as personal names, like the -ō suffix. Some examples she provides are ambarō 'type of bream fish', spārō 'storage space beside mast on a boat', and sīflindō 'a type of eel'. Thus, not only do Kumzari incorporate animals and landscapes into their own names and nicknames—which are the prime markers of one's personal identity—but there is also a linguistic connection between these semantic features of Kumzar's ecology and the morphology of personal names.

8.0. Sardine Fishing, Boating Technology, and Goat Husbandry: Equipment, Labour, and Decoration in Kumzari

Fishing and date cultivation have long been the primary seasonal sources of income for Kumzari villagers. Labour in Kumzar has traditionally revolved around the sea and been shaped by the changing weather and seasons. Indigenous fishing knowledge of the Musandam region, and Kumzar in particular, has received some attention in scholarship (Musallam et al. 2006; Al-Anbouri, Ambak, and Jayabalan 2011; Al Jufaili 2021). However, one study which included interviews with fisherman from all over Oman (who had at least thirty years of experience in the sardine and anchovy fisheries) left out the Musandam region completely (Al-Jufaili 2011).

Kumzar is well-known in Oman for its long history of sardine and tuna fishing. In Kumzari, the 'sardine season' is called *ṭyāḥ*. The sardine season stretches from September (*mā naʾ*) to April (*mā čār*), with December (*mā dwāẓda*) and January (*mā yak*) being its peak, as the colder weather of 'winter' (*dimistan*) provides the most favourable conditions. In May (*mā panj*), after the sardine season, residents of Kumzar head to Khasab (*Xāṣab*) to harvest dates during the 'searing heat' (*ẓuqqum*)[11] at the 'beginning of summer' (*daymē*).[12] The 'summer migration' is called *ḥuwwil*. Sardines are used by Kumzari villagers as food for humans and livestock, bait (*gīm*), and also fertiliser. Sardines are carried in Kumzar in an *anda* a 'round woven mat with handles used for carrying sardines'. Outside of Musandam, the main markets for sardines in Oman are located in Muscat (*Maškat*), Al-Batinah, and Dubai in the UAE (*āmarātō*).

---

[11] 'Warmth' or 'heat' in general in Kumzari is *garm* (as in Persian), while the adjective *garmaǧ* is used for 'hot'.

[12] When I was in Kumzar, I noticed that many houses had at least one air conditioner (*kandēšin*).

The coastal waters of the Sultanate of Oman have six sardine species. This striking variety may "indicate greater diversity of environmental habitats when compared to the other sardine-anchovy systems" (Al-Jufaili 2002). This diversity "allows or perhaps encourages speciation" (Al-Jufaili et al. 2006). Further, seasonal shifts in winds triggered by changes in the atmospheric pressure of the Indian Ocean cause reversals of the current along the East African coast that similarly affect Oman and Iran (Sheppard 2000, 920). It is possible that the diversity of sardine species in Oman is related to the "migration of fish to the north during the southwest monsoon and southward during the southeast monsoon" (Al-Jufaili et al. 2006). The sandy coast in the north, around Al-Batinah, yields many sardines, whereas shark and tuna fish tend to be caught along the "rocky coastlines of the Gulf of Oman along Musandam" (El Mahi 2000, 99). Longitudinal environmental data is still needed for understanding fluctuations in Oman's sardine catches, and the effects of ocean currents and the monsoon cycle on sardine communities in Oman.

For sardine fishing, fishermen in Kumzar use traditional beach and purse seines, which require little effort and are set out close to shore. In Oman in general, beach seines (modified gillnets) are the most popular method for catching sardines. Such a 'gillnet' (*li kūkū*) can require about a dozen people to set and collect. However, as I witnessed in Kumzar, most boat crews fishing for sardines use about two to four net handlers. A gillnet catches the 'gills' (*ǧmūt*) of a fish in the mesh when it tries to back out of the net. A sardine catch can yield approximately forty tons a day.

Kumzari has a number of words related to fish netting. *Say* is a 'traditional fishing net', *lē* is a general term for 'fishing nets, *kurraf* is a 'deep-sea fishing net', and *qbēl* a 'sardine net' in particular. Traditional 'large' fishing nets are referred to as *ābat*, *jārif*, and *šābak*. There also a variety of terms for different types of fishing nets (well defined in Kumzari, but still unknown to outsiders), such as *bān*, *ṭarḥ*, *sāğa*, and *ṣēram*. There are also several net-related terms, such as *fars* 'fishing net thread' and *miḥḥ* 'seine net rope'. The parts, or sections, of nets and ropes have specific terms. For example, *likkit* 'main section of a net', *nāxē* 'beginning of a fishing net rope', and *qādam* 'end of a fishing net rope'. These specific terms for parts of the rope mirror the phenomenon of specific words being used to refer to different sections of the beach.

Netting is not the only technology that Kumzari fisherman use to catch fish. In addition to net fishing, Kumzari fishermen also use 'fish traps' (*ābāʾ*), as well as 'metal fish traps' (*dūbāy*) and 'a small wire fish cage' (*gargur*). Other fishing equipment includes: *ṣāmur* 'a stone weight for fishing', *markūʾī* 'a fish caller', and *kībal* 'buoy'. There are a number of terms in Kumzari related to buoys: *qālub* 'a large buoy', *rammul* 'a small buoy', *qarʾa* 'a middle buoy in a fishing net', *bōya* 'a large plastic buoy', *karb* 'a buoy', but also the 'thick end of a palm branch'. In Musandam, buoys are used not just for fishing, but also to control marine tourist traffic. For instance, mooring buoys are installed at Telegraph Island, which tourists use as a dive site, yet these two buoys are not sufficient for the number of boats that arrive during the weekends.

As the acts of anchoring and hooking play important roles in fishing and boating, Kumzari has terms for different kinds of anchors and hooks: a general term is *langal* 'anchor', while *qanḥē* is a 'small anchor' and *nittar* a 'stone anchor'. *Msaww* is a 'fishing net weight' and *sinn* a 'fishing net anchor'. Other terms related to fishing include: *jām* 'hooked', *mnaxx* 'large hook', *nišbil* 'fishing line', and *ṣēram* 'container for fresh fish'.

Kumzari words used to describe labour related to fishing refer to the construction and movement of boats, the manipulation of nets, and the preparation of fish. Fishing is, of course, a communal endeavour that requires many roles, such as a *ṭrādīn* 'motorboat driver', *nijjar* 'boatbuilder', *diryiʾīn/diryiʾīnē* 'fisherman', and *nōxada* 'captain'. Kumzari also has a word for 'fishing instructions': *ṭālab*. Traditionally, a spotter is also used in the nearby cliffs to help fishermen reach their catch. The Kumzari verb *līmē* 'gesturing to call someone far away' attests to the bodily signals and coordination necessary when communicating across the land and sea without the aid of modern technology.

The act and labour of fishing is very much defined by directionality. Fishermen must go toward and into the water, stay for a period of time in the water waiting for the catch, and then return to the shore. The Kumzari word for 'departure' (*jēl*) is also used for 'the laying out of fish nets', an act which marks 'leaving' to go fishing. In traditional daily life in Kumzar, 'departing' almost always meant leaving to go fishing—thus, the two are understandably linked. The Kumzari word for the act of 'sitting in a boat waiting for fish' is *ṭalʾit*. Thus, the stasis of fishing and experience of anticipation of a catch is captured in a single word—instead of just assumed under a generic term like *fishing*. The verb to 'trap fish' is *ābā*,[13] while *quṣrō* is the word for 'pulling in nets'. This is done with the help of a *mintab*, a 'hooked stick used for pulling in fish nets'. While *ḥamya* is the general verb for 'docking' or 'beaching', the deverbal *gamaga* is used to describe the action of 'going onto the shore quickly to remove a boat from the water and store it on the beach'. This term captures the movement and speed of returning a boat to shore. Perhaps more work is needed to explore articulations in Kumzari of the storage and maintenance of fishing equipment.

While there are many Kumzari words to describe the labour and equipment of fishing, there are also words that refer to the preparation of fish after the act of fishing. For example, catch can be described as *dīr* 'a slit fish', *gannit* 'a stack of dried fish', *ṣaḥnē* 'crushed dried sardines', *qāša* 'drying fish', *tik* 'the slitting of fish', *kālak* 'fish cheek', *ūmit* 'dried sardines'. Just as there is a specific word for fishing instructions in Kumzari (*ṭalab*), the term *māya* is used for specifically for 'payment for fishing'. The traditional diet in Kumzar is primarily made up of locally sourced ingredients from Kumzar's marine environment. Some popular dishes in Kumzar include *mēčūrī* 'fish soup', along with fish-derived condiments and sauces like *sāwaraǧ* 'fish brine condiment' and *qaššad* 'shark sauce'.

---

[13] See *bā* 'trap fish, pull in (IMPV)' and *tābā* 'trap fish (IMPF)'.

Figure 2: Boats on Display in Khasab Castle (Photo: Cathy Birdsong Dutchak)

Boating is the traditional bedrock of Kumzari livelihood, culture, and migration. As Kumzar is accessible only by boat, boating is the prime mode of transportation for venturing outside the village, which is why boating has played such a prime role in the navigation, trade, and identity of the people of Kumzar (Vosmer 1997; Weismann et al. 2014; Ghidoni and Vosmer 2021). A 'vessel' in general is *abrit*, while a 'motorboat' is *ṭrājē* or *ṭarrādē*. Kumzari speakers refer to a *dhow*, a large traditional boat in Oman and throughout the Persian Gulf, as *būm* and *lanj*. A 'type of short *dhow*' in Kumzari is *dādrō*, and a 'rowboat' is *ōra*. In Arabic, the traditional boats of the Musandam Peninsula used for seine fishing, along with coastal trading, smuggling, fishing, pearling, and fighting, are called *battil bahwy*, *battil qarib*—or *selek* (Agius 2002, 111)—and *zarūqa*.

A *battil* is a double-ended fishing vessel with a low pointed prow, high sternpost, and projections. The *battil bahway* is of medium size, the *battil qarib* is slightly larger, and the *zarūqa* is a smaller version of the *battil* with a deeper forefoot. Kumzari also refers to this style of boat, which is unique to the Musandam Peninsula, as *battil*, with *salq* being the 'type of large *battil*' and *z̧ōraqa* being the smallest version. The bow and stern of a *battil* traditionally featured a stitched method of binding the planks with coconut thread (Weismann et al. 2014). Several such boats are on display in Khasab Castle (*Kālat Zēranī*). General Kumzari words for the parts of a boat include: *āšyō* 'mast beams across boat deck', *dastur* 'lower sail crossbar', *dōl* 'mast', *ērisin* 'oar', *ōz̧ar* 'sail', *sāxī* 'bow of boat', *sikkē* 'stern', *sikkan* 'rudder', *kaʾnağ* 'cross-beam', *tēlan* 'inner railing of a boat', *z̧gurda/z̧burda* 'sheer strake', *xišš* 'side of a boat', *xiz̧mītō* 'stem-post', *dār bandirōʾō* 'ship's flagpole', *bandēra* 'ship's flag', *bandōlō* 'mast box', and *māyikan* 'handle on a traditional boat'. The Kumzari word for the 'back of a boat" is *dūm*, which is also used for 'tail', and the 'wake of a boat' is *āwga*. The Kumzari words *xurṭ* 'a stable thing' and *durb* 'an unstable, wavering thing' are usually used to describe the condition of a boat in the water. Kumzari words related to stability and stasis (such as the aforementioned *ṭalʾit* 'sitting in a boat waiting for fish') capture the necessary balance and patience required for the act of fishing.

Figure 3: Cowrie shell decoration in Khasab (Photo: Cathy Birdsong Dutchak)

In Kumzar and the Musandam Peninsula in general, a *battil* is often ornamented with bands of cowrie-shell decoration around the prow, rudder, or false sternpost. In Kumzari, this 'cowrie chain' is called a *zarzur*, whereas a single 'cowrie shell' is a *pakkis*. Agius (2007, 104) recounts: "I was told by my informants in Kumzar that the decoration of cowrie shells around the tall stern fins of a *battil bahwi* is to commemorate a wedding in the village." Similarly, palm fronds and "tassels (*kasht*) are hung from the *zaruka* steamhead in Kumzar" (Agius 2007, 103). It is "generally understood that the pendulous decorations such as tassels, flags, umbrellas, shells, ostrich eggs and feathers serve as amulets to guard the boat against the evil eye," much like the bridle ornaments of Arabian camels (Agius 2007, 104). In the Kumzari language, a "goatskin hung on the prow of a boat" is referred to as *pōṣṭ sīnōʾō*. It is still the custom today to "sacrifice a sheep or goat at the launching of a boat or ship," after which "the flayed goat skin is dressed on the stemhead—such as the stempost of a *battil karib* at Kumzar, Musandam Peninsula" (Agius 2007, 102–3). The goatskin decoration is intended to ward off *afrit* 'evil spirits', *banjāʾī* 'evil', and *ḥassa* 'misfortune' in general. Throughout the Sultanate of Oman, beliefs about the *šūmē čōmē* 'evil eye' and magic are prevalent, and Kumzar is no exception. In fact, Kumzari contains several words for someone competent in magic: *ṣāḥar* 'sorcerer', *arḍī* 'powerful sorcerer', and *jinjāwir* 'master sorcerer'.

In the traditional culture of Kumzar, goatskin is not just used for boating decoration, but also for churning. A goatskin used for churning is called *mašk* (as in Persian), whereas elsewhere in Oman, like Dhofar, a goatskin for churning is called *qirbah* and/or *sqa*. In Kumzar, these goatskins are usually large enough to allow for the churning of 10–12 kg of yoghurt and water, though some may be even larger. A goatskin from Dhofar in the Sultanate of Oman is in the collection of the British Museum (object number As1985,18.4). Donated in 1978, it is accompanied by the following text:

> The water bag (*qirbah*) continues to be the most reliable means of storing water and milk for many families in remote regions of the country [Oman]. It is hung inside a dwelling or from the branch of a tree, and is carried on the side of the camel when travelling.... Along the desert coast, camel and goat milk is often more plentiful than fresh water, and is a critical component of the local diet. Buttermilk (*laban*), which is particularly favoured, is made in a large leather churning bag (*sqa*) suspended from a tripod or tree

branch, and rocked back and forth. (Richardson and Dorr, 2003, 373)

Goatskin churning bags are closed at the bottom with stitched and embroidered leather, while an opening is left at the top through which the bags can be filled, emptied, or stirred with a churning stick. A cord allows it to be suspended from a tree branch for the churning process or hung for storage or migration on a hook or camel. This traditional churning technology can be found in photographic and archival records from around the Persian-speaking world, such as Iran and Afghanistan, as well as in Palestine, Egypt, Iraq, Gilgit-Baltistan, and Socotra in Yemen.

Goat husbandry is another traditional practice and livelihood of the Kumzari people. Goat Island (*Jēẓurtō*) has traditionally served as a seasonal grazing ground. In Kumzari, a 'goat' is *gōsin*. There are also specific words for goats at different stages of development: *bukrit* 'newborn goat', *xāšar* 'young goat', and a *dēbaḥit* 'full-grown male goat'. However, in children's speech, a goat is *taḥḥa*. Relatedly, the interjection used by goat herders to call a goat to come is *taḥḥ* or *tayʾ tayʾ tayʾ*. Similarly, the interjection to call sheep (*kapš*) is: *taʾ taʾ taʾ*.[14] The act of 'catching goats' (*ḥayš*) is performed by a *ḥayyiš* 'goat catcher'. A *rāʾī* is a 'person who raises goats'. When not grazing, goats are kept in a 'goat pen' (*ẓēribit/sandaqa/innit*). A 'sloping well for watering goats' is *ḥisī* or *ḥusī*. Kumzari also has terms for a 'wily goat' (*furī*) and a 'stupid goat' (*agī*). While goatskin is used to decorate the traditional boats of Musandam, goat hair is used for the fashioning of a special kind rope (*tēxa*).

---

[14] The interjection to call cats is *taktūk* and *takū*.

Traditionally, Kumzari villagers would bring goats to the coastal bays of Goat Island *(Jazirat al Ghanam)* to graze after rainfall. As Lorimer (1908, 577) explains: "Jazirat-al-Ghanam is totally barren and devoid of water; but the people of Kumzar, to whom it belongs, send goats here for grazing after rain." The remains of a World War II Naval Signal Station still exist on Goat Island, vestiges of the island's modern entanglements in regional and global conflicts. Today, Goat Island is the command centre for Oman's surveillance of the Strait of Hormuz. The Musandam Naval Base, opened in 1986, and its radar posts are overseen by hundreds of Omani marines and sailors in addition to the British Royal Navy (Kostiner 2009, 197). In addition to interviewing via radio every ship that passes through the strait, the Omani military and its British and American partners also use the island as a listening post to conduct surveillance on the Islamic Republic of Iran.

Goat Island is just one element in Oman's and Great Britain's sprawling ecosystem of militarism in the Strait of Hormuz. There are only a few dozen local inhabitants left on the barren island, which has no natural water resources. The base has led to the displacement of some in the surrounding area, such as the relocation of the population of the village of Qabal on the east coast of Musandam for the construction of a military installation (Dickey 1986). The environmental effects of these ecosystems of military surveillance are not currently known, but they are certainly harming the environment—through the use of large quantities of oil alone. Prince William and then UK Minister of Defense Ben Wallace visited the naval base on Goat Island, and Great

Britain has conducted joint exercises with Omani troops on the island (including for mountain warfare practice). Today, the island administratively belongs to the Wilaya al-Khasab of Musandam Governorate.

Figure 4: Goatskin decorating a *battil* (Photo: Jacques Van Dinteren)

9.0. Date Plantations in Khasab: Palm Cultivation and Coastal Migration in Kumzari

In the summertime, Kumzari villagers travel to Khasab to tend to their date plantations. This migration includes the 'mountain Bedouin' (*kōʾī*) of Kumzar—Shihuh families who speak Arabic and, due to constant droughts, have moved down from the mountainside into the village of Kumzar (and even learned Kumzari). In Khasab, Kumzari villagers live in their own neighbourhood 'quarter' (*hārtō*), called Harat al-Kumzari in Arabic, near the sea. The date palm is the primary agricultural crop in the Sultanate of Oman; half of the dates that the country's seven million palm trees produce are used for human consumption, and the other half for animal feed. In fact, one type of date palm in Oman is called 'Al Khasab', which is treated with hand pollination as opposed to the mechanical pollination of varieties like Khalas.

The date palm (*muğ*) plays an important role in the daily life of Kumzaris. Accordingly, Kumzari has many words 'pertaining to the date palm' (*maxlēdī*). There is not just one 'category of dates' (*sayr*), but many different categories and thus various types, such as: *baṣrī, bağl, qaṣ ṭābayya, qa jannur, qa jaʾfar, qa šurbē, qa ṣumrē, lūlū, mēdiq, kilwiskit, mijnaẓ, nāğal, qēṣarit, ēl mātarī, xār xnēẓī, qaḍḍuḥ, qašš, qaš fāras, qaš ḥābaš, qaš mqālaf, qaš xuršid,* and *xṣāb*.[15] The *jujube* (aka 'red date') is *knār*, while the yellow-golden date is *qērin*. Kumzari has singular terms for many parts of the date palm, such as *pīš* 'date palm frond or leaf', *līf* 'date palm root strands', *gurd* 'midrib of palm frond', *wagẓ* 'tip of a palm frond's midrib', and *qišʾan* 'date palm bark'.[16] *Pang* is used for the poker at the top of a palm tree, as well as for 'sword'. 'Date palm pollen' (*nābat*) is made from the 'male date palm' (*faḥl*). For irrigation in Khasab, plantations use a regular 'irrigation channel' (*indīyē/andīyē*) system as well as the *fālaj* 'channel' irrigation system used throughout Oman.

There are a number of environmental issues related to palm cultivation in Oman in general. The main issues that plague date palm production are a shortage of labour, the use of traditional methods of cultivation that are not as efficient as mechanical methods, and unsatisfactory post-harvest handling and marketing approaches. For example, in the traditional practice of

---

[15] *Qāqā* is how children refer to a 'date' in Kumzari.

[16] 'Bark' in general is *faqqaš*, a word which can also be used for the 'shell of an egg' or 'peeling skin'.

cultivation in Khasab, Kumzari villagers use basin irrigation, which is a low-cost method, but relatively less efficient than other irrigation methods, leading to more water loss from runoff and evaporation. Further, twenty-five percent of all dates produced in Oman is wasted every year (Al-Yahyai and Khan 2015, 9) due to poor quality, as a number of date growers are unaware of the rigorous export standards. Palm cultivation is also affected by diseases and pests. Dubas bug and red palm weevil are "the main biotic factors that affect date quality and yield in Oman" (Al Yahyai and Khan 2015). The word for 'date palm sickness' in Kumzari is *šēṣ*.

Dates in Kumzari can be described in various stages of growth and preservation. Beginning as *ḥābabō* 'tiny green date seeds', a date palm progresses to the stage of being a *sarm* 'sapling'. Some terms for dates at various stages include: *ğēt* 'young white date fruit', *king* 'ripening date', *arṭab* 'fresh date', *arma* 'a date in a preserved stage' and *ḥāšaf* 'dried-out dates'. A 'ream' or 'branch of dates' is *ōš*. The 'harvesting' (*gadda*) of dates and 'palm leaf cutting' (*šakasa*) are not the only labour related to the date palm tree, as Kumzari villagers in Khasab use the gathered palm leaves to create an assortment of essential structures, aids, and objects.

Many everyday objects in Khasab and Kumzar are fashioned from various parts of the palm tree. By 'braiding' (*suffū*), 'weaving' (*saffa*), and pounding the palm leaves, Kumzari women produce all kinds of 'palm work' (*suffit/tūrāṣ*), such as 'palm thatch' (*d'ān*), 'palm floor mat' (*smēt*), 'palm back support' (*ḥābul*), 'palm frond broom' (*mayšaṭṭa*), and 'palm fibres pounded into twine' (ḥakka). In Kumzari, a 'palm-frond shelter' is a *sirg*, whereas in Arabic these traditional airy summer homes constructed to escape the scorching heat are called *barasti* (or *arish*). These structures were traditionally used by the mountain dwellers of Kumzari who travelled to Khasab to harvest dates. Other popular date products include 'date syrup' (*dūš*), which is produced in a special 'date syrup basket' (*tak*). After the 'hot, dry weather' (*ḥēriq*) of summer, Kumzaris begin their 'autumn migration' (*ḥōṭir*) back to Kumzar. These eco-cultural coastal migrations (Dostal 1972) are a cultural adaptation to the seasonal changes of the climate and environment. Almost the entire population of Kumzar participates in these seasonal migrations.

10.0. Conclusion

As important as it is for Kumzari speakers to enjoy a sustainable future and for Kumzari to thrive as a language, it is equally important for the environment, animal species, and plant life in and around Kumzar to be protected and preserved. As the traditional stewards of the tip of the Musandam Peninsula, Kumzari speakers must be at the centre of any efforts to preserve the fragile ecosystems and biodiversity in and around Kumzar. The Kumzari language is symbiotically tied to the environment of Kumzar in its nuanced identification of animal and plant species, articulation of natural marine phenomenon, and understanding of specific weather patterns. Accordingly, the erosion of Kumzari as a language threatens not just the future of this unique language and community, but also the region's natural environment and non-human organisms.

Kumzari's biolinguistic diversity and Kumzar's biological diversity necessitate more rigorous ecological analyses as well as increased protection of its ecologies and coastographies. To halt the destruction of the natural environment and prevent the loss of Kumzari terms for the region's diverse plant and animal species and climate patterns, there is a pressing need for the people of Kumzar, along with eco-minded and ethical linguists, to work alongside biologists and ecologists to identify and preserve Musandam's biodiversity. Further cooperation might include nurturing sustainable, rather than destructive, tourist development, and pioneering technological advances, such as using wastewater to supply the nutrients necessary to produce algae and using the sugar-filled waste material from date farming as an organic energy source for the production of algae (Darley 2022) to create a circular economy.

Efforts to preserve the Kumzari language must also consider the needs of the people of Kumzar in relation to their environment. The ecological turn has enabled the humanities to "contribute to building a more ecological civilization where people meet their physical needs, their needs for wellbeing, and their need to find meaning, in ways which protect and enhance the ecosystems that life depends on" (Stibbe 2021a, 7). The pay for fishing (especially sardine fishing) is low, and due to commercial fishing, many local fish stocks have been exhausted. Thus, the livelihoods of Kumzar villagers must be secured, in addition to the ecosystems on which they depend to survive. Establishing the Musandam Peninsula as a Biosphere Reserve under UNESCO's Man and the Biosphere (MAB) Programme would help to support harmonious and sustainable interactions between biodiversity conservation efforts and the socio-economic well-being of Kumzari villagers.

The underwater environment of Kumzar is especially deserving of more ecological analysis. While we know limited terms for shells and coral, like *maḥḥar* 'oyster', *jō'ar* 'pearl', *gišr* 'coral', *dām* 'a type of coral', and words for some echinoderms, like 'sea cucumbers' (*kēr pāčak*) and 'sea urchins' (*lumba*), more research is needed to identify the shells and the flora of the seabed, most likely with the help of conchologists and malacologists. In fact, sea cucumber is a delicacy on the Musandam Peninsula, and sea urchins are the most abundant invertebrate in Musandam. Further, as the stars have always been central to navigation, researchers might inquire more into Kumzari celestial terminology, such as names of constellations—like *kandarkas* for 'Orion's belt'.

Additional research is needed to explore olfactory terminology related to nature. For instance, the verb *xalafa* is used to say something, namely water, 'smells bad'. Also deserving of further exploration is the use of certain materials in interactions with animals, such as 'birdlime' (*manṣab*), an adhesive used in trapping birds, and materials made from animals, such as 'fish oil wood sealant' (*ṣill*). Future studies may also identify medicinal plants (such as *barg* 'a medicinal leaf'), trees,[17] berries, and flora in general.

---

[17] Several trees have been identified by English speakers, such as *bādam* 'nut tree' and *ṣumr* 'a type of acacia tree', but more scientific identifications are needed.

Kumzari is not just a 'language' (*majma*) and socio-cultural-tribal-clan identity, but a way of coastal living—a way of 'being' in nature and the world. Thus, the preservation of Kumzari is as much an ontological concern as it is an environmental one. A language is not an object, but a human endeavour to "create new worlds" (Pennycook 2004). Linguistic analyses embedded in ecopsychology might further explore the psychological dimensions of Kumzari (O'Dell fc), the construction of subjectivity and understandings of self in relation to nature in Kumzari culture, and environmental ethics in traditional Kumzari culture. An ecopsychological analysis can also further uncover how ecocultural factors shape important aspects of Kumzari cognition and social interdependence. Similarly, further ecocritical analyses of Kumzari oral literature will likely reveal more about how the aqua environment of Kumzar is expressed and constructed in stories about the sea, such as fishing and sailing songs, folktales, wedding songs, *qāwals*, work songs, proverbs (*matal*), and lullabies. In passing down the Kumzari language to the youth of Kumzar, attention might also be paid to the central role of ecology in language education.

As environmental crises are reflected through language, more work is needed to excavate how the current environmental crises of Kumzar are being expressed in language and narratives. Furthermore, the impact of the COVID-19 'plague' (*dayit*) on the villagers and ecosystem of Kumzar is still unknown. However, the coronavirus crisis stands to produce "new stories and, some would argue, a new civilization that combines radical views on language, environment, and ecolinguistics" (Zhou 2021, 470) and is founded in bio-ecological awareness. As Stibbe (2021a, 2) explains, due to the global pandemic, "there has never been a more urgent time or greater opportunity to find new stories" for "[w]e are now in a position where the old stories are crumbling due to coronavirus and the increasingly harmful impacts of climate change and biodiversity loss." Now is the time for a radical embodied ecolinguistics (Steffensen and Cowley 2021) to lie the foundation for an ecologically minded future in Kumzar rooted in the bio-ecological awareness and eco-languaging of Kumzari. The future of Kumzari—and the abundant animal and plant species in Kumzar—depend on it.

References

Aboelezz, Mariam. 2022. 'Translating Piracy: On the Origin of the Arabic words Qurṣān/Qarṣanah'. *British Library/Qatar Foundation Partnership*. https://blogs.bl.uk/asian-and-african/2022/08/translating-piracy.html

Abram, David. 1996. *The Spell of the Sensuous: Perception and Language in a More-than-Human World*. New York: Vintage.

Agius, Dionisius. 2007. 'Decorative Motifs on Arabian Boats: Meaning and Identity.' In *Natural Resources and Cultural Connections of the Red Sea*, edited by Janet Starkey, Paul Starkey, and Tony Wilkinson, 101–10. Oxford: British Archaeological Reports International (Series 1661).

Aitchison, Charles Umpherston. 1929–1933. *Collection of Treaties, Engagements and Sanads Relating to India and Neighbouring Countries*. Vol. VII. Calcutta: Govt. of India Central Publications Branch.

Allday, Louis. 2014. 'The British in the Gulf: An Overview'. *Qatar Digital Library*. https://www.qdl.qa/en/british-gulf-overview

Almojil, Dareen. 2021. 'Local Ecological Knowledge of Fisheries Charts Decline of Sharks in Data-Poor Regions'. *Marine Policy* 132/3: 104638.

Alexander, Richard, and Arran Stibbe. 2014. 'From the Analysis of Ecological Discourse to the Ecological Analysis of Discourse'. *Language Sciences* 41: 104–10.

Al-Ghanim, Kaltham, and Janet C. E. Watson. 2021. 'Language and Nature in Southern and Eastern Arabia'. *European Journal of Multidisciplinary Studies* 6/1: 109–19.

Al-Jahdhami, Said. 2013. 'Kumzari of Oman: A Grammatical Analysis'. PhD dissertation, University of Florida.

Al-Jufaili, Saud Musallam, Adnan Rashid Al-Azri, and Sulaiman Salim Al-Shuaily. 2006. 'A Preliminary Investigation on the Omani Sardines and Anchovies Stock Fluctuation: Recommendations for Future Studies'. *Pakistan Journal of Biological Sciences* 9: 1073–82.

Al Jufaili, Saud, and Omar Al-Jahwari. 2011. 'The Omani Coastal Traditional Sardine Fishery 1994–2007: A Review'. *Journal of Agricultural and Marine Sciences* 16/1: 1–12.

Al-Kumzari, Ali H. A. 2009. 'Kumzārī Lexicon and Grammar Notes'. MA thesis. Ḥāratu Kumzāryan.

Al-Mahmoud, Abdulaziz. 2011. *Al-Qurṣān*. Doha: Bloomsbury Qatar Foundation Publishing.

———. 2013. *The Corsair*. Translated by Amira Noweira. Doha: Bloomsbury Qatar Foundation Publishing.

Al-Maktum, Shaykh Maniʾ ibn al-Shaykh Rashid. 'A Map of Pearl Banks in Persian Gulf' [13r] (1/2), British Library: India Office Records and Private Papers, IOR/R/15/1/616, f13, in Qatar Digital Library.
https://www.qdl.qa/archive/81055/vdc_100023403859.0x000019

Al Naqeeb, Khaldoun. 1987. *Society and State in the Gulf and Arab Peninsula*. Oxfordshire: Routledge.

Anonby, Erik J. 2008. 'Stress-induced Vowel Lengthening and Harmonization in Kumzari'. Paper presented at the *1st International Conference on Languages and Dialects in Iran*, University of Sistan and Baluchestan, 28–31 October.

———. 2010. 'Kumzarītī [Kumzari alphabet chart]'. MA thesis, Leiden University.

Anonby, Erik J., and Christina A. van der Wal Anonby. 2011. *Ktēb majma Kumzārī [Kumzari Dictionary]*. Khasab: Xanagho Kumzari.

Anonby, Erik J., and Pakzad Yousefian. 2011. *Adaptive Multilinguals: A Survey of Language on Larak Island*. Uppsala: Uppsala University Press.

Anonby, Erik, Simone Bettega, and Stephan Procházka. 2022. 'Demonstratives in Musandam Arabic: Distinctive Archaisms and Innovations'. *Arabica* 69/6: 675–702.

Anonby, Erik, and Abdul Qader Al Kumzari. Forthcoming. 'A Typology of Fish Names in Kumzari'. *Harvesting the Sea in Southeastern Arabia, vol. I*, edited by Janet C. E. Watson, Miranda J. Morris, and Erik Anonby. Cambridge: Cambridge Semitic Languages and Cultures.

Balfour, Edward. 1885. *The Cyclopaedia of India and of Eastern and Southern Asia*. Third Edition. London: B. Quaritch.

Balfour-Paul, Glen. 1994. *The End of Empire in the Middle East: Britain's Relinquishment of Power in Her Last Three Arab Dependencies*. Cambridge: Cambridge University Press.

Bang, Jorgen, and Wilhelm Trampe. 2014. 'Aspects of an Ecological Theory of Language'. *Language Sciences* 41: 83–92.

Bastardas-Boada, Albert. 2017. 'The Ecology of Language Contact: Minority and Majority Languages'. In *The Routledge Handbook of Ecolinguistics*, edited by Alwin Fill and Hermine Penz, 26–40. London: Routledge.

Bauman, Andrew, John Burt, David Feary, Elise Marquis, and Paolo Usseglio. 2010. 'Tropical Harmful Algal Blooms: An Emerging Threat to Coral Reef Communities?' *Marine Pollution Bulletin* 60: 2117–22.

Bayshak, Maryam S. 2002. 'Are there Traces of Sassanian in the Language of the Shihuh, and is Kumzari among the Affected Varieties? The Shihhi Dialect in the Light of Linguistic Science'. *Al-Khaleej* (Arabic edition) 8541: 12–17.

Belgrave, Charles. 1966. *The Pirate Coast*. London: G. Bell & Sons.

Bento, Rita, David A. Feary, Andrew S. Hoey, and John A. Burt. 2017. 'Settlement Patterns of Corals and other Benthos on Reefs with Divergent Environments and Disturbances Histories around the Northeastern Arabian Peninsula'. *Frontiers in Marine Science* 4.

Biddulph, John. 1907. *The Pirates of Malabar and an Englishwoman in India Two Hundred Years Ago*. London: Smith, Elder & Co.

Burke, Lauretta, Katie Reytar, Mark Spalding, and Allison Perry. 2011. 'Reefs at Risk, Revisited.' Washington, D.C.: World Resources Institute.

Burt, John, Hanneke Van Lavieren, and David A. Feary. 2014. 'Persian Gulf Reefs: An Important Asset for Climate Science in Urgent Need of Protection'. *Ocean Challenge* 20: 49–56.

Burt, John A., S. Coles, Hanneke van Lavieren, Oliver Taylor, Elayne Looker, and K. Samimi-Namin. 2016. 'Oman's Coral Reefs: A Unique Ecosystem Challenged by Natural and Man-related Stresses and in Need of Conservation'. *Marine Pollution Bulletin* 105/2: 498–506.

Calvet, Louis Jean. 2006. *Towards an Ecology of World Languages.* Translated by Andrew Brown. Cambridge: Polity Press.

Castelier, Sebastian, and Quentin Müller. 2017. 'Omani Fishermen Play their Part in Destructive Global Shark Trade'. *Middle East Eye,* April 18. https://www.middleeasteye.net/features/pictures-omani-fishermen-play-their-part-destructive-global-shark-trade

Castelier, Sebastian. 2020. 'Tracking the Global Fin Trade: Shark Fishing in Oman'. *Al Jazeera,* March 11. https://www.aljazeera.com/features/2020/3/11/tracking-the-global-fin-trade-shark-fishing-in-oman

Coles, Stephen L. 2003. 'Coral Species Diversity and Environmental Factors in the Arabian Gulf and the Gulf of Oman: A Comparison to the Indo-Pacific Region'. *Atoll Research Bulletin* 507.

Cook, Andrew S. 1990. *Survey of the Shores and Islands of the Persian Gulf 1820–1829.* Gerrards Cross: Archive Editions.

Couto, Hildo Honório do. 2014. 'Ecological Approaches in Linguistics: A Historical Overview'. *Language Sciences* 41: 122–28.

———. 2018. 'Ecosystemic Linguistics'. In *The Routledge Handbook of Ecolinguistics*, edited by Alwin Fill and Hermine Penz, 149–61. London: Routledge.

Crampton, Jeremy W., and Stuart Elden (eds). 2007. *Space, Knowledge, and Power: Foucault and Geography*. Aldershot, UK: Ashgate.

Crouzet, Guillemette. 2019. 'The British Empire in India, the Gulf Pearl and the Making of the Middle East'. *Middle Eastern Studies* 55/6: 864–78.

Darley, George Charles. 2022. 'Algae the Key as KAUST Seaweed Biotech Aims to Boost Kingdom's Fisheries'. *Arab News*, February 8. https://www.arab-news.com/node/2020451/business-economy

Davies, Charles E. 1997. *The Blood Red Arab Flag: An Investigation into Qasimi Piracy, 1797–1820*. Exeter: University of Exeter Press.

Dawdy, Shannon Lee, and Joe Bonni. 2012. 'Towards a General Theory of Piracy'. *Anthropological Quarterly* 85/3: 673–99.

Dent, Felix, and Shelley Clarke. 2015. 'State of the Global Market for Shark Products'. *FAO Fisheries and Aquaculture Technical Paper No. 590*. Rome: Food and Agriculture Organization of the United Nations. https://www.fao.org/3/i4795e/i4795e.pdf

Dickey, Christopher. 1986. 'Va. Firm Has Big Role in Oman'. *Washington Post*. March 24.

https://www.washingtonpost.com/archive/politics/1986/03/24/va-firm-has-big-role-in-oman/5b5df7f9-a476-4dee-be29-717ac6480979

Dostal, Walter. 1972. 'The Shihuh of Northern Oman: A Contribution to Cultural Ecology'. *The Geographical Journal* 138 (Jan–Dec): 1–7.

Dubuisson, Patricia R. 1975. 'Qasimi Piracy and the General Treaty of Peace (1820)'. MA thesis, McGill University.

———. 1978. 'Qāsimi Piracy and the General Treaty of Peace (1820)'. *Arabian Studies* 4: 55.

Eliasson, Stig. 2015. 'The Birth of Language Ecology: Interdisciplinary Influences in Einar Haugen's *The Ecology of Language*'. *Language Sciences* 50: 78–92.

Fill, Alwin. 2001. 'Ecolinguistics: State of the Art 1998'. In *The Ecolinguistics Reader: Language, Ecology and Environment*, edited by Alwin Fill and Peter Mühlhäusler, 43–53. London: Continuum.

Finke, Peter. 2018. 'Transdisciplinary Linguistics: Ecolinguistics as a Pacemaker into a New Scientific Age'. In *The Routledge Handbook of Ecolinguistics*, edited by Alwin Fill and Hermine Penz, 406–19. London: Routledge.

'FO 464/42: 1955 [Jan 01–1955 Dec 31]: Arabia: Buraimi Arbitration Case; Miscellaneous Documents, Volume 3'. Arabia's Gulf Digital Archives.
https://www.agda.ae/en/catalogue/tna/fo/464/42

Fukuda, Sadashi. 1992. 'Omani Maritime Trade and the Indian Residents of Muscat in the 18th and the Beginning of the 19th Centuries'. *Orient* 28: 1–16.

Ghidoni, Alessandro, and Tom Vosmer. 2021. 'Boats and Ships of the Arabian Gulf and the Sea of Oman Within an Archaeological, Historical and Ethnographic Context'. In *The Arabian Seas: Biodiversity, Environmental Challenges and Conservation Measures*, edited by Laith A. Jawad, 957–89. Cham, Switzerland: Springer.

Graham, Gerard S. 1967. *Great Britain in the Indian Ocean: A Study of Maritime Enterprise 1810–1850*. Oxford: Clarendon Press.

Halliday, Michael Alexander Kirkwood. 2001 [1990]. 'New Ways of Meaning: The Challenge to Applied Linguistics'. In *The Ecolinguistics Reader: Language, Ecology and Environment*, edited by Alwin Fill and Peter Mühlhäusler, 175–202. London: Continuum.

Harré, Rom, Jens Brockmeier, and Peter Mühlhäusler. 1999. *Greenspeak: A Study of Environmental Discourse*. London: Routledge.

Haugen, Einar. 1972. *The Ecology of Language*. Palo Alto, CA: Stanford University Press.

———. 1987. *Blessings of Babel: Bilingualism and Language Planning—Problems and Pleasures*. Berlin: De Gruyter Mouton.

Hawley, Donald. 1970. *The Trucial States*. London: George Allen & Unwin Ltd.

Hightower, Victoria Penziner. Forthcoming. 'The Single Story: Reclaiming the Narrative About Sea Violence in the Lower Gulf Emirates'. In *Muslim Storytelling, Seafaring, and Travel Writing the Arabian Seas, the Persian Gulf, and the Indian Ocean*, edited by Nuha Alshaar, Beate Ulrike La Sala, and David Wilmsen. Leiden: Brill.

Holes, Clive. 2004. *Modern Arabic: Structures, Functions, and Varieties*. Washington, D.C.: Georgetown University Press.

Hopper, Matthew S. 2015a. 'Antislavery and Empire: Paradoxes of Liberation in the Western Indian Ocean.' In *Slaves of One Master: Globalization and Slavery in Arabia in the Age of Empire*, 142–80. New Haven, CT: Yale University Press.

———. 2015b. 'Pearls, Slaves, and Fashion'. In *Slaves of One Master: Globalization and Slavery in Arabia in the Age of Empire*, 80–104. New Haven, CT: Yale University Press.

International Ecolinguistics Association. 2020. https://www.ecolinguistics-association.org

Jabado, Rima W., Saif M. Al Ghais, Waleed Hamza, and Aaron Henderson. 2014. 'The Shark Fishery in the United Arab Emirates: An Interview Based Approach to Assess the Status of Sharks'. *Aquatic Conservation: Marine and Freshwater Ecosystems* 25/6: 800–16.

Jabado, Rima W., Saif M. Al Ghais, Waleed Hamza, and Mahmood S. Shivji. 2015. 'Shark Diversity in the Arabian/Persian Gulf Higher than Previously Thought: Insights based on Species Composition of Shark Landings in the United Arab Emirates'. *Marine Biodiversity* 45/4: 719–31.

Jabado, Rima W. et al. 2015. 'The Trade in Sharks and their Products in the United Arab Emirates'. *Biological Conservation* 181: 190–98.

Jabado, Rima W. et al. 2018a. 'Troubled Waters: Threats and Extinction Risk of the Sharks, Rays and Chimaeras of the Arabian Sea and Adjacent Waters'. *Fish and Fisheries* 19: 1043–62.

Jabado, Rima W. et al. 2018b. 'Low Abundance of Sharks and Rays in Baited Remote Underwater Video Surveys in the Arabian Gulf'. *Scientific Reports* 8: 15597.

James, William. 2002 [1827]. *The Naval History of Great Britain, Volume 5, 1808–1811*. London: Conway Maritime Press.

Jayakar, Atmaram S. G. 1902. 'The Shahee Dialect of Arabic'. *Journal of the Bombay Branch of the Royal Asiatic Society* 21: 246–77.

Kelly, John Barrett. 1968. *Britain and the Persian Gulf, 1795–1880*. Oxford: Clarendon Press.

Kleinen, John, and Manon Osseweijer (eds.). 2010. *Pirates, Ports, and Coasts in Asia: Historical and Contemporary Perspectives*. Singapore: ISEAS-Yusof Ishak Institute.

Kostiner, Joseph. 2009. *Conflict and Cooperation in the Gulf Region*. New York: Springer.

Kravchenko, Alexander. 2016. 'Two Views on Language Ecology and Ecolinguistics'. *Language Sciences* 54: 102–13.

Li, Jia, Sune Vork Steffensen, and Guowen Huang. 2020. 'Rethinking Ecolinguistics from a Distributed Language Perspective'. *Language Sciences* 80: 101277.

London, British Library, 'Trigonometrical Plan of the Backwater at Ras Al Khyma'. By Lieut. J. M. Guy, drawn by M. Houghton. IOR/X/3685.

London, British Library, 'Trigonometrical Survey of Core Alladeid on the Arabian side of the Gulf of Persia. By Lieuts J. M. Guy and G. B. Brucks, H. C. Marine. Drawn by Lieut. M. Houghton, H.C.M.' IOR/X/3693.

London, British Library, 'Trigonometrical Plan of the Harbour of El Biddah on the Arabian Side of the Persian Gulf. By Lieuts J. M. Guy and G. B. Brucks, H. C. Marine. Drawn by Lieut. M. Houghton'. IOR/X/3694.

London, British Library, 'Survey of the Western Shore of the Persian Gulf in 1820/21 by Captain Philip Maughan and Lieutenants John Michael Guy and George Barnes Brucks'. IOR/F/4/676/18677.

London, British Library, 'File 2902/1916: Treaties and Engagements between the British Government and the Chiefs of the Arabian Coast of the Persian Gulf'. IOR/L/PS/10/606. Qatar Digital Library.

Lorimer, John Gordon. 'Gazetteer of the Persian Gulf Oman and Central Arabia: Kumzar'. *Gazetteer of Arabia Vol. I* [645] (694/1050). London: British Library (India Office Records and Private Papers). IOR/L/MIL/17/16/2/1, in Qatar Digital Library. https://www.qdl.qa/archive/81055/vdc_100023909214.0x00005f

Malcolm, John. 1828. *Sketches of Persia, From the Journals of a Traveller in the East.* 1st edition. London: J. Murray.

McDonald, Kevin. 'European Piracy in the Indian Ocean'. In *Oxford Research Encyclopedia of Asian History*. Oxford: Oxford University Press. https://oxfordre.com/asianhistory/view/10.1093/acrefore/9780190277727.001.0001/acrefore-9780190277727-e-679

McKenzie, Robin. 1997. 'Downriver to Here: Geographically Spatial Deictics in Aralle-Tabulahan (Sulawesi)'. In *Referring to*

Space: Studies in Austronesian and Papuan Languages, edited by Gunter Senft, 39–51. Oxford: Oxford University Press.

Middleton, Drew. 1986. 'On Vital Strait, Omani "Traffic Cops"'. *New York Times*, December 22nd.

Moyse-Bartlett, Hubert. 1966. *The Pirates of Trucial Oman*. London: Macdonald.

Mühlhäusler, Peter. 2019. 'Revisiting Greenspeak'. In *The Second Cognitive Revolution: A Tribute to Rom Harré*, edited by Bo Allesøe Christensen, 81–88. Switzerland: Springer Nature.

Mühlhäusler, Peter, and Adrian Peace. 2006. 'Environmental Discourses'. *Annual Review of Anthropology* 35, 457–79.

Notarbartolo di Sciara, Giuseppe, and Rima Jabado. 2021. 'Sharks and Rays of the Arabian Sea and Adjacent Waters'. In *The Arabian Seas: Biodiversity, Environmental Challenges and Conservation Measures*, edited by Laith Jawad, 443–77. Cham, Switzerland: Springer.

O'Dell, Emily Jane. 2020. 'Yesterday is Not Gone: Memories of Slavery in Zanzibar and Oman in Memoirs, Fiction, and Film'. *Journal of Global Slavery* 5: 357–401.

'Oman Notices to Mariners.' 2016 (January 28). p. 9 (English, Arabic). https://members.mod.gov.om/ar-OM/RNO/HydrographicOceanicServices/Documents/notice2016/mon1/OMAN%20N2M%2001-16.pdf#page=20

Onley, James. 2004. 'The Politics of Protection in the Gulf: The Arab Rulers and the British Resident in the Nineteenth Century'. *New Arabian Studies* 6: 30–92.

———. 2009a. 'Britain and the Gulf Shaikdoms, 1820–1971: The Politics of Protection'. *CIRS Occasional Paper No. 4*. Doha:

Center for International and Regional Studies Georgetown University School of Foreign Service in Qatar.

———. 2009b. 'The Politics of Protection: The Arabian Gulf Rulers and the Pax Britannica in the Nineteenth Century'. *LIWA: Journal of the National Center for Documentation and Research* 1/1: 25–89.

Owfi, Fereidoon, Mahnaz Rabbaniha, S. Al-Obeid Mehana, and Faezeh Mahichi. 2015. 'Biodiversity and Distribution Patterns of Coral Reef Ecosystems in ROPME Sea Area (Inner part: Persian Gulf-Iranian waters)'. *Survey in Fisheries Sciences* 1: 21–26.

Palmer, Bill. 2002. 'Absolute Spatial Reference and the Grammaticalisation of Perceptually Salient Phenomena'. In *Representing Space in Oceania: Culture in Language and Mind*, edited by Giovanni Bennardo, 107–57. Canberra: Pacific Linguistics.

Pearson, Michael N. 1981. *Coastal Western India: Studies from the Portuguese Records.* Cambridge: Cambridge University Press.

Pennycook, Alastair. 2004. 'Language Policy and the Ecological Turn'. *Language Policy* 3/3: 213–39.

Peszko, Magdalena. 'Important Work: The British 1820 Survey that Charted the Gulf for the First Time'. *Qatar Digital Library.* https://www.qdl.qa/en/important-work-british-1820-survey-charted-gulf-first-time

Prange, Sebastian R. 2013. 'The Contested Sea: Regimes of Maritime Violence in the Pre-Modern Indian Ocean'. *Journal of Early Modern History* 17/1: 9–33.

Al-Qāsimī, Sulṭān Muḥammad. 2016. *The Myth of Arab Piracy in the Gulf*. London: Routledge.

Richardson, Neil, and Marcia S. Dorr. 2003. *The Craft Heritage of Oman*. Vol. 2. Dubai: Motivate Publishing.

Roche, Gerald J. 2022. 'The World's Languages in Crisis (Redux): Toward a Radical Reimagining for Global Linguistic Justice'. *Emancipations: A Journal of Critical Social Analysis* 1/2, Article 8.

Rubin, Aaron D. 2010. *The Mehri Language of Oman*. Leiden: Brill.

Sato, Shohei. 2016. 'Pirates' Turned Sovereign States, 1819–1964'. In *Britain and the Formation of the Gulf States: Embers of Empire*. Manchester: Manchester University Press.

Sheline, Annelle. 2020. 'Oman's Smooth Transition Doesn't Mean its Neighbors Won't Stir Up Trouble'. *Foreign Policy*, January 23. https://foreignpolicy.com/2020/01/23/omans-smooth-transition-saudi-arabia-uae-mbs-stir-up-trouble

Sheppard, Charles. 2000. *Seas at the Millennium an Environmental Evaluation*. Warwick: University of Warwick.

Skjærvø, Prods Oktor. 1989. 'Languages of Southeast Iran: Lārestānī, Kumzārī, Baškardī'. In *Compendium Linguarum Iranicarum*, edited by Rüdiger Schmitt, 363–69. Wiesbaden: Ludwig Reichart.

Souter, David, Serge Planes, Jérémy Wicquart, et al. (eds). 2021. 'Status of Coral Reefs of the World: 2020 Report'. *Global Coral Reef Monitoring Network (GCRMN) and International Coral Reef Initiative (ICRI)*. https://doi.10.59387/WOTJ9184

Starkey, David. 1990. *British Privateering Enterprise in the Eighteenth Century*. Exeter Maritime Studies. Liverpool: Liverpool University Press.

———. 1994. 'Pirates and Markets'. In *The Market for Seamen in the Age of Sail*, edited by Lewis R. Fischer, 59–80. Liverpool: Liverpool University Press.

Steffensen, Sune Vork. 2007. 'Language, Ecology and Society: An Introduction to Dialectical Linguistics'. In *Language, Ecology and Society: A Dialectical Approach*, edited by Jorgen Christian Bang and Jorgen Døør, 3–31. London: Continuum.

Steffensen, Sune Vork, and Stephen Cowley. 2021. 'Thinking on Behalf of the World: Radical Embodied Ecolinguistics'. In *The Routledge Handbook of Cognitive Linguistics*, edited by Xu Wen and John R. Taylor, 723–36. London: Routledge.

Steffensen, Sune Vork, and Alwin Fill. 2014. 'Ecolinguistics: The State of the Art and Future Horizons'. *Language Sciences* 41: 6–25.

Stibbe, Arran. 2012. 'Ecolinguistics and Globalization'. In *The Handbook of Language and Globalization*, edited by Nikolas Coupland, 406–25. Singapore: Wiley-Blackwell.

———. 2014. 'An Ecolinguistic Approach to Critical Discourse Studies'. *Critical Discourse Studies* 11/1: 117–28.

———. 2021a. *Ecolinguistics: Language, Ecology and the Stories We Live by*. 2nd edition. London: Routledge.

———. 2021b. 'Ecolinguistics as a Transdisciplinary Movement and a Way of Life'. In *Crossing Borders, Making Connections: Interdisciplinarity in Linguistics*, edited by Allison Burkette and Tamara Warhol, 71–88. Boston: De Gruyter Mouton.

Story, G. M., William J. Kirwin and J. D. A. Widdowson. 1990. *Dictionary of Newfoundland English*. Toronto: University of Toronto.

Suzuki, Hideaki. 2018. 'Chapter 3: The Making of the "Joasmee" Pirates: A Relativist Reconsideration of the Qawāsimi Piracy in the Persian Gulf'. In *In the Name of the Battle against Piracy*, edited by Atsushi Ota, 69–96. Leiden: Brill.

Sweet, Louise. 1964. 'Piracy or Polities? Arab Societies of the Persian or Arabian Gulf, 18th Century'. *Ethnohistory* 11/3: 265–76.

Teller, Matthew. 2014. 'The Hardship Posting to End All Hardship Postings'. *BBC News*. 25 October. https://www.bbc.com/news/blogs-magazine-monitor-29761017

Thomas, Bertram. 1929. 'The Musandam Peninsula and Its People the Shihuh'. *Journal of the Royal Central Asian Society* 16/1: 71–86.

———. 1930. 'The Kumzari Dialect of the Shihuh Tribe (Musandam), Arabia, and a Vocabulary'. *Journal of the Royal Asiatic Society* 62/4: 785–854.

———. 1931. *Alarms and Excursions in Arabia*. London: George Allen & Unwin Ltd.

UNEP: United Nations Environmental Programme. 2017. 'Global Environment Outlook: Environment for Development'. Nairobi: UNEP.

van der Wal Anonby, Christina. 2010. 'The Mixed Persian/Arabic Heritage of Kumzari'. *Leiden Institute for Area Studies Seminar*. Leiden: Leiden University.

———. 2013. 'Traces of Arabian in Kumzari'. *Forty-sixth Seminar for Arabian Studies (London, 26–28 July 2013)*. London: The British Museum.

———. 2014. 'Traces of Arabian in Kumzari'. *Proceedings of the Seminar for Arabian Studies* 44: 137–46. http://www.jstor.org/stable/43782857

———. 2015. *A Grammar of Kumzari: A Mixed Perso-Arabian Language of Oman*. Leiden: Leiden University.

———. 2019. 'Kumzari'. In *The Languages and Linguistics of Western Asia: An Areal Perspective*, edited by Geoffrey Haig and Geoffrey Khan, 625–58. Berlin: De Gruyter Mouton.

Verne, Jules. 1895. *Captain Antifer*. New York: R. F. Fenno.

Vosmer, Tom. 1997. 'Indigenous Fishing Craft of Oman'. *The International Journal of Nautical Archaeology* 26/3: 217–35.

Weismann, Nobert, Eric Staples, Alessandro Ghidoni, Tom Vosmer, Piotr Dziamski, and Lilli Haar. 2014. 'The Battīl and Zārūqah of Musandam, Oman'. *International Journal of Nautical Archaeology* 43/2: 413–35.

Willis, John Thabiti. 2016. 'A Visible Silence: Africans in the History of Pearl Diving in Dubai, UAE'. In *Museums in Arabia*, edited by Karen Exell and Sarina Wakefield, 34–50. London: Routledge.

Wilson, Arnold Talbot, Sir. 1928. *The Persian Gulf: An Historical Sketch from the Earliest Times to the Beginning of the Twentieth Century*. Oxford: Clarendon Press.

———. 1954. *The Persian Gulf*. London: Routledge.

Woodbridge, David, Mariam Aboelezz, and Tahani Abu Shaban. 2021. '"Piracy" in the India Office Records:

Some Historical Context'. *Qatar Digital Library*. https://www.qdl.qa/en/piracy-india-office-records-some-historical-context.

World Resources Institute. 2020. 'Coral Reefs: Persian Gulf and Gulf of Oman: Importance, Status and Outlook for Coral Reefs.' *Resource Watch.* https://resourcewatch.org/dashboards/coral-reefs-persian-gulf-and-gulf-of-oman

Al-Yahyai, Rashid, and Mumtaz Khan. 2015. 'Date Palm Status and Perspective in Oman'. In *Date Palm Genetic Resources and Utilization*, edited by Jameel am Al-Khayri, Shri Mohan Jain, and Dennis V Johnson, 207–40. New York: Springer.

Zhou, Wenjuan. 2017. 'Ecolinguistics: Toward a New Harmony'. *Language Sciences* 62: 124–38.

———. 2021. 'Ecolinguistics: A Half-century Overview'. *Journal of World Languages* 7/3: 481–86.

Zwemer, Samuel M. 1902. 'Three Journeys in Northern Oman'. *The Geographical Journal* 19: 54–64.

THREE SHEHRET TEXTS: BUILDING WITH FLORA*

Janet C. E. Watson, Andrea Boom, Amer al-Kathiri, and Miranda J. Morris

1.0. Introduction

Traditionally the people of Dhofar enjoyed a close relationship with the natural world (Watson and Boom, in press). Local flora was used for food, fodder, building, medicines, and beautification. Several factors have impacted the use of local materials for traditional activities. Urbanisation has increased by over 70 percent since the 1970s: with many no longer living and working in the natural environment, MSAL community members have

---

* We thank our funders, the Leverhulme Trust, for supporting the Documentation and Ethnolinguistic Analysis of Modern South Arabian project (RPG-2012-599) from 2013 to 2016, during which time the texts presented in this chapter were collected, and for funding a Major Research Fellowship (MRF-2018-121) for Watson in 2019–2023, during which time the texts were transcribed and translated and the chapter was written; ELAR for archiving the texts; the Commonwealth Scholarship Commission for funding the second author's PhD; our consultants, Azad Musallam Ali al-Kathiri, Ahmad Suhayl Hardan, Mhud Saeed Ayrun, Said Baquir, Saeed al-Mahri, Umm Said, and Umm Muhammad; and an anonymous reviewer of this volume.

become alienated from a once intimate knowledge of the local ecology; the development of towns has involved building with new materials, including cement, breeze blocks and plastic; and the natural environment has itself changed as a result of overgrazing, changes in the monsoon rains patterns, and climate change. Recent research has shown a 33 percent decrease in vegetation cover in Dhofar between 1978 and 2018, caused to a significant degree by increased livestock herd sizes (Ball and Tzanopoulos 2020): between 1982 and 2012, populations of cattle, camels, and goats increased by at least 275 percent, 170 percent, and 96 percent, respectively (Ball et al. 2020). The texts presented in this chapter speak of a world that was once the norm in Dhofar and show a depth of local knowledge that younger generations of MSAL speakers no longer possess. Our aim in this paper is to present these unrehearsed texts as evidence of such local expertise and of the collaborative ways in which people worked in the hope that future research in linguistic anthropology and social geography will investigate the extent to which legacy linguistic material can assist in re-establishing close links between humans and the local ecology.

1.1. The Texts and the Speakers

For this chapter, we selected three texts describing the construction and materials involved in building shelters that had been collected during the Leverhulme-funded *Documentation and Ethnolinguistic Analysis of Modern South Arabian* (DEAMSA) (RPG-2012-599). The Shehret archive is hosted, along with archives of Mehri, Ḥarsūsi, Hobyōt, and Baṭḥari, by ELAR and the audio of the texts can be accessed by typing the file name, provided here at the beginning of each text, into the search box at the link: www.elararchive.org. It is hoped that further work will be conducted both by us and by others on the audio and audio-visual texts collected during the DEAMSA project. The texts examined here were recorded on Olympus LS-11 digital audio recorders in Dhofar in lossless wav. format 44.1 kHz. The speakers, noted by code names, are members of three different tribes: Shahri (J004), al-Kathiri (J019), and Hakli (J020). J004 was in his late 30s, J019 in his 50s, and J020 in his early 40s at the time of recording. J004 lives in the central mountains in Halkot; J019 lives in, and was raised around, Jufa, in Eastern Dhofar; J020 was raised in Gabgabt in the central mountains, but during his adult life has spent significant periods around Dhalkut towards the Yemeni border with Oman. J020's speech patterns, however, are closer to those of Central Shehret than Western Shehret; thus, he has /b/ rather than /w/ as cognate of historical *w. None of the speakers reported speaking or hearing difficulties and the speech of all was considered by other Shehret speakers, including the third author, to be representative of the language.

Transcription was conducted using the free-download annotation tools *ELAN* and *Praat* (Boersma and Weenink 2017). The texts were transcribed from the audio in broad phonemic transcription in *ELAN* and then vowel qualities and stress were checked in *Praat*. This means that words are not transcribed in their lexeme form, but in their contextual form, resulting in occasional differing vowels and stress marks across different tokens of the same lexeme. Stress marks are given as acute accents on stressed vowels where words have more than one vowel. A forward slash (/) indicates a pause in the text.

The first and fourth authors conducted the transcription and translation in consultation with the third author. The second author was responsible for §2.0. Descriptions of the flora mentioned in the texts were taken from Miller and Morris (1988) and from our consultants during fieldwork conducted as part of the second author's PhD study. The Latin botanical terms were taken predominantly from Miller and Morris (1988) and checked against *Plants of the World Online* (2022). Where particular flora had traditional uses beyond building, these are mentioned in §2.0.

1.2. Shehret Phonemic Inventory

The consonantal inventory for the Central and Eastern varieties of Shehret we examine is given in Table 1 (overleaf). There are three particularly interesting points regarding the consonant system of Shehret within Modern South Arabian: the alveolo-palatal fricatives, /š̃, ṣ̃, ž̃/, which are produced with salient lip protrusion (Bellem and Watson 2017) and are the cognates of the post-alveolar fricatives, /š, ṣ, ž/, in the other Modern South Arabian languages; the voiced lateral /ź/, which most frequently occurs as an allophone of /l/, but may also function as a separate phoneme, as in *nuź* 'indigo'; and the pre-aspirated sonorants, /ʰl, ʰm, ʰn, ʰr/, which occur in the offset to word-final stressed syllables in a

Table 1: Shehret consonantal phoneme table

	labial	dental	alveolar	post-alveolar	alveolo-palatal	palatal	velar	uvular	pharyngeal	glottal
plosive	b		t d ṭ				k g¹ ḳ			
fricative	f	ṯ ḏ ṯ̣	s z ṣ	š	s̃ z̃ ṣ̃			x ġ	ḥ ʕ	h ʔ
lateral fricative			ś ź ṣ́							
lateral sonorant			ʰl l							
nasal	ʰm m		ʰn n							
rhotic			ʰr r							
glide	*w²					y				

closed set of function words and a few content words (Watson et al. 2023). Restricted to Central and Eastern varieties of Shehret (Al-Maʕšani 2014), the pre-aspirated sonorants lose their breathiness in utterance-medial position, particularly but not exclusively, before vowels or before 'unbreathed' (emphatic or voiced) consonants (Watson et al. 2023). The sonorant portion of both pre-aspirated and non-pre-aspirated sonorants is typically silent in utterance-final position (Watson et al., in press). The sets of

---

[1] Among some speakers in East and Central Dhofar, /g/ has the reflex /ʤ/, transcribed in the texts below as /j/.

[2] w is a historical phoneme in Central and Eastern Shehret, hence *w in this table.

function and content words with breathy sonorants are given below in Tables 2 and 3.

Table 2: Shehret function words with final pre-aspirated sonorants

Words	Gloss
aġá^{h}l	'below'
bū^{h}n	'here'
ḏa^{h}n ~ ḏo^{h}n ~ ḏohú^{h}n	'this (M)'
ḏi^{h}n ~ ḏihú^{h}n	'this (F)'
ḏokú^{h}n	'that (M)'
hu^{h}n	'there'
iźá^{h}n ~ iźó^{h}n ~ iźohú^{h}n	'these'
iźokú^{h}n	'those'
lḥokú^{h}n	'there'
mənhú^{h}m	'of them (M)'
mənkú^{h}m	'of you (MPL)'
mənsέ^{h}n	'of them (F)'
mu^{h}n	'who'
nḥa^{h}n	'we'
olohú^{h}n	'over there'
sε^{h}n	'they (F)'
šu^{h}m	'they (M)'
tε^{h}n	'you (FPL)'
tu^{h}m	'you (MPL)'
ṭa^{h}n	'like this'

Table 3: Shehret content words with final pre-aspirated sonorants

Words	Gloss
ʕi^{h}n	'eye; source'
dʕi^{h}n	'areas of rocky plain'
ḏo^{h}r	'blood'
egmí^{h}l	'the camels'
ε^{h}r	'land (as opposed to sea)'
ḥa^{h}l	'time; pressed oil'
ḳu^{h}n	'horn; mountain peak'
mġe^{h}r	'frankincense trees'
ri^{h}m	'tall; long'
sε^{h}m	'poison'
ṣo^{h}r	'Sur [place name]'
śḥε^{h}r	'green mountains'
ṭi^{h}m	'garlic'
yu^{h}m	'day; sun'

Shehret has a large number of vowels in comparison to Mehri, Ḥarsūsi, Baṭḥari, and Hobyōt; however, several of the surface vowels are allophones of other vowels. The short vowels are *i*, *e*, *ɛ*, *ə*, *a*, *o*, and *u*, of which [ə] is generally restricted to unstressed syllables, [i] and [u] are frequently allophones of /e/ and /o/, respectively, in the environment of nasals, and [a] is frequently an allophone of /ɛ/ (Rubin 2014; Dufour 2016) in the environment of back consonants. The long vowels *ī*, *ē*, *ɛ̄*, *ā*, *ō*, *ɔ̄*, and *ū* occur phonemically in loan words and a few native words, and may result from sibilant–V(–guttural) or liquid–vowel metathesis, or from elision of intervocalic /b, m, y, *w/. Where intervocalic /m/ is elided, the resulting long vowel is nasalised. This is represented in the texts below with a superscript tilde, as in *ĩ*. Non-phonemic utterance-final post-consonantal vowels (usually [ɛ]~[e]) are noted in the text when they occur. Notes are provided in the first text in particular for interesting phonetic features: utterance-final post-consonantal vowels, possibly to ensure the consonant is sounded in the case of final sonorants; the realisation of utterance-medial words with final pre-aspirated sonorants; the glottalisation of final non-pre-aspirated sonorants in utterance-final position; silent utterance-final sonorants; and pre-glottalisation of 'unbreathed' obstruents.

2.0. Traditional Use of Flora for Building in Dhofar

This section describes the vegetation used in building two types of shelters: those for humans (*stɔ́rta*) and those for livestock (*dĩ́ṣáf*). It begins with a brief explanation of the data followed by a description of the process of building the shelters and goes on to describe the plants and trees used for building. Numbers in round brackets refer to line numbers in the texts in §3.0.

The recordings describe the process of constructing buildings and which plants were used. The Shehret plant names were cross-checked with one of our older female Shehret language consultants and some of the information about how they are used also comes from her. The Latin names and descriptions of uses of the plants are from Miller and Morris (1988) and *Plants of the World Online* (*POWO*) (2022). Classification was again cross-referenced through a public international image database; while this is not scientific validation, it does indicate broad acceptance of the botanical nomenclature.

Traditional houses were called *strit*, plural *stɔ́rta* in Shehret. They were circular buildings with walls made of stones, about the height of a man (J020 1.17). A hole was dug for the support pillar, *nṣəbét*, plural *nṣɛb* (1.19), made from tree trunks (1.20). This was stabilised using stones (1.23) and plastered with clay (1.48). For larger *strit* buildings there were more than one of these pillars (1.21). The roof was made from crossbeams, *mšábkəf* (1.8; J019 2.5), interwoven and layered with a variety of other plants and materials (1.36–37) to keep out rain during the monsoon period, *xorf,* and to provide shade the rest of the year (1.38). There were variations in how the houses were built (1.40)—some plants used are more readily available in some regions than in others. However, the general pattern of a circular building with a thatched roof supported by one or more roof-bearing pillars was universal across Dhofar except at the east end of the coastal plain. The ruins of buildings for people and livestock byres can still be found in Dhofar today. Our consultant told us that the way these were built meant they could last a lifetime, were very well insulated, and were well-suited to the needs of the people.

The plants used depended somewhat on whether the *strit* was to be built on the sea-facing slopes, the coastal plain, or on the plateau above the fog forests. The following is a description of the plants mentioned in the texts, their Shehret name, their botanical name in Latin, where they grow in Dhofar, how they were used in the construction of buildings and finally, some other notable uses the plants had.

> **muṭín**—wild olive; *Olea europaea* (Miller and Morris 1988, 216; also for further uses)

Wild olive was once plentiful on the sea-facing slopes of the escarpment mountains, but over-harvesting has led to a steep decline in numbers. The tree was regularly harvested to produce the support beam, *nṣɛb* (2.3), and the roof beams, *mšábkəf* (2.5), of shelters (cf. also Tabook 1997, 36–37). It was considered the best wood available for this type of work, but grows only on the southern slopes of the escarpment, so would have been substituted for other wood in regions to the north. The wood was dried by tempering it in embers to remove the bark (2.14), which made it more resistant to insects.

In addition to being used for *strit* building, wild olive was used to make herding staffs (*xóṭrók*, plural *xaṭérək*) (Tabook 1997, 38), and the ashes from burning the wood were used as fertiliser. Bees love the tree's flowers, and the resulting honey was highly prized. Cultivated varieties of this tree produce olives, but the trees in Dhofar do not produce edible olives; only goats eat their fruit.

> *soġót*—*Anogeissus dhofarica* syn. *Terminalia dhofarica*[3] (Miller and Morris 1988, 102)

Anogeissus dhofarica is endemic to Dhofar. Historically it has been the dominant species in the escarpment forests and is still prolific today. In the past, the wood of this tree would be prepared by drying for two to three months then soaking through the monsoon season and drying again. After this, the bark would be removed and it would be ready for use as support pillars, *nṣɛb* (2.5), for a *strit* building or as crossbeams, *mšábkəf* (2.11), for the roof. Tabook (1997, 62) describes the green branches of *soġót* being used for building the roofs of shelters as well.

One of our consultants describes this tree as the 'miracle tree' because it has so many medicinal and practical uses. It is still used today as medicine and as a cleansing wash, particularly for women. This tree has traditionally also been a very important livestock fodder, especially leading into the monsoon season, when grazing is scarce. It was also used for making tools.

> *xĩr*—*Ormocarpum dhofarense* (Miller and Morris 1988, 172)

This shrub is endemic to Dhofar and can be found both on the sea-facing slopes of the escarpment and in some north-flowing wadis. It was traditionally used in *strit* construction for the curved doors and as the slim, whippy branches, *śírín*, woven into the roof (3.10). It was also used in construction of summer shelters of

---

[3] This tree is categorised as *Terminalia* by POWO (2022), but according to Said Baquir (p.c.), the people of Dhofar still regularly refer to it as *Anogeissus*.

bowed branches covered with cloth (1.52) because the branches are long and supple. This shrub has also been an important fodder in the past.

ġárád—Grewia bicolor (Miller and Morris 1988, 284)

This shrub grows throughout the escarpment mountains and around permanent water sources in the drier areas. Similar to *xĩr*, *Ormocarpum dhofarense*, this shrub has long, supple branches used for making doors and weaving into the roofs of *strit* buildings.

The branches were also traditionally used for hand-tools and weapons, as well as for constructing baby cradles. It also produces edible fruit and leaves, which were an important food source.

ʿĩṭét[4]—Cordia perrottettii (Miller and Morris 1988, 72)

This tree/shrub grows where there is water, whether that is a permanent water source or rainfall. It has wood that is similar in quality to that of the *muṭín*, *Olea europaea*, but will grow in places the *muṭín* trees will not—i.e., where there is little or no rainfall. The wood is resilient and close-grained, making it good for support pillars, *nṣɛb*, in *strit* and *dáḳəf* buildings (2.15, 2.4). It has also been used for tool-making in the past.

sábxíḏ—Cordia ovalis (Miller and Morris 1988, 70)

This shrub grows across the southwestern region of the Arabian Peninsula with Dhofar as its eastern-most reaches. It is smaller than *ʿĩṭét*, and produces edible fruit. Because of the fruit, its wood

---

[4] Given as *ʿáyṭít* in Miller and Morris (1988) and by some of our consultants. The third author, based on his own consultants, gives it as *ʿĩṭét*.

was less often exploited. Its wood is also not of as good a quality as that of ՙitét.

ՙišót—possibly *Indigofera oblongifolia* (Miller and Morris 1988, 170)

This shrub grows in drier areas of the coastal plains east of Mirbat. It grows to the height of a man and the branches can be used to make a herding staff, *xóṭróḳ*, carried by herdsmen traditionally from the age of twelve (Tabook 1997, 38). Before the introduction of metal fish traps, it also served for the construction of fish traps for the people living on the plains.

šoʾ—unknown

According to our consultants, this plant rarely grows in Dhofar today because it is too dry. Due to lack of an image, we were unable to identify it. It is said to be a plant similar to ՙitét, but the wood was not as useful. This is likely to be another species of *Cordia,* possibly the one described in Miller and Morris (1988, 70) as follows: "Another unnamed and possibly new species of *Cordia* is found on Jebel Samhan and may occur in other similarly dry areas of Dhofar."

ḥárśũt—*Grewia tenax* (Miller and Morris 1988, 284)

This shrub grows in the drier areas of Dhofar on the north side of the escarpment mountains. Similar to *ġárád*, *Grewia bicolor*, and *xĩr*, *Ormocarpum dhofarense*, this shrub would be used for the door and the small, whippy branches, *śírín* (3.10), woven into the roof. This shrub was also an important food source in the drier areas where it grows.

ʿaṭréʾ—*Cissus quadrangularis* (Miller and Morris 1988, 289)

This is a climber that grows throughout Dhofar and indeed much of the tropical world. It is characterised by rectangular-shaped stems that are bare for much of the year. According to our consultant, it was used for keeping grass on top of *strit* roofs even in the wind. The stems are not eaten by livestock, so by encouraging the plant to grow up the walls and over the roof of a *strit* building, the other, more edible layers of the roof were protected from livestock as well. It was also prized as a shade-enhancer in trees that on which it climbed.

The new leaves during the monsoon period were eaten by livestock. The sap is very irritating to human skin, but could be used to clean out infected wounds on pack animals and to treat mastitis in livestock.

xfot—*Blepharispermum hirtum* (Miller and Morris 1988, 106)

This shrub is endemic to Dhofar and grows in the lower altitudes of the escarpment. It was one of the dominant species in monsoon forests in the past. Our consultant says it was used in the roofs of *strit* buildings, but the wood is not as strong as the *Olea europaea*, so it was less desirable for long-term buildings. It was also valued as firewood, because it would burn even when damp.

3.0. The Texts

3.1. Text 1

20131212_ShehretCJ_J020_buildingstret

(1.1)   *tókhob lókum ʿáfɛ́t ḏaʰn he aḥmɛd ɛr shɛl*
        Good day. This is me, Ahmad ber Shayl

(1.2)   ɛr mḥād ɛr ʿaysɛ ɛr ḥardān / ḥalū́ṭel lókumɛ[5] / išḥáyr

ber Mhad ber Ayse ber Hardan. I am going to tell you today

(1.3)   b-ɛstrít / estɔ̄́rta ʿáyun źók ź ixódəmsən yɔ̄

about *strit* construction, the buildings that people used to make,

(1.4)   istɔ̄́rta yixódəmsən yɔ̄ / ɛ́nfɛ̄́tɛ[6] / yibġíd yɔ̄ yilɔ̄́d ʿádɔ̄́t

the buildings that people make; first people go and cut down suitable timber.

(1.5)   yibġíd eṣ́órəḥ

They go to the shrubbed slopes,

(1.6)   ɛ-šɛh de-ḥótərf ʿar ū́ś́ɛ́t ḍ-o tīlójš ū́ś́ɛ́t lo her ol-ʿod yixórb hérúʾ(m)[7]

that they keep the livestock out of so that they don't destroy the trees.

(1.7)   eṣ́órḥ de-ḥótərf ʿar ū́ś́ɛ́t ḍ-o tīlójš lo / yilɔ̄́d mɛ̄́š

The shrubbed foothill area that they keep livestock out of—they cut from it

(1.8)   nṣɛb / b-īlɔ̄́d mɛ̄́š mšábkəf

supporting pillars, and they cut roof beams from it

(1.9)   b-īlɔ̄́d mɛ̄́š sírʔ(n)[8]

and they cut long slim branches from it.

(1.10) bə-her ber aġeyj flo ġāj lɔ̄d u-ber / id-ūlm her ʿádɔ̄́t kálǝs

And when the man or men have cut, they prepare all the timber.

---

[5] Non-phonemic, utterance-final, post-consonantal vowel.

[6] See footnote above.

[7] Non-pre-aspirated sonorants are typically pre-glottalised and articulated silently in utterance-final position (Watson et al., in press).

[8] See footnote above.

(1.11) *yihótf ʿak̲ iẑók iẑ šóhum bə-yɔ̄ iẑ ḥóṣór yiʿū̃r nḥáʰn ḥa-nḥád̲ár / strít / bə-ʿájan tókum tik̲rḗ tu(n)*

They fetch wood from there that they have, and people come along. They say, we are building a *strit* and we want you to help us.

(1.12) *bə-yɔ̄ yik̲írəb ṭáṭóhu(m)*

And people help each other.

(1.13) *bə-ġāj mənhúm⁹ iẑ ber mágrób yʿū̃r yɔ̄ d̲an¹⁰ d̲ílín yiŝbír yiḥád̲ər / ed̲ílín yijódor / yiġórb / d̲ahún*

And some men are well known [for being able to build]. They will say so-and-so knows how to build. So-and-so knows how to build walls, that one.

(1.14) *yízḥúm yiŝún eyɔ̄ b-īxódəm yɔ̄ kal / fáxra*

They come and see the people and people all work together.

(1.15) *yixódəm énfḗt jídórɛ¹¹ / d̲e-fédnîʔ(n)¹² / yiŝírekš hes ḥūk̲át*

First, they make the walls from stones. They make it circular.

---

⁹ Pre-aspirated sonorants lose their breathiness in utterance-medial position, particularly before vowels or 'unbreathed' (voiced or emphatic) consonants (Watson et al. 2023; in press).

¹⁰ See footnote above.

¹¹ Non-phonemic, utterance-final, post-consonantal vowel.

¹² Non-pre-aspirated sonorants are typically pre-glottalised and articulated silently in utterance-final position (Watson et al., in press).

(1.16) šɛh de stɔ́rta íti mənsɛ́ʰn / mənsɛ́ʰ(n)[13] / stɔ́rta / ʿámḳúti / mənsɛ́n[14] nṣíníti

Some *strit* buildings are large, some are medium, and some are small.

(1.17) yixódəm ejódere[15] / ɛd ber hes miṣír ḏe-ġeyʾj[16]

They build the wall until it is the height of a man

(1.18) flo ġaṣ́ xɛ́riʾ(n)[17] / mit er ejódórɛ[18]

or a little lower. When they have built the walls,

(1.19) yizḥím bə-ʿádɔ́t / yizḥím bə-nṣəbétʰ / ʿámḳɛ́t

they bring suitable timber, they bring the central pillar,

(1.20) baʿlét érš́únta

the one with side branches.

(1.21) b-estɔ́rta mənsɛ́n íti yikín bísən zēd mən nṣəbét ṭit mən nṣəbét ṭrut bə-zɛ́ʾd

And the large *strit* buildings have more than one supporting pillar and sometimes more than two,

(1.22) li-ḳídárɛ[19] / éstrít

according to the size of the *strit* building.

---

[13] Assimilation of /n/ to /s/.

[14] Pre-aspirated sonorants lose their breathiness in utterance-medial position.

[15] Non-phonemic, utterance-final, post-consonantal vowel.

[16] Pre-pausal glottalisation of 'unbreathed' (voiced or emphatic) consonant here and below.

[17] Non-pre-aspirated sonorants are typically pre-glottalised and articulated silently in utterance-final position.

[18] Non-phonemic, utterance-final, post-consonantal vowel.

[19] Non-phonemic, utterance-final, post-consonantal vowel.

(1.23) ḥaṣ ṭer ɛd-ḥofór hes ʕak ʕamk̲ b-érṣún lis rḥim fédnín ber riṣ lis m-boh bə-m-boh inʕót tənhɛzhéʾz

When they have dug out (a hole) for it in the middle and secured it well by piling stones around it here so that it doesn't wobble,

(1.24) yizḥím b-ĩšábkəf / yɔ́kaʕhum ʕak erṣúntɛ́s aʕálíta

they bring the roof beams. They put them in its upper branches.

(1.25) b-ĩxódəm b-ĩsójən ḥof / ɛ-ṹškáf / yisójənš eṭer jídór

and they work, they interweave the tip(s) into the roof beams and criss-cross them over the walls.

(1.26) hes / ɛd yik̲ólbs l-ɛṭánə hes k̲ɛ́dər / mənṭíh

They make it like this, [in the shape of] a pot, on top.

(1.27) mit ɛr sójún iẓahún ɛ-ber / u-bə-ṭer ɛ̃šábkəf b-áḥtóʾ(l)

when they have interwoven those and laid them over the roof beams, they tie them in place.

(1.28) yiḥóṭəl / ɛd yóbḏorhum rḥim mən o yinhɛzhéʾz

They bind them. They know how to do it so that it doesn't wobble.

(1.29) yizḥím / bə-ssírɛʾ(n) / yiḥóṭi bóhum

Then they fetch long slim branches. They tie them in place.

(1.30) yiḥóṭi bóhum l-ĩšábkəf iẓahún ɛd īkəlóbəs

They tie them to those roof beams so that they make it

(1.31) his táʕmɛr / ḏa-bɛk śśon ḥánít iẓ

as you would say, so that you have such-and-such

(1.32) iẓ ínɛh šũ̃əš / iẓ sok

that, what's its name? So, they are closely enmeshed

(1.33) ḥaṭɛ berót hes táʕmɛr d-ĩsíks rḥiʾ(m)

above, so that as you would say, it is well locked down.

(1.34) mit éttəmím ḏahúne[20]
When they have finished that

(1.35) ḥaṭɛ ḏahún bə-sɔ̄r ḏahún bə-ssírín iẑahú^h(n)[21]
above with this long slim branch, with those long slim branches

(1.36) iẓḥím bə-śaʿr
they bring hay.

(1.37) b-iẓḥím / b-irɔ́ṣ́áf lis b-irṣíṣ lis mənṭíh
They bring [it] and press it down and place it in layers above

(1.38) ino / ino l-xlel / o-mən xorf
so that it won't leak during the monsoon period.

(1.39) b-irɔ́ṣ́af ṭírəs
And they tie that (i.e., the whole roof) down with rocks.

(1.40) bə-yɔ̄ kō dē bə-xadmáśś[22]
And people all have their own way of working.

(1.41) de mənhúm[23] / yiʿū̃r nirɔ́ṣ́áf / her ber aṣólḥan o śóhum jíẑéd iẑ elhóti b-ejíẑéẑ[24] ẑahún
Some people say we weigh the roof down with rocks and when we have done it well and they have hides of cows and those hides

(1.42) yifíḳí bóhum / her o-ʿod ol-áxxaʾ(l)
they cover it with them so that it [the roof] won't leak.

---

[20] Non-phonemic, utterance-final, post-consonantal vowel.

[21] Sonorant element of pre-aspirated sonorant silent in utterance-final position (Watson et al. 2023; Watson et al., in press).

[22] Assimilation of /t/ to /š/.

[23] Lacks pre-aspiration, perhaps because speaker does not feel he has completed the utterance.

[24] Assimilation of /d/ to /ẑ/.

(1.43) bə-de yifóḳa bə-hérmíti ź

And some people cover with vegetation that

(1.44) yikín ber d-ū́ləm eśáʕr bə-hérmíti ź

they have got ready, dried grass and vegetation that,

(1.45) iź də-reṣṣóhum kal rḥiʾ(m)

that they lay down neatly in layers

(1.46) ɛd ĩśórks / yóṣlaḥs kā́ləs / mit éttəmím mən xúnáṭ

until they finish it, they make it all good. When they have finished from outside,

(1.47) yɔ́jaḥ ʕámḳəs mən ḥā́ḳál yinḥíṣ̌əs

they go into it [the building] and inside they do the plastering.

(1.48) de yinḥṓṣ̌ bə-ṭʕór

Some plaster with clay.

(1.49) bə-de yikín də-xódəm ṭer ṣárfét / də-wáḍaʕ / b-irṓṣ̌ad olohún yɔ̃ḳaʕ / yínṣ̌óf śaʕr

And some work on an area of flat bedrock and [...] and weigh it with rocks there and then put, spread out hay.

(1.50) yinṣ̌íf / śaʕr ḍahún u-mġor yɔ̃ḳaʕ ṭírəs ḥaṣírt

They spread out that hay and then they put fibre matting on top,

(1.51) o tforḥ ʕar / ʕar tšə̃f

and all you want to do is lie down and sleep.

(1.52) b-ixódər ʕámḳis mən ġál[25] mən ʕámḳəs / mən ḥā́ḳáʾ(l)

They use [it] to make shade inside from below and from above.

---

[25] The pre-aspirated sonorant loses breathiness, particularly before 'unbreathed' (voiced or emphatic) consonants and vowels.

(1.53) yišíreke[26] / flo / hes táʿmɛr śóṭrór / flo xóṭók̩ šúmɛ[27]

They make it or, as you could say cloths or clothes, they,

(1.54) iźan ɛ-ksbḗʰt[28]

those that were clothes

(1.55) min ʿámk̩əs ʿad ik̩olóbəs / o ʿok hɛt śśun o sírín b-o śśun źahún / tik̩təlób lɛ-ṭaʰn / ṭílélɛ[29]

from inside so that they make it such that you don't see the long, slim branches or those (other) things; it becomes just a place of shade

(1.56) b-ikín əd-škəlíl ʿak̩ eṭoŕób o-yíhbi ʿak̩ aʿántɛ́k b-o śe mənṭíh

so that you can protect yourself among the sticks and nothing will fall into your eyes from above.

(1.57) b-ixódəm / yišérek múššəd / ɛ-ɔ́ʾb

And they work, they make something to block the gap for the door.

(1.58) bə-dḗtmím éstrít yixódəm də-ʿod díṣ̌áf / bə-ḥáḏrîʾ(n)[30]

When they have finished the *strít* building, they go on to build byres and pens

(1.59) her ū̃śḗt

for the livestock.

---

[26] Non-phonemic, utterance-final, post-consonantal vowel.

[27] Non-phonemic, utterance-final, post-consonantal vowel.

[28] Heavily pre-aspirated final /t/.

[29] Non-phonemic, utterance-final, post-consonantal vowel.

[30] Utterance-final /n/ pre-glottalised and articulated silently (Watson et al., in press).

(1.60) *yiġólḳ akter*[31] */ ediṣ̌áf ɛxádím ter ṣárfét / ḏe-her ḏ-ijórf mġóra mənsér ū́ś̌ét*

They look more ... the byres are built on an area of flat bedrock so that they can (i.e., more easily) muck out after the livestock.

(1.61) *yiġólḳ her ṣárfét*

They look for an area of flat bedrock.

(1.62) *bə-yixódəm edáḳəf hes yiḥótf ṭahún b-īlɔ́d ʿádɔ̄́thum her díṣ̌áf b-edáḳəf o ykin / yiʿdól ḥaṭíh hes estrít lo / ɛ-yɔ́ lo*

And they build the byre. When they have smoothed [that area], they cut down suitable timber for the byres and a byre won't be as high as a *strit* building for people.

(1.63) *yikín də-ġóttaṣ xɛ́rín lɛ́kən / yɔ́saʿanš*

It will be a bit smaller, but they make sure it is wide enough

(1.64) *her / her ū́ś̌ét / bə-ḏaʰn šɛh yikín beš enṣɛ́b mɛ́kən*

for the livestock and it will have lots of supporting pillars;

(1.65) *o ṭit b-o ṭrut yikín nṣɛb*

not one or two, there will be [lots of] pillars.

(1.66) *iź her təślɛ́lən ḏihún ʿádɔ̄́t ḏihún bə-tšérkənš*

When those poles have been carried, they make it.

(1.67) *u-mit ɛ́tmím edáḳəf her elhóti íti / īšírek / ḥáḏór*[32]

And when they have finished the byre for the big cows, they make smaller pens

(1.68) *her šiṭár eníṣúʾn / ź-īhulɔ́hum élhúʰ(n)*

for the small female calves into which they put them for the night.

---

[31] Arabic.

[32] Tabook (1997, 62).

(1.69) b-īšírek ġódɛʾ ṭaʰn her

And they will make a depression like that for,

(1.70) b-eġódɛʾ hóhum kal her éstrít bə-her eyś bə-her edáḳəf

they have a depressed area for all of them, for the *strit* building and for the byre.

(1.71) b-īźáʰn sɛn istɔ́rta ź īxódəm yixódəmsən ʿayún źók būʰ(n)

And that is about the *strit* buildings that people used to build here.

(1.72) bə-ḥayyākum allāh[33]

May God keep you well.

3.2. Text 2

20131027_ShehretEJ_J019_buildingshelters

(2.1) edī́ṣ́éf / b-estɔ́rta

Livestock byres and *strit* buildings

(2.2) tkinən bə-šḥɛ́r[34] o ykin śe bə-ṣolót lo

are in the mountains. They are not found in the eastern area [east from Mirbat to Hadbin].

(2.3) edī́ṣ́éf yilɔ́d hóhəm ġēj ʿádɔ̃t mən ɔ̃tʔ(n) / bə-sġót / bə-xī̃ʔ(r)

For byres, men cut suitable timber from *Olea europaea* (wild olive) and *Anogeissus dhofarica* and *Ormocarpum dhofarense*.

(2.4) bə-her ber šóhum ʿádɔ̃t bə-nṣɛ́ʾb / yišérek ɛnfɛ́t nṣɛʾb

And when they have timber and pillars. First, they make the supporting pillars,

(2.5) u-mġórɛ ɛ̃šábkəf

and then they do the roof beams,

---

[33] Arabic.

[34] Pre-aspirated sonorant loses breathiness utterance-medially.

(2.6) u-mġórɛ juśí

and then they collect whippy, green branches to interleave between the larger ones to make roofing.

(2.7) jóśɛ jóśɛ jóśó / ṭóròb ḳíṭinúʾ(n)

They collect whippy, green branches, slender pieces of timber.

(2.8) u-mġor ínέ(t)[35] śśəʕóroʾ(n)

Then the women collect dried grass.

(2.9) b-efoḳḗn bə-śaʕr manṭíh / ṭer éstrít

They cover it [the roof] with dried grass from above on the *strit* building

(2.10) bə-ṭer edáḳəf / b-īkín dáḳəf b-īkín strít / bə-xaṭḗrəḳ

and on the byre. It could either be a byre or a *strit* building. And... and (as for) herding staffs.

(2.11) yɔ̄ yilɔ́d xaṭḗrḳ / šímti ź-hérmít

People cut herding staffs. The names of the trees?

(2.12) ɔ̃ṭʾ(n) / yilɔ́d mɛ̃s yɔ̄ xóṭróḳ

[are] *Olea europaea*. People cut from them to make a herding staff,

(2.13) b-her ber lɔ́dəš yiḳbíš ʕaḳ śɔ́ʾṭ

and when they have cut it, they fire-harden it in the embers of a fire,

(2.14) bə-her ber kɛ̄š yiḳósər ʕãš eḳέśrót bə-ykin xóṭróḳ

and when they have fire-hardened it in the embers, they remove the bark, and it becomes a herding staff.

(2.15) ɔ̃ṭʾ(n) / bə-ġáráʾd / bə-ʕíṭét / bə-śábxíʾd / bə-ʕíšót / bə-šoʾ

The wild olive, *Olea europaea* and *Grewia bicolor* and *Cordia perrottettii* and *Cordia ovalis* and *Blepharis dhofarensis* and *šoʾ*

---

[35] Partial assimilation to /ś/.

(2.16) bə-ḥárśū́t

and *Grewia tenax*.

(2.17) ḏanúh ykin mɛnhúm xaṭɛ́rək lɛ́kən o lɛ́br iẓók rḥā̃t lo / rḥā̃t bass ɔ̃ṭʔ(n)

Those are the ones they make herding staffs from but those aren't as good as those other ones. The best is the wild olive,

(2.18) b-eġarád b-eʕiṭét / źan[36] rḥā̃t

then *Grewia bicolor* and *Cordia perrottettii*. Those are good,

(2.19) bə-sérohəm ḥárśū́t

followed by *Grewia tenax*.

3.3. Text 3

20131008_ShehretCJ_J004_makingcowshelters

(3.1) mḥū̃d ber ʕáyrún / ʕáyun źok / ʕáyun źok yɔ̄ o śóhum o śe ḥanít tɛ́búḵ b-o śe smī̃t[37] b-o śe smī̃t məndún ašjār[38]

Muhammad ber Ayrun. In the past, in the past, people didn't have-whatsit-breeze blocks. They had no cement, only trees

(3.2) b-ašjār iẓohún yilɔ́d ašjār iẓokún b-iśírek ediṣ́áf

and those trees, they cut down trees and made the byres.

(3.3) b-iśírek diṣ́áf b-iśírek stɔ́rta

They made byres and *strit* buildings for people.

(3.4) estɔ́rta her yɔ̄ / yɔ́jaḥ ʕámḵisən yɔ̄

The *strit* buildings for people, people went into them

(3.5) b-iśī́f ʕámḵisən / b-ediṣ́áf her ū́śɛ́t her ɛ́lhótī

and slept in them and the byres were for livestock, for cows.

---

[36] /n/ assimilates to /r/.

[37] English 'cement'. Repeated below.

[38] Arabic. Repeated several times below.

(3.6) *b-edišáf ykin beš ɛd kun dáḳəf eb ykin beš nṣɛb mɛ́kən*

And the byres, if it was a big byre—it would have lots of pillars.

(3.7) *b-ɛd kun dáḳəf nísán ykin beš nṣɛb mɛ́kən lo*

And if it was a small byre there wouldn't be many pillars

(3.8) *bə-her ḥa-yxódum yɔ̄ dáḳəf yibġíd yɔ̄ her ʿaśīrét ġēj bə-flo ʿáśəri ġēj b-īlɔ́d ʿádɔ̄t*

and when people were going to build a shelter, ten or twenty men would go and chop suitable timber

(3.9) *ʿádɔ̄t yilɔ́d enṣɛ́b*

suitable timber, they would chop for pillars

(3.10) *ʿádɔ̄t yilɔ́d enṣɛ́b / b-īlɔ́d ɛ̃šábḳəf b-īlɔ́d sírín*

suitable timber, they would chop down timber and roof beams and whippy, green branches for thatching

(3.11) *b-iḏɔ́lhəm bə-her ber ʿaḳ ɛ̃nzíl yihófər her enṣɛ́b*

and they would carry them and when they were back home, they would dig holes for the posts.

(3.12) *yiḥófər her enṣɛ́b ʿaḳ ʿamḳ ɛ-dáḳəf*

They would dig holes for the pillars in the middle of the byre.

(3.13) *ykin ber jódór edáḳəf ber jódórš múfri*

They would have built the walls of the byre; they would have built double walling.

(3.14) *ber jódór dáḳəf də-kun eb b-ɛd-kun nísán b-ɛd kun dáḳəf eb / yhófər her enṣɛ́b mɛ́kən ʿaḳ ʿamḳ ɛ-dáḳəf*

And the walls of the byre would be big or small. If the byre was big, they would dig holes for lots of pillars in the middle of the byre,

(3.15) *b-iśólá ṭíriš b-ɛ̃šábḳəf*

and they would place the beams on top.

(3.16) bə-min ṭer ε̃šábḳəf yišórək erɩ́krékɛ³⁹
On top of the beams, they would put soft soil.

(3.17) u-mġor yšérek sɩ́rín
And then they would put small, whippy, green branches [on top].

(3.18) bə-her ber šérek sɩ́rín ber šérek erkərék
After they had put the whippy, green branches on top and placed soft soil,

(3.19) yifíḳe liš bə-śaʕr ʕayún źok / nā́ṣa ol-ʕad śe śaʕr lo yifíḳe liš bə-ṭorū́ʾ(l)⁴⁰
they would cover it with dried grass. That was in the past. Now people don't have dried grass, so they roof it with tarpaulin.

(3.20) bə-nā́ṣənu ol ʕad de d-ɩ̄šérok de dišā́f iź ʕayún źok lo məndún ṭad ṭaʾd / ṭad ṭaʾ(d)
Now no one makes byres like in the past, apart from the odd one.

(3.21) nā́ṣan yišírek ṭḗbúḳ
Now they use breeze blocks.

(3.22) b-ɩ̄šírek smɩ̄t / b-ɩ̄šírek albóḥ bə-šínkó / bə-blḗwət⁴¹
They use cement and [commercial] planking and corrugated iron and plywood.

(3.23) lɛ́kən ʕayún źok yšérek edā́ḳəf ār ašjār
But in the past, they made byres just from trees.

(3.24) b-edā́ḳəf εšjār tkosš šɛ̄ʾ(l)
A byre made from wood you would find cool.

---

[39] Non-phonemic, utterance-final, post-consonantal vowel.
[40] From English 'tarpaulin'.
[41] From English 'plywood'.

(3.25) *tkoss ɛ́kət ɛ-ḥarr*[42] *ṣɛ̄ˀ(l)*

In the hot period, you would find it cool.

(3.26) *b-ɛ́kət ɛ-ḥɔ̄r júnú*

and in the cold period you would find it to be shelter.

(3.27) *lináh ykin*

because it would be

(3.28) *l-iṭabīˁah*[43] *l-iṭabīˁah / ɛd kun ṣɛ̄l [sic] ɛd kun ḥɔ̄r*

adapted to the environment, the environment. If it was cold, if it was cold weather,

(3.29) *ykin júnɛ́ b-ɛd kun ɛdək*[44] *ykin ḥánít*

it would be sheltered and if it was stifling and close, it would be such-and-such.

(3.30) *ykin ṣɛ̄ˀ(l) / bə-linah ḥanít iź ašjār*

It would be cool because of that whatsit—natural wood.

(3.31) *bə-din eṭabīˁat*[45] *ɛ-yɔ̄ ɛ-sɛh bə-śḥɛʰr*

And that was the way people lived in the mountains.

(3.32) *ɛ-sɛh bə-śḥer ˁayún źok / éstrít*

That was the way in the mountains at that time, making a building for people

(3.33) *éstrít tkin mən stɔ́rta yišíf ˁámḳísən yɔ̄*

A *strit* was of.... Buildings people would sleep in,

(3.34) *b-iṣúnf bísən bə-śaˁr*

and they would cover them with thatch

---

[42] Arabic.

[43] Arabic. Repeated twice below.

[44] Good example of lenited /k/, realised as velar fricative.

[45] Arabic.

(3.35) *b-īkin ʿámḳísən ʿɔ́rś b-īśíf ʿámḳísən yɔ́*

they would have a raised area in them, and people would sleep in them.

(3.36) *b-edáḳəf her ū̃śḗt*

And the byre was for livestock.

(3.37) *bə-ḏan ɛ-šɛh ḥal / nā́ṣan ol ʿod īśérɛksən yɔ́ lo / edī̃ṣ́áf íźanúh ʿad īśérɛkhəm yɔ́ lo / nā́ṣan ṭad ṭaʾ(d)*

And that was how it was. But now, no one makes them anymore. Those byres aren't built anymore, just the odd one,

(3.38) *ġeyj ġeyʾj / ġeyj ġeyj bə-šḗʰr*

the odd man, the odd man in the mountains

(3.39) *tkoss ed-īśérɛk dáḳəf ɛ-ʿádɔ́t*

you would find making byres from timber.

(3.40) *ʿádɔ́t yiśtūm yiśtūm ʿádɔ́t ū̃ṭíʾ(n)*

They would buy suitable timber of olive wood

(3.41) *her kúnút ʿádɔ́t muṭín hárdét ū̃ṭín hárdét*

and if the timber were of olivewood, they would be strong. Olivewood is hard wood.

(3.42) *yíśtūm ʿádɔ́t d-írót mən zəbḗn*

They would buy well-seasoned wood,

(3.43) *b-ixédəm beš dáḳəf / b-īkín ḏahún dáḳəf ṣ́ḗl bə-tərtāḥ*[46] *beš ū̃śḗt*

and build a byre from it. The byre would be cool and the livestock would feel happy in it.

(3.44) *nā́ṣan edī̃ṣ́áf íź-səmīt / muśḗt ol ərtɔ́ḥót bóhum lo*

Now byres are made from cement and animals don't like them.

(3.45) *tkin smīt jíśfśíf*

The cement would be rough,

---

[46] Arabic.

(3.46) *b-ol ərtɔ́ḥót bóhum lo b-īkín ɛdək*⁴⁷

and they wouldn't be happy. It is stifling.

(3.47) *šínkó / bə-blḗwət / yikín ɛdk*

Corrugated iron and plywood are stifling.

References

Al-Maʿšanī, Aḥmad 2014. *Muʿjam Lisān Ẓufār: Jibbāli–ʿArabīFfaṣīḥ*. Muscat.

Ball, Laurence, Doug MacMillan, Joseph Tzanopoulos, Andrew Spalton, Hadi Al Hikmani, and Mark Moritz. 2020. 'Contemporary Pastoralism in the Dhofar Mountains of Oman'. *Human Ecology* 48: 267–77. https://doi:10.1007/s10745-020-00153-5

Ball, Laurence, and Joseph Tzanopoulos. 2020. 'Livestock Browsing Affects the Species Composition and Structure of Cloud Forest in the Dhofar Mountains of Oman'. *Applied Vegetation Science* 23/3: 363–76.

Bellem, Alex, and Janet C. E. Watson. 2017. 'South Arabian Sibilants and the Śḥerēt ś̃-š̃ Contrast. In *To the Madbar and Back Again: Studies in the Languages, Archaeology, and Cultures of Arabia Dedicated to Michael CA Macdonald*, edited by Laïla Nehmé and Ahmad Al-Jallad, 622–44. Leiden: Brill.

Boersma, Paul, and David Weenink. 2017. *Praat: Doing Phonetics by Computer*. https://www.fon.hum.uva.nl/praat/

Dufour, Julien. 2016. 'Recherches sur le verbe subarabique modern'. Habilitation sous la direction de M. Gilles Authier, EPHE. Paris: École pratique des hautes études.

---

⁴⁷ Lenited /k/, realised as velar fricative.

Miller, Anthony, and Miranda J. Morris. 1988. *Plants of Dhofar: Traditional, Economic and Medicinal Uses*. Diwan of Royal Court, Sultanate of Oman: The Office of the Adviser for Conservation of the Environment.

POWO. 2022. 'Plants of the World Online. Facilitated by the Royal Botanic Gardens, Kew'. http://www.plantsoftheworldonline.org/

Rubin, Aaron D. 2014. *The Jibbali (Shaḥri) Language of Oman: Grammar and Texts*. Studies in Semitic Languages and Linguistics 72. Leiden: Brill.

Tabook, Salim Bakhit Salim. 1997. 'Tribal Practices and Folklore of Dhofar, Sultanate of Oman'. PhD thesis, University of Exeter.

Watson, Janet C. E., and Andrea Boom. In press. *Modern South Arabian: Appraising the Language–Nature Relationship in Dhofar*. Proceedings of NACAL 2019.

Watson, Janet C. E., Barry Heselwood, Amer al-Kathiri, Abdullah al-Mahri, and Gisela Tomé Lourido. In press. 'Silent sonorant articulations in Mehri and Shehret'. In *Rarities in Phonetics and Phonology: Evolutionary, Structural, Typological and Social Dimensions*, edited by Cormac Anderson, Natalia Kuznetsova, and Shelece Easterday. Berlin: Language Science Press.

Watson, Janet C. E., Barry Heselwood, Gisela Tomé Lourido, and Amer al-Kathiri. 2023. 'Pre-aspirated Sonorants in Central and Eastern Shehret, a Modern South Arabian language'. *20th International Congress on Phonetic Sciences, Prague*.

ASPECTS OF THE PHONOLOGY AND MORPHOLOGY OF SAUDI VARIETIES OF ARABIC

Stuart Davis, Wafi Alshammari, Musa Alahmari, and Mamdouh Alhuwaykim

1.0. Introduction

Various Saudi subvarieties of Arabic are known to display certain unusual linguistic features with respect to aspects of their phonology and morphology. Such features may be archaic features of Arabic that have long disappeared in other varieties or substrate features, but other unusual features may be innovations. An example of an archaic feature is the persistence of a lateral fricative pronunciation of historical *ḍād* still found in the southwestern area of ʿAsīr and Saudi Tihāmah, as documented in such works as Watson and Al-Azraqi (2011) and Al-Wer and Al-Qahtani (2016). This is best understood as an archaic feature that is consistent with Sībawayh's description of the sound (Watson and Al-Azraqi 2011, 426). An example of a substrate feature is the nasal definite article which occurs in Faifi Arabic (Alfaifi and Behnstedt 2010; Alfaifi and Davis 2021) and other varieties of southwestern Saudi Arabic (Prochazka 1988; Behnstedt 2016).

Watson (2018) views the nasal definite article in these varieties as reflecting a non-Arabic Semitic substrate (see also Al-Jallad 2021). While various Saudi varieties preserve ancient features, innovation is also present. One example of an innovation in some Saudi varieties is the presence of word-initial consonant clusters. While some varieties, such as Urban Hijazi Arabic, do not allow initial clusters, quite a few varieties of Saudi Arabic do allow such clusters, such as Najdi Arabic (Abboud 1979; Ingham 1994) and the southwestern Saudi dialect described in Alahmari (2018). That the presence of word-initial clusters is an innovation can be gleamed from the observation that they may be quite limited in some varieties, as in a subvariety of Faifi Arabic discussed in Alfaifi and Davis (2021); word-initial clusters seem to first arise diachronically from the extension of the process of high vowel deletion to word-initial syllables, an environment where deletion is blocked in many dialects (such as in Urban Hijazi).

With this as background, in this chapter we will highlight some unusual features of the phonology and morphology of various Saudi varieties of Arabic that are either unexamined or have not been studied in detail, and to consider whether they are archaic features or reflect internal innovation. An important aspect of our article, though, will be the detailed description of the phenomena that we will be considering. The descriptions are based on native speaker intuition in consultation with other speakers of the same dialect. In §2.0 of this chapter we focus on an unusual productive morphological augmentative witnessed in Ha'ili Arabic of the northern Najdi region (Alshammari and Davis 2019), which includes forms like *klaab* 'dog (augmentative)' for *kalb* 'dog' (where bold indicates pharyngealisation), *šwaaʕir* 'poet (augmentative)' for *šaaʕir* 'poet', and *sraawiil* 'pants (augmentative)' for *sirwaal* 'pants', where augmentative indicates largeness and sometimes awkwardness (as in Sifianou 1992). The Haʔili Arabic pattern will be described in detail, focusing on its morphophonological realisation. In §3.0 we describe and analyse the 2nd person masculine singular possessive pronoun, focusing on a southwestern Arabian variety (Alahmari 2018). In this variety, the 2nd person masculine singular possessive suffix alternates between -*k*, -*ka*, and -*ak* as witnessed by examples such as *kutub-k* 'your books', *malik-ka* 'your king', and *baab-ak* 'your door'. As far as we are aware, this three-way allomorphic variation is unusual. In §4.0, we discuss final degemination along with stress shift, which appears to be fairly widespread among Najdi and northwestern Saudi Arabic varieties, especially as witnessed in disyllabic words that end in an underlying geminate, as illustrated by the difference between *ḥagg* 'a truth' and *íl-ḥag* 'the truth', with stress on the definite article, or in the elative, as exemplified by *áxaf* 'lighter' with initial stress, where most dialects have *axáff*. Focusing on a dialect spoken in Sakaka City (Alhuwaykim 2018), the details of the degemination pattern are presented and analysed, including the lack of degemination (and stress shift) in derived contexts (e.g., *sikát-t* 'I kept silent'). We then analytically unify degemination with the occurrence of word-final vowel shortening (and stress shift) in disyllabic words that end in a long vowel. We conclude in §5.0 with a summary of the paper.

2.0. The Morphological Augmentative in Northern Najdi/Haʾili Arabic

In this section we describe in detail a unique productive morphological augmentative pattern found in Haʾili Arabic as spoken by the Shammar group. The Shammar group falls under the subdialect of Northern Najdi in the division of Najdi Arabic found in Ingham (1994). The data presented in this section are mostly from Alshammari and Davis (2019) and are supplemented by the native intuition of the first author of that work (who is the second author of the present chapter). A pertinent discussion of the morphological augmentative can be found in Assuwaida (1997), who relates the formation of the augmentative to the older dialect of *Tayy*, which goes back to the pre-Islamic era. The uniqueness of the Tayy dialect is emphasised by Al-Jallad (2013) and the distinctiveness of the Arabic of the Shammar group from other Northern Najdi varieties is emphasised by Ingham (1982).

In presenting the morphological augmentative we will also show the corresponding diminutive forms. Haʾili Arabic possesses a morphological diminutive and there is an analytical issue as to whether the Haʾili augmentative is derived directly from the corresponding diminutive or, like the diminutive, is derived directly from a corresponding base noun. That is, for example, is the augmentative for 'dog', *klaab*, derived from the diminutive *kleyb* or from the noun *kalb* 'dog'? In our description of the augmentative, though, we will maintain that the diminutive serves as the base for the augmentative and we will provide reasons for this position. The issue of the relationship between an augmentative and a diminutive is briefly discussed by Sifianou (1992, 157) for

Modern Greek, where she mentions that the occurrence of an augmentative in a language suggests the presence of a diminutive. The diminutive in Haʾili Arabic is similar to the pattern found in Classical Arabic and in other varieties of Peninsular Arabic (e.g., Holes 1984), but with some diachronic phonological changes largely predictable based on the Classical Arabic diminutive; see Zewi (2006) and Gadoua and Davis (2019) for overviews of the diminutive across different Arabic varieties and see Alshammari and Davis (2019) for a description of the diminutive in Haʾili Arabic.

In (1)–(4) of Table 1 below, we show the diminutive and augmentative of words whose base form is a monosyllabic noun. The base noun is given in the leftmost column with the word pattern indicated as either CVCC in (1), CVGG in (2), where GG is a geminate, CVVC in (3), and CCVVC in (4); the diminutive is shown in the second column, the corresponding augmentative in the third column, and the English gloss in the rightmost column (note also that bold indicates pharyngealisation; a full stop indicates a syllable boundary; long vowels are transcribed as a sequence of two identical vowel letters).

Table 1: Diminutives and Augmentatives of monosyllabic word forms

(1) CVCC word	Diminutive	Augmentative	Gloss
(a) kalb	kleyb	k**laab**	'dog'
(b) gird	greyd	g**raad**	'monkey'
(c) wajh	wjeyh	**wjaah**/wjaah	'face'
(2) CVGG word	Diminutive	Augmentative	Gloss
(a) xadd	xdeyd	x**daad**	'cheek'
(b) ḥagg	ḥgeyg	ḥ**gaag**	'right'
(3) CVVC word	Diminutive	Augmentative	Gloss
(a) baab	bweyb	b**waab**	'door'
(b) naar	nwey.r-ah	n**waa.r**-ah	'fire'
(c) daar	dwey.r-ah	d**waa.r**-ah	'clay house'
(d) raas	rweys	**rwaas**	'head'
(e) faas	fweys	**fwaas**	'hatchet'
(4) CCVVC word	Diminutive	Augmentative	Gloss
(a) graad	gray.yid	**graa**.yid	'tick'
(b) ḥjaab	ḥjay.yib	ḥ**jaa**.yib	'veil'
(c) ftaat	ftay.yit	—	'crumbs'

The augmentative of monosyllabic nouns in (1)–(4) seems to be based on the diminutive form, with the diphthong in the first syllable of the diminutive (*ey* or *ay*) simply replaced with the long pharyngealised vowel that we transcribe as long **aa**. The remainder of the augmentative is exactly the same as the diminutive, although pharyngealisation from the augmentative vowel may show limited spreading onto neighbouring phonemes, as indicated by the bold in the transcription (the details of pharyngealisation spread in Ha'ili Arabic is left for future research). The argument for viewing the augmentative as deriving from the diminutive is based not only on the simplicity of the description, but also on the observation that irregularities of the diminutive are encountered in the augmentative, as seen in (3b) and (3c), where the same suffix that occurs in the diminutive also occurs in the augmentative. Furthermore, there occur diminutive forms without a corresponding augmentative, as in (4c), but not vice-

Phonology and Morphology of Saudi Varieties of Arabic 143

versa. It should be noted that the presence of pharyngealisation in the augmentative sometimes leads to phonological contrast, as in the pair *klaab* 'dog, plural' versus *kḷaaḅ* 'dog, augmentative', but sometimes to homophony, as in the example *graad* 'monkey augmentative' in (1b), which is also the noun meaning 'tick' seen in (4a).

The next set of data in (5)–(11) of Table 2 illustrates the augmentative (and diminutive) forms for a wide variety of different types of disyllabic nouns (note: * indicates an ungrammatical form).

Table 2: Diminutives and Augmentatives of disyllabic word forms

(5)	CV.CVC word	Diminutive	Augmentative	Gloss
(a)	*ga.lam*	*gleym*	*gḷaam*	'pen'
(b)	*ʕi.jil*	*ʕjeyl*	*ʕjaal/ʕjaal*	'calf'
(6)	CV.CVC word	Diminutive	Augmentative	Gloss
(a)	*šaa.ʕir*	*šwey.ʕir*	*šwaa.ʕir*	'poet'
(b)	*naa.g-ah*	*nwey.gah/ nwey.ḍʕah*	*nwaa.gah/ *nwaa.ḍʕah*	'camel (F)'
(7)	CVC.CVC word	Diminutive	Augmentative	Gloss
(a)	*dir.ham*	*drey.him*	*draa.him*	'Dirham'
(b)	*ʕan.bar*	*ʕney.bir*	*ʕnaa.bir/ ʕnaa.bir*	'dungeon'
(c)	*ʕil.b-ah*	*ʕley.b-ah*	*ʕḷaa.b-ah*	'can'
(8)	CV.CVVC word	Diminutive	Augmentative	Gloss
(a)	*ki.biir/ tˁi.biir*	*kbay.yir/ tˁbay.yir*	*kbaa.yir/ *tˁbaa.yir*	'big'
(b)	*ki.taab*	*ktay.yib*	*ktaa.yib*	'book'
(c)	*ṣi.ġiir*	*ṣġay.yir*	—	'small'
(d)	*ḥa.nuun*	*ḥnay.yin*	—	'kind, compassionate'
(9)	CV.C-ah word	Diminutive	Augmentative	Gloss
(a)	*sa.n-ah*	*snay.y-ah*	*snaa.y-ah/ snaa.y-ah*	'year'
(b)	*ma.r-ah*	*mray.y-ah*	*mṛaa.y-ah*	'woman'

(10)	CVC.CVVC word	Diminutive	Augmentative	Gloss
(a)	sir.waal	srey.wiil	sraa.wiil	'pants'
(b)	ṣil.ṭaan	ṣley.ṭiin	ṣlaa.ṭiin	'Sultan'
(c)	xab.baaz	xbey.biiz	xbaa.biiz	'baker'
(d)	maj.nuun	mjey.niin	mjaa.niin/ mjaa.niin	'crazy'
(11)	CCV.C-ah word	Diminutive	Augmentative	Gloss
(a)	nxa.l-ah	nxey.l-ah	nxaa.l-ah	'palm tree'
(b)	wri.g-ah	wrey.g-ah/ wrey.ǰ-ah	wraa.g-ah/ *wraa.ǰ-ah	'paper'

Again, as in Table 1, the augmentative is formed from the diminutive by replacement of the diphthongal nucleus of the first syllable of the diminutive with the long pharyngealised vowel *aa*, which triggers subsequent pharyngealisation spread. Concerning the optionality of pharyngealisation in the augmentative in the forms in (5b), (9a), and (10d), as well as in (1c) above, pharyngealisation can be optionally blocked in the presence of a palatal-type consonant—although this does not account for the optionality shown in (7b). The data items in (6b), (8a), and (11b) are interesting in that these words show optional affrication of velar stops in the diminutive; the corresponding augmentative cannot surface with affrication. This suggests an antagonistic relationship between affrication and pharyngealisation. With respect to semantics, examples like (8c) and perhaps (8d) show that a word signifying smallness cannot be made into an augmentative, but (8a) shows that a word that expresses largeness can have a diminutive form. This difference supports the observation that the augmentative is based on the diminutive (though semantics may also contribute to this difference).

A final set of data of base words consisting of three syllables is shown in (12) below in Table 3, where the augmentative seems to be formed from the diminutive by replacing the diphthongal nucleus of the first syllable with the long pharyngealised vowel ***aa*** and the remaining syllables preserve identity with the corresponding syllables of the diminutive.

Table 3: Diminutives and Augmentatives of trisyllabic word forms

(12)	Trisyllabic word	Diminutive	Augmentative	Gloss
(a)	siy.yaa.**rah**	swey.rii.r-ah	swaa.rii.r-ah	'car'
(b)	mir.jey.ḥah	mrey.jii.ḥ-ah	mra(a).jii.ḥ-ah	'swing'
(c)	ʿan.kə.buut	ʿney.ki(i)b	ʿnaa.ki(i)b/ ʿnaa.ki(i)b	'spider'
(d)	**bar**.naa.mij	**brey**.nii.mij	**braa**.nii.mij	'programme'

The presence of a morphological augmentative in Haʾili Arabic raises a number of questions. There is a question of the consideration of the semantics and pragmatics of the augmentative in a more thorough manner than what we present here. Also, there is the issue of the morphological relationship between the augmentative and the diminutive, where we maintain that the former is based on the latter, but this would require further and more detailed argumentation than what we have presented. The question that we want to briefly address here concerns the matter of whether the occurrence of a productive morphological augmentative is a recent innovation or a preservation of a truly archaic feature of Haʾili Arabic. Augmentatives are rarely discussed in Arabic, since they are typically expressed periphrastically, using a phrase of two or more words as in the Standard Arabic example *bayt kabiir* 'a big house'. Assuwaida (1997) argues for the antiquity of the augmentative in Haʾili Arabic by providing evidence that it is part of the older dialect of *Tayy* (Haʾil region, modern-day Saudi Arabia), going back to the pre-Islamic era. He provides evidence from poetry and place names that display the augmentative pattern. Two examples that he gives are *ʿuwaariḍ* and *tuwaarin* (although we note that in the contemporary dialect the /u/ in the first syllable would not be pronounced, given the diachronic loss of unstressed high vowels in initial syllables). Assuwaida (1997) notes that *ʿwaariḍ* is the name of a lone-standing mountain located in front of *twaarin*, which is a castle in the Aja mountains in Tayy. Assuwaida's discussion leads us to conclude that the morphological augmentative is both an archaic feature of Haʾili Arabic as spoken by the Shammar group, who descend from the ancient Arab *Tayy* tribe, (Al Rasheed 1991; Fattah and Caso 2009) and a feature that has probably always been geographically limited within the Arabian Peninsula. It is possible that it historically derived from the diminutive in pre-Islamic times as an ancient innovation, but its persistence into a contemporary dialect is truly noteworthy. (see Goitein 1960 for the occurrence of diminutives and augmentatives in Yemeni Jewish Arabic, where diminutives can be used with augmentative meaning).

3.0. The Possessive Suffix /-k/ in a Southwestern Dialect of Saudi Arabic

The masculine singular second person possessive (or genitive) suffix has the reflex *-ka* in standard varieties of the language, such as Classical Arabic and Modern Literary Arabic (Cowan 1958), as exemplified by the word *kitaabu-ka* 'your (MS) book (NOM)'. In dialects, such as Cairene Arabic, that lack case endings, the realisation of this possessive suffix shows allomorphy between *-ak* and *-k*, where the latter occurs only after words that end in a vowel, such as *abuu-k* 'your father' or *ʿašaa-k* 'your dinner'; all other forms take *-ak*, such as *balad-ak* 'your country', *rigl-ak* 'your leg', and *kitaab-ak* 'your book'. The allomorph *-ak* is also suffixed to feminine words that end in *tā marbūṭa*, such as *ṭaalib-t-ak* 'your student (F)', whose non-possessive realisation is *ṭaaliba*. The most straightforward analysis of the allomorphy in a dialect like Cairene is to posit /-ak/ as the underlying form of the 2nd person masculine singular possessive suffix and to have a rule that deletes the /-a/ of the suffix when it occurs immediately after a vowel. Feminine words that end in an orthographical *tā marbūṭa* would be analysed as either ending in an abstract /t/ or in a *t* introduced as part of the possessive construction of feminine word forms.

When we turn to Saudi varieties of Arabic, the allomorphy between *-k* and *-ak* (or *-ik*) has been discussed by Ingham (1982; 1994), especially with respect to Central Najdi Arabic. Here we find a pattern and an analysis that is quite different from the Cairene pattern briefly described above. Ingham (1982, 96) notes that in the central area of the Najdi Arabic region, suffixes like /-ak/ lose their vowel when they follow a syllable ending in VC (i.e., a short vowel followed by a single consonant). Examples include *naxal-k* 'your (MS) palms' and *walad-k* 'your (MS) son', where the suffix is just *-k*, but in other phonological environments the vowel surfaces, as in *beet-ak* (or *beet-ik*, depending on the subvariety) 'your (MS) house'. This differs not only from Cairene Arabic, but also from Urban Hijazi Arabic, as briefly discussed in Al-Essa (2019, 161), where the 2nd person masculine singular possessive suffix is given as *-ak*, but the corresponding

2nd person feminine singular possessive suffix is reported as having the allomorphs *-ik* after a word-final consonant and *-ki* after a word-final vowel. With this as background, in this section we consider specifically the allomorphy of the 2nd person masculine singular possessive suffix in an understudied Southwestern Saudi Arabian (SSA) variety spoken in the area of Northern Tihama, which, as reported in Alahmari (2018), shows unusual three-way allomorphy between *-k*, *-ak*, and *-ka*. We will detail their distribution and provide argumentation for *-k* being the underlying form of the suffix (we do not discuss the separate problem of the 2nd person feminine singular possessive suffix, which involves a different set of issues and does not always pattern like its masculine counterpart).

The distribution of the 2nd person masculine singular possessive suffix in SSA is straightforward, but interesting because it attests the three allomorphs *-k*, *-ak*, and *-ka*, which makes it somewhat different from other varieties. The allomorphs are predictable depending on the nature of the last syllable of the noun to which it attaches. The analytical questions are which variant of the allomorph constitutes the basic or underlying form; how are the other variants derived; and what might be the diachrony of the allomorphy? In our view, the basic or underlying form of the suffix in SSA is just /-k/. To see this, we must consider the range of data that is shown below. A main observation is that the allomorphy is predictable based on the nature of the last syllable of the base. To illustrate this, first consider the base words in (13) that end in a final CVC syllable (the base word is in the left column, the 2nd person masculine singular suffixed form is in the middle column, and the gloss is on the right; the full stop indicates a syllable boundary).

Table 4: Possessive formation for stems ending in CVC

(13)	Base word	Suffixed form	Gloss
(a)	/kutub/	ku.tubk	'your books'
(b)	/walad/	wa.ladk	'your son'
(c)	/balad/	ba.ladk	'your country'
(d)	/galam/	ga.lamk	'your pen'
(e)	/maktab/	mak.tabk	'your desk'
(f)	/ṣaaḥib/	ṣaa.ḥibk	'your friend'

Here we see that the suffixal allomorph -k can attach to words that end in a single consonant. The result is a final consonant cluster ending in k. Since SSA allows for a word-final voiceless consonant to be preceded by any other consonant, the final cluster in word forms like that shown in (13) is phonotactically permissible. However, the generalisation for when the allomorph -k occurs is not that the base word ends in a single consonant, but that it ends in a CV(C) syllable. This is made clear by the forms in (14) where a long vowel precedes the final consonant in the base word (the forms in the rightmost column with an asterisk are ungrammatical).

Table 5: Possessive formation for stems ending in CVVC

(14)	Base word	Suffixed form	Gloss	Ungrammatical alternative
(a)	/baab/	baa.bak	'your door'	*baabk
(b)	/beet/	bee.tak	'your home'	*beetk
(c)	/xaal/	xaa.lak	'your uncle'	*xaalk
(d)	/jiiraan/	jii.raa.nak	'your neighbours'	*jii.raank

These forms make clear the role of syllable weight in determining allomorphy. If we consider the example in (14a), /baab/, the ungrammatical output *baabk is not disallowed because of the final cluster, since the final cluster *bk* occurs in (13a), *kutubk*. Rather, a word-final consonant cluster after a long vowel, as in the righthand column in (14), is ruled out because it results in an extra-heavy CVVCC syllable. Since this is not phonotactically permitted, the allomorph that surfaces is *-ak*.

The role of final syllable weight in the determination of allomorph is also made clear by word forms that end in a consonant cluster or a word-final geminate. These words always take the allomorph *-ak*, as shown in (15) and (16).

Table 6: Possessive formation for stems ending in CVCC

(15)	Base word	Suffixed form	Gloss	Ungrammatical alternative
(a)	/bint/	bin.tak	'your daughter'	*bintk
(b)	/uxt/	ux.tak	'your sister'	*uxtk
(c)	/ahl/	ah.lak	'your family'	*ahlk
(d)	/nafs/	naf.sak	'yourself'	*nafsk

Table 7: Possessive formation for stems ending in CVGG

(16)	Base word	Suffixed form	Gloss	Ungrammatical alternative
(a)	/rabb/	rab.bak	'your god'	*rabbk
(b)	/umm/	um.mak	'your mother'	*ummk
(c)	/jadd/	jad.dak	'your grandfather'	*jaddk
(d)	/ʕamm/	ʕam.mak	'your uncle'	*ʕammk
(e)	/maḥall/	ma.ḥal.lak	'your place'	*ma.ḥallk

In both (15) and (16), the suffixation of the allomorph *-k* would lead to an extra-heavy syllable ending in three consonants, as shown in the rightmost column; such forms are avoided and the allomorph *-ak* surfaces. If we reference moraic theory for the analysis of Arabic along the lines of Watson (2002), Mahfoudhi (2005), Davis and Ragheb (2014), and Alahmari (2018) specifically for SAA, a short vowel would comprise one mora, a geminate consonant one mora, a long vowel would be two moras, and a coda consonant (other than one in word-final position) would also constitute one mora. Given this moraic structure, the generalisation for the occurrence of the allomorph -ak is that it attaches to a final-syllable that is bimoraic. The allomorph -k cannot attach to such a syllable since it would create an extra-heavy (i.e., trimoraic) word-final syllable; such syllables are prohibited in many Arabic dialects.

Given the patterning whereby the allomorph -ak attaches to a word-final heavy (bimoraic) syllable, the other allomorph -k can be analysed as suffixing to a word-final light syllable (i.e., a monomoraic syllable), as shown in (13). Recall that a word-final consonant is not moraic, so that a final CVC syllable as in the word ku.tub 'books' would be monomoraic (or light). In the suffixed output of word forms like ku.tub-k 'your books' in (13a), the final syllable becomes bimoraic (heavy), with the vowel u of the final syllable contributing one mora and the immediately following consonant b contributing another; the suffix -k does not add weight. Further evidence that the suffix -k attaches to word-final light syllables come from base words that end in a final CV. Consider the data in (17).

Table 8: Possessive formation for stems ending in CV

(17)	Base word	Suffixed form	Gloss
(a)	/abu/	a.buuk	'your father'
(b)	/axu/	a.xuuk	'your brother'
(c)	/ʕaša/	ʕa.šaak	'your dinner'
(d)	/ġada/	ġa.daak	'your lunch'

Here, as in many other dialects of Arabic, the allomorph -k is suffixed to a vowel-final word, with subsequent vowel lengthening of the final vowel. While some analyses have argued that the final vowel is underlyingly long in such forms (e.g., McCarthy 2005), Alahmari (2018) specifically argues that the final vowels in the SSA words in (17) are underlyingly short, which is in agreement with Watson's (2002) view on the final vowel length problem in Arabic (the details of which are beyond the scope of the current chapter).

A set of data related to the word forms in (17) are words that are marked with the feminine ending *tā marbūṭa*, shown in (18), where in isolation the word ends in the short suffixal vowel -*a*, but in possessive forms the phoneme *t* occurs immediately after the short vowel, which can be viewed as a linker to the following morpheme. When the 2nd person masculine singular possessive morpheme is suffixed to such a word, the allomorph -*k* occurs and clusters with the *t*, as in (18).

Table 9: Possessive formation with stems ending in *tā marbūṭa*

(18) Base word	Gloss	Suffixed form	Gloss
(a) *ra.ga.b-a*	'neck'	*ra.ga.batk*	'your neck'
(b) *jad.d-a*	'grandmother'	*jad.datk*	'your grandmother'
(c) *ʿam.m-a*	'aunt'	*ʿam.matk*	'your aunt'

The possessive forms shown in (18) are completely regular in the sense that the allomorph -*k* attaches to a final light syllable, whether we take that syllable to be vowel-final ending in a short -*a* (a final CV syllable) or abstractly ending in /C-at/ where the final /t/ is not pronounced in unaffixed forms.

Given the presentation so far in this section, that the allomorphy between -*k* and -*ak* is determined by the weight of the final syllable to which it is suffixed, whereby -*k* attaches to monomoraic final syllables and -*ak* to bimoraic ones, the data shown below in (19) are unexpected, where a third allomorph appears, -ka, rather than the expected -k.

Table 10: Possessive formation with the suffix -ka

(19)	Base word	Suffixed form	Gloss	Ungrammatical alternatives
(a)	/malik/	ma.lik.ka	'your king'	*ma.likk *ma.li.k-ak
(b)	/samak/	sa.mak.ka	'your fish'	*sa.makk *sa.ma.k-ak
(c)	/maalik/	maa.lik.ka	'your owner'	*maa.likk *maa.li.k-ak
(d)	/maslak/	mas.lak.ka	'your path'	*mas.lakk *mas.la.k-ak

What the base word forms shown in (19) all have in common is that the final syllable is CV*k*, that is, a word-final light (monomoraic) syllable ending in *k*. The expected allomorph based on the discussion above for a word like *samak* 'fish' in (19b) should be **samakk*, but this does not occur. The clear reason for this is the avoidance of a derived bimorphemic word-final geminate. While such geminates can occur in SSA (e.g., *sakat-t* 'I fell silent'), they are avoided for the 2nd person masculine singular possessive suffix (although forms like *ma.lik-k* 'your king' do occur in other Saudi varieties, such as the northwestern variety discussed in Alhuwaykin 2018). Given the avoidance of the derived word-final bimorphemic geminate-k in (19), one might expect the correct output for the words in (19) to have the allomorph -*ak*, resulting in a form like **samak-ak* 'your fish' for (19b), but recall from the above discussion that -*ak* attaches only to word forms that have a final bimoraic syllable. The base for the hypothetical **samak-ak* would be *sa.mak* with a word-final light CVC syllable. Consequently, a third allomorph surfaces only for base words that have CVk as its final syllable. This allomorph is -ka, which we would maintain, is an archaic form that survives in this specific context.

A final set of data that is supportive of the analysis offered here comes from base words where the final syllable is bimoraic with k as the word-final consonant. The pertinent data are shown in (20).

Table 11: Possessive forms of words with final /k/ in a bimoraic syllable

(20)	Base word	Suffixed form	Gloss	Ungrammatical alternatives
(a)	/mulk-k/	mul.kak	'your possession'	*mulkk *mulk.ka
(b)	/šeek-k/	šee.kak	'your check' (borrowing)	*šeekk *šeek.ka
(c)	/šakk-k/	šak.kak	'your doubt'	*šakkk *šakk.ka

Since the stems to which the 2nd person masculine singular possessive suffix attaches in (20) consist of a single heavy (bimoraic) syllable, the allomorph that occurs is -ak, which attaches to word-final bimoraic syllables. As shown in the rightmost column, the suffixing of either of the other allomorphs would create extra-heavy (trimoraic) syllables and would be phonotactically problematic. Thus, we maintain that the distribution of the allomorphs of the 2nd person masculine singular possessive suffix is for the most part weight-based, with -ak attaching to any base word whose final syllables is bimoraic and -k attaching to base words whose final syllable is monomoraic, unless the final syllable is CVk, in which case the allomorph is -ka.

In considering the questions concerning which allomorph is the underlying form of the 2nd person masculine singular possessive suffix (from a synchronic perspective) and what the diachrony might be, we would maintain, as argued for in Alahmari (2018), that in SAA the synchronic underlying form of the suffix is /-k/, without a vowel. The clearest evidence for this comes from the data in (13), where base words end in a final CVC syllable, as in *kutub* 'books'. Here, any of the three allomorphs are phonotactically possible, which includes the correct output *kutubk* as well as the unattested **kutubak* and **kutubka*. The fact that the correct output is *kutubk* strongly suggests that the underlying form is just /-k/, since there would be no reason for the low vowel to delete from a synchronic perspective if the underlying forms were either /-ak/ or /-ka/. We refer the reader to Alahmari (2018) for a formal analysis of the allomorphy within Optimality Theory. If we maintain that the underlying form of the suffix is /-k/, then the rule that inserts the vowel *-a* in such forms as *bint-ak* from underlying /bint-k/ would probably be morphophonological in order that the vowel quality be *a*. It may be possible to maintain a purely phonological account of the vowel insertion for the data shown in (14)–(16) and (20), but the specific argumentation for that is beyond the scope of this chapter.

With respect to the diachrony, that is, which allomorph may reflect a more archaic form of the language, a case can be made that the *-ka* allomorph that appears only on word forms like in (19), which end in a final CV*k* syllable, is actually an archaic form reflecting what is found in Classical Arabic. One could speculate that the loss of suffixal *-ka* in Saudi dialects relates to the loss of an earlier case system in the dialects. Based on this, a form like *malik-ka* 'your king' in SSA could be viewed as a remnant from a possible earlier form, such as **malikV-ka* (where V is a vocalic case marker), whereby this case ending has been diachronically lost. The persistence of -*ka* in SSA in just this one environment can be understood as due to specific avoidance of a word-final derived geminate; the allomorph did not change to -*ak* since in SSA -*ak* attaches only to bimoraic syllables. Thus, one could argue that the presence of the third allomorph -*ka* is an archaism among contemporary Saudi varieties. As far as we are aware, SSA is unusual among contemporary spoken Saudi varieties in maintaining three allomorphs, -*k*, -*ak*, and -*ka*, for the 2nd person masculine singular possessive suffix rather than two, -*k* and -*ak* (or -*ik*), as in many other Saudi varieties.

4.0. Final Degemination and Stress Shift in the Attuwair Dialect of Arabic

The special properties of geminate consonants in Arabic have been discussed for a variety of phenomena, including stress assignment by Watson (2002) for Sanʿani Arabic, first language acquisition by Ragheb and Davis (2014) for Cairene Arabic, and mora timing by Khattab and Al-Tamimi (2014) for Lebanese Arabic. All these studies demonstrate the saliency of geminate consonants for Arabic phonology. One way that this saliency is manifested is by the attraction of stress to a word-final syllable ending in a geminate consonant, which occurs in most dialects of Arabic, and the attraction of exceptional stress to syllables closed by a geminate in southwestern Arabian dialects of Arabic, which include Sanʿani Arabic (Watson 2002) and the southwestern variety of Northern Tihama detailed by Alahmari (2018; 2020). In both these varieties, primary stress falls on the first syllable of the word *dáw.wart* 'I/you (MS) looked for', where the first syllable is closed by a geminate consonant; this pattern is exceptional, since normally CVCC final syllables attract stress regardless of the nature of the preceding syllable, as in the example *gam.bárt* 'I/you (MS) sat', where the first syllable is closed but not by a geminate. The stress-attracting nature of geminate consonants might be an areal feature of southwestern Arabia, but we think that it is an understudied part of the stress system of Arabic dialects more generally.

Given the saliency of geminate consonants for Arabic phonetics and phonology, it may be somewhat surprising to find cases of degemination. One common case of degemination in Arabic, discussed in Farwaneh (2009), occurs when an underlying geminate comes immediately before another consonant; this is exemplified by Levantine /kull-hum/, which is realised as *kul.hum* 'all of them'. This can be contrasted with Cairene *kul.lu.hum*, where epenthesis occurs rather than degemination. A second type of degemination that occurs in some Arabic dialects is word-final degemination. This is characteristic of the Sudanese varieties discussed by Ali (2014; 2015). In the Hamar subdialect of Sudanese Arabic, not only is there word-final degemination, but more generally, the final consonant in a word-final cluster deletes. What is interesting is that the final degemination and final cluster reduction do not entail a shift of stress. The consequence of this is that the Hamar dialect distinguishes *kál.lam* 'he told' from *kal.lám* 'I told' (from underlying /kallam-t/) totally on the basis of stress location.

With this as background, an unusual feature that is found in various varieties of Najdi Arabic and in northwest Arabia, though little discussed, is the degemination of word-final geminates with concomitant stress shift off the final syllable, as in the example *á.ham* 'more important', where most other dialects have *a.hámm*. However, this does not happen when the word-final geminate is bimorphemic, as in *si.kát-t* 'I kept silent', where there is no stress shift or final degemination. In this section, based on Alhuwaykim (2018), we will detail this phenomenon in one sub-variety, spoken in the village of Attuwair *iṭṭ.weer*, which is a Bedouin-influenced dialect within the boundaries of Sakaka City (Aljouf) in northwestern Saudi Arabia, north of where Northern Najdi Arabic is spoken, according to Ingham's (1994) classification of Najdi subdialects. In this section, we present the pertinent data from Attuwair Arabic, offer a descriptive analysis of the phenomenon, and suggest that while it is an innovative feature of Arabic, it is most likely an older innovation.

In Attuwair Arabic in northwest Saudi Arabia and also in at least some varieties of Najdi Arabic there is a phenomenon of the degemination of word-final geminate consonants. However, before presenting the data that illustrate this, we first consider what we view as a related phenomenon: the shortening of word-final long vowels in CVV base words upon prefixation, as exemplified in (21).

Table 12: Final shortening of long vowels in CVV words upon prefixation (with prefix in bold)

(21)	Word	Gloss		Word	Gloss
(a)	maa	'water'	(a')	**íl**.ma (note: máa-kum)	'the water'
(b)	daa	'sickness'	(b')	**íd**.da	'the sickness'
(c)	zii	'costume'	(c')	**íz**.zi	'the costume
(d)	jaa	'he came'	(d')	**má**a.ja	'he did not come'
(e)	fii	'there is'	(e')	**má**a.fi	'there is not'
(f)	lii	'for me'	(f')	**má**a.li	'there isn't for me'

The data in the left-hand column in (21a–f) show lexical items that have the shape CVV and carry stress when pronounced in isolation or as unaffixed. The prefixal data in the right-hand column are interesting in that they show that the definite article prefix in (21a'–c') and the negative prefix in (21d'–f') are part of the prosodic word to which they attach and attract stress. When this occurs, as shown, the vowel of the base word is short. The most straightforward analysis is the shortening of a word-final vowel upon prefixation with concomitant stress shift to the first syllable. While one can argue whether the data in (21) really reflect word-final vowel shortening in disyllabic words (21a'–f') or an alternative analysis of vowel lengthening when the word is realised as monosyllabic in isolation (21a–f) (and when a suffix is added, as in máa.kum 'your (PL) water'), a parallel phenomenon occurs with word-final geminates: they are realised as geminates in word forms that are monosyllabic (and when a suffix is added), but they shorten (i.e., degeminate) when word-final in disyllabic forms. This is shown by the data in (22), when a prefix is added to a monosyllabic word that ends in a geminate, and in (23), which shows disyllabic comparative (i.e., elative) forms that typically end in a geminate consonant in most other dialects of Arabic with word-final stress.

Table 13: Degemination of final geminates in CVGG words upon prefixation (with initial stress)

(22)	Word	Gloss		Word	Gloss
(a)	ʕamm	'uncle'	(a')	íl.ʕam (note: ʕám.m-i)	'the uncle'
(b)	hamm	'distress'	(b')	íl.ham	'the distress'
(c)	ḥubb	'love'	(c')	íl.ḥub	'the love'
(d)	ḥagg	'truth'	(d')	íl.ḥag	'the truth'
(e)	jaww	'weather'	(e')	íl.jaw	'the weather'
(f)	fayy	'shadow'	(f')	íl.fay	'the shadow'
(g)	damm	'blood'	(g')	fíi.dam	'there is blood'
(h)	/jaa-yamm/		(h')	jáa.yam	'he came to'
(i)	/maḥall/		(i')	má.ḥal	'place, grocery store'

Table 14: Degemination of final geminates in segmentally monomorphemic words (elative forms)

(23)	Other dialects	Attuwair	Gloss
(a)	a.šádd	á.šad	'stronger'
(b)	a.xáff	á.xaf	'lighter'
(c)	a.hámm	á.ham	'more important'
(d)	a.ʕámm	á.ʕam	'more general'
(e)	a.ḥágg	á.ḥag	'more entitled to'

In the left-hand column of (22), the data in (22a–g) show monosyllabic word forms that end in a geminate consonant where the geminate consonant is pronounced. It is clear from the suffixal forms of these words, such as ʕám.m-i 'my uncle' shown in (22a), that these base words end in final geminates. However, when a prefix is placed before these base words, such as the definite article prefix as in (22a′–f′), the word-final geminate consonant undergoes degemination and stress shifts to the first syllable. The data shown in (22g–i) show that degemination (and stress shift) also occurs with other prefixes besides the definite article. Just as interesting is the observation on comparative (elative) form of roots, where the last two consonants are identical, as in (23). These comparatives typically have final geminates with stress on the final syllable in most dialects of Arabic, as shown in the left-hand column of (23). In the Attuwair dialect (and in various Najdi varieties as well) there is degemination of the final consonant, with stress appearing on the initial syllable.

At first glance, the phenomenon reflected by the data in (22) and (23), which involves the metrical shortening of the final syllable and stress shift to the initial syllable, may seem somewhat reminiscent of an observation from Ingham's (2008, 330) work on Najdi Arabic about how the definite article attracts stress. He notes, "The stress rules of the dialect also lead to stressing of the definite article *ál-* preceding nouns of the form CvC or CvCvC, as in *álbil* 'the camels', *álwalad* 'the boy', *álhawa* 'love'" (See also Watson 2011, 902 on this). However, while the attraction of stress to the definite article might explain the data in (22a′–f′), where final degemination would be seen as a consequence of stress shift, it does not really explain the elative data in (23) nor the degemination seen in (22i). Moreover, the definite article in Attuwair Arabic does not always attract the stress, as can be seen in an example like *il.má.ḥal* 'the place, grocery store', where stress is on the penultimate syllable, as it would be in a word like *mid.rí.sah* 'school'. Furthermore, if a monosyllabic noun ends in two different consonants, then no stress shift occurs when the definite article is added, as exemplified by *il.ʕílm* 'the knowledge, news', where stress remains on the final syllable despite the presence of the definite article.

If the motivation for final degemination (22)–(23) and final vowel shortening (21) is not the stressing of the definite article (or other prefix), then what is the motivation? Here we suggest that there is a constraint that is active in Attuwair Arabic against having a moraic element at the end of a word that would result in a bimoraic stressed syllable. The practical result of this avoidance would either be the shortening of a final long vowel or degemination of a final geminate. This would not apply to monosyllabic word forms, like the data in the left-hand column of (21) and (22), since it would result in a (subminimal) monomoraic word form, for example *ma 'water' instead of *maa* or *ʕam 'uncle' instead of *ʕamm* (see Alhuwykim 2018 for an Optimality Theory analysis that offers a formal analysis with ranked constraints). The evidence that the constraint in Attuwair Arabic against having a moraic element at the end of a word that would result in a bimoraic stressed syllable comes from apparent exceptions in which there is no degemination. Consider the two examples shown below in (24).

(24) No degemination (and no stress shift) if the word-final geminate is morphologically derived

   (a) /sakat-t/ → *si.kátt* 'I kept silent'
   (b) /malak-k/ → *mi.lákk* 'your (MS) king'

Both words in (24) end in a final geminate, but there is no degemination. The difference between the two words in (24) and the final geminate in the words in (22) and (23) which undergo degemination is that in (22) and (23) the final geminate is underlyingly moraic, whereas in (24a–b) the final geminate is derived (sometime referred to as a 'fake' geminate). In (24a), the word-final geminate-t that surfaces comes about through the concatenation of two different morphemes: a root-final /t/ followed by the inflectional 1st person suffix /-t/. Neither of these consonants is underlyingly moraic, so no degemination (i.e., avoidance of a word-final mora) occurs. Similarly, the word-final geminate-k in (24b) comes about through the concatenation of the final /k/ root morpheme for *malak* with the 2nd person masculine singular possessive suffix -k. Neither of these is underlyingly moraic, so there is no word-final mora in (24b). This view that it is a word-final mora that is lost in the degemination process (and in the vowel shortening process) is further supported by the lack of stress shift in words ending in a consonant cluster as shown in (25).

(25) No stress shift (or mora loss) in words ending in two different consonants:

(a) la.ʿáb-t   'I played'
(b) il.ʿílm   'the knowledge/news'

There is no stress shift or word-final mora loss in the two words in (25) because the word-final consonant in these words is not moraic. The second syllable retains its stress because it is a heavy (bimoraic) syllable, but the word-final consonant is not moraic. A final type of evidence for the view that stress shift results from the demoraification of a word-final consonant (if it is moraic), as in (22) and (23), or the demoraification of a word-final long vowel, as in (21), comes from the observation that no word-final degemination occurs if the final geminate is preceded by a long vowel. This is shown by the two examples in (26).

(26) No degemination in word-final CVVGG syllables
  (a) *il.jáadd*   'the serious (M)'
  (b) *il.ʕáamm*   'the general/public'

The last syllable in each of the examples in (26) is trimoraic. These final syllables have a long vowel which is two moras and a final geminate which adds the third mora. If degemination were to occur, the final syllable would still be heavy because of the long vowel maintaining the stress. Words in Attuwair Arabic that have a final CVVC syllable receive stress on that syllable, as illustrated by such words as *bi.ʕíid* 'distant' and *il.ʕáam* 'the (last) year'. Consequently, degemination in (26) would still leave stress on the final syllable, meaning that word-final degemination (and vowel shortening) only occur if it would result in a stress shift.

To summarise our descriptive analysis, an underlying word-final long vowel shortens, as in (21), and an underlying word-final geminate degeminates, as in (22)–(23), only if the outcome is an unstressed monomoraic final syllable. That is, there is avoidance of stressing a word-final bimoraic syllable that ends in a moraic element (see Alhuwaykim 2018 for a formal Optimality Theory analysis).

There are a number of larger questions that word-final degemination in Attuwair Arabic relate to. First, as a theoretical issue, final degemination as illustrated in this section is best understood on the view that geminate consonants are underlyingly moraic. This explains why there is no degemination in (24a–b), when the surface geminate is derived from two different morphemes: there is no underlying geminate in these word forms, so degemination (i.e., demoraification) cannot occur. This supports the view that geminates are underlyingly moraic in Arabic, as maintained by Davis and Ragheb (2014) and Khattab and Al-Tamimi (2014). Second, is the issue of the geographical isogloss of final degemination in Saudi Arabian varieties of Arabic and whether it always occurs alongside final vowel shortening, as in (21). While our focus has been on Attuwair Arabic in northwest of Saudi Arabia, somewhat north (and west) of northern Najdi Arabic as delimited in Ingham (1994), we are aware that word-final degemination is also characteristic of at least some varieties of Najdi Arabic. However, we do not know what the isogloss of final degemination might be and if the specific details as presented here for Attuwair Arabic are exactly the same or different in other varieties that witness final degemination. A final matter concerns whether word-final degemination is an archaic feature of Attuwair (and Najdi) Arabic or an innovation reflecting an internal development. While we have no direct evidence bearing on it, we suggest that final degemination in Attuwair (and Najdi) Arabic is an innovation specific to an area of Saudi Arabia that includes Sakaka City and at least parts of the Najdi region, but degemination is probably not a recent innovation, given that it seems to be fairly widespread. These matters are in need of further research.

5.0. Conclusion

In this chapter we have presented an abundance of data reflecting unusual phenomena in understudied dialects of the Arabian Peninsula, specifically morphological augmentatives in Northern Najdi/Haʔili Arabic, the distribution of the allomorphs of the second person masculine singular possessive suffix in a southwestern Saudi Arabian dialect (Northern Tihama), and final degemination and stress retraction in Attuwair, Sakaka City Arabic. For each case we have presented detailed data illustrating the phenomenon and have offered a descriptive analysis. We have also discussed the question as to what extent the phenomena presented here reflect archaic features, be it substrate or older forms of Arabic, or just reflect Arabic-internal developments. In all the cases presented, data come from the intuitions of native speaker linguists in consultation with other speakers of the same dialect. While some may consider this manner of data compilation less than rigorous, it is nonetheless important for native speakers to carry out such work because data can be gathered quickly and can lead to research questions regarding the verification of the data, their status as internal developments or archaic forms, and their contemporary sociolinguistic manifestations.

References

Abboud, Peter. 1979. 'The Verb in Northern Najdi Arabic'. *Bulletin of the School of Oriental and African Studies* 42/3: 467–99.

Alahmari, Musa. 2018. 'An Optimality-Theoretic Analysis of Some Aspects of the Phonology and Morphology of a Southwestern Saudi Arabian Arabic Dialect'. PhD dissertation, Indiana University.

———. 2020. 'Stress Assignment and Foot Construction in a Southwestern Saudi Arabian Dialect'. In *Perspectives on Arabic Linguistics XXXII*, edited by Elly van Gelderen, 11–33. Amsterdam: John Benjamins.

Al-Essa, Aziza. 2019. 'Phonological and Morphological Variation'. In *The Routledge Handbook of Arabic Sociolinguistics*, edited by Enam Al-Wer and Uri Horesh, 151–68. London: Routledge.

Alfaifi, Abdullah, and Peter Behnstedt. 2010. 'First Notes on the Dialect of Ǧabal Fayfā (Jazan Province/Saudi Arabia)'. *Zeitschrift für Arabische Linguistik* 52: 53–67.

Alfaifi, Abdullah, and Stuart Davis. 2021. 'An Examination of the /m-/ Definite Article in Upper Faifi Arabic'. *Zeitschrift für Arabische* Linguistik 73: 36–52.

Alhuwaykim, Mamdouh. 2018. 'Aspects of the Phonology of Northwestern Saudi Arabic Dialect: An Optimality-Theoretic Analysis'. PhD dissertation, Indiana University.

Ali, Abdel-Khalig. 2014. 'Syllabification and Phrasing in Three Dialects of Sudanese Arabic'. PhD dissertation, University of Toronto.

———. 2015. 'Prosodic Domains of Syllabification Sudanese Arabic'. In *Perspectives on Arabic Linguistics XXIX*, edited by Hamid Ouali, 33–54. Amsterdam: John Benjamins.

Al-Jallad, Ahmad. 2013. 'Arabia and Areal Hybridity'. *Journal of Language Contact* 6: 220–42.

———. 2021. 'The History of the *am-* Definite Article: South Arabian or Arabic?'. *Zeitschrift für Arabische Linguistik* 73: 53–70.

Al Rasheed, Madawi. 1991. *Politics in an Arabian Oasis: The Rashidis of Saudi Arabia*. New York: I. B. Tauris Publishers.

Alshammari, Wafi, and Stuart Davis. 2019. 'Diminutive and Augmentative Formation in Northern Najdi/Ha'ili Arabic'. In *Perspectives on Arabic Linguistics XXXI*, edited by Amel Khalfaoui and Youssef Haddad, 51–73. Amsterdam: John Benjamins.

Al-Wer, Enam, and Khairia Al-Qahtani. 2016. 'Lateral Fricative ḍād in Tihāmat Qaḥtān: A Quantitative Sociolinguistic Investigation'. In *Perspectives on Arabic Linguistics XXVII*, edited by Stuart Davis and Usama Soltan, 151–69. Amsterdam: John Benjamins.

Assuwaida, Abdul Rahman. 1997. *An-Nakhatu at-Ta'iyyatu fi al-Lahjati al-Ha'iliyyah* [The Tayy Flavour in the Ha'ili Dialect]. Ha'il, Saudi Arabia: Dar al-Andalus li-l-Nashr wa-l-Tawzī. [Arabic]

Behnstedt, Peter. 2016. *Dialect Atlas of North Yemen and Adjacent Areas*. Leiden: Brill.

Cowan, David. 1958. *Modern Literary Arabic*. Cambridge: Cambridge University Press.

Davis, Stuart, and Marwa Ragheb. 2014. 'Geminate Representation in Arabic'. In *Perspectives on Arabic Linguistics* XXIV–

XXV, edited by Samira Farwaneh and Hamid Ouali, 3–19. Amsterdam: John Benjamins.

Farwaneh, Samira. 2009. 'Toward a Typology of Arabic Dialects: The Role of Final Consonantality'. *Journal of Arabic and Islamic Studies* 9/4: 82–109.

Fattah, Hala, and Frank Caso. 2009. *A Brief History of Iraq*. New York: Hermitage.

Gadoua, Abdulhamid, and Stuart Davis. 2019. 'Diminutive Formation in a Libyan Dialect with Some Phonological Implications'. In *Perspectives on Arabic Linguistics* XXXI, edited by Amel Khalfaoui and Youssef Haddad, 31–49. Amsterdam: John Benjamins.

Goitein, Shlomo D. 1960. 'The Language of Al-Gades: The Main Characteristics of an Arabic Dialect Spoken in Lower Yemen'. *Le Muséon* 73: 351–94.

Holes, Clive. 1984. *Colloquial Arabic of the Gulf and Saudi Arabia*. London: Routledge and Keegan Paul.

Ingham, Bruce. 1982. *North East Arabian Dialects*. London: Kegan Paul International.

———. 1994. *Najdi Arabic: Central Arabian*. Amsterdam: John Benjamins

———. 2008 'Najdi Arabic'. In *Encyclopedia of Arabic Language and Linguistics* III, edited by Kees Versteegh, 326–34. Leiden: Brill.

Khattab, Ghada, and Jalal Al-Tamimi. 2014. 'Geminate Timing in Lebanese Arabic: The Relationship between Phonetic Timing and Phonological Structure'. *Laboratory Phonology* 5: 231–69.

Mahfoudhi, Abdessatar. 2005. 'Moraic Syllable Structure and Edge Effects in Arabic'. In *Perspectives on Arabic Linguistics XVII–XVIII*, edited by Mohammad Alhawary and Elabbas Benmamoun, 27–48. Amsterdam: John Benjamins.

McCarthy, John. 2005. 'The Length of Stem-final Vowels in Colloquial Arabic'. In *Perspectives on Arabic Linguistics XVII–XVIII*, edited by Mohammad Alhawary and Elabbas Benmamoun, 1–26. Amsterdam: John Benjamins.

Prochazka, Theodore, Jr. 1988. 'Gleanings from Southwestern Saudi Arabia'. *Zeitschrift für Arabische Linguistik* 19: 44–49.

Ragheb, Marwa, and Stuart Davis. 2014. 'On the L1 Development of Final Consonant Clusters in Cairene Arabic'. In *Perspectives on Arabic Linguistics XXVI*, edited by Reem Khamis-Dakwar and Karen Froud, 263–81. Amsterdam: John Benjamins.

Sifianou, Maria. 1992. 'The Use of Diminutives in Expressing Politeness: Modern Greek Versus English'. *Journal of Pragmatics* 17/2: 155–73.

Watson, Janet C. E. 2002. *The Phonology and Morphology of Arabic*. Oxford: Oxford University Press.

———. 2011. 'Dialects of the Arabian Peninsula'. In *The Semitic Languages*, edited by Stefan Weninger, Geoffrey Kahn, Michael Streck, and Janet Watson, 897–908. Berlin: de Gruyter.

———. 2018. 'South Arabian and Arabic Dialects'. In *Arabic Historical Dialectology: Linguistic and Sociolinguistic Approaches*, edited by Clive Holes, 316–34. Oxford: Oxford University Press.

Watson, Janet C. E,. and Munira Al-Azraqi. 2011. 'Lateral Fricatives and Lateral Emphatics in Southern Saudi Arabia and Mehri. *Proceedings of the Seminar for Arabian Studies* 41: 425–31.

Zewi, Tamar. 2006. 'Diminutive'. In *Encyclopedia of Arabic Language and Linguistics* I, edited by Kees Versteegh, 637–40. Leiden: Brill.

DISTAL AND PROXIMAL RELATIVE PRONOUNS IN CENTRAL FAIFI ARABIC*

Abdullah Alfaifi

This paper provides preliminary evidence that relative pronouns in Central Faifi Arabic can possibly denote distality and proximity.[1] The paper contextualises relative pronouns in Central Faifi Arabic by providing a general overview of relative pronouns, with a focus on relative pronouns in Modern Written Arabic and some Arabic dialects. Central Faifi Arabic has three pairs of relative pronouns: *ḏī* and *ḏā*, *tī* and *tā*, and *awḏī* and *awḏā*. The members of each pair, which differ in only the quality of the final vowel, have been previously regarded as free variants.

Through a series of tasks performed by fifteen Central Faifi Arabic native speakers, this paper shows that relative pronouns in Central Faifi Arabic are not always in free variation and that they can indicate distality and proximity in the presence of an adverb of place, e.g., *ḥawla* 'there', *ṯamma* 'there'. In other words,

---

* I would like to thank Stuart Davis from Indiana University, Bloomington, for his extensive feedback on this paper. An earlier version of this paper was presented at Janet Watson's *Language and Nature in South Arabia Workshop* at the University of Leeds. This paper benefited greatly from the comments of the attendees, to whom I also extend my thanks.

[1] The classification of the dialect as 'Central' is based on Alfaifi (2022).

adverbs of place in the dialect draw out a possible historical distinction between the relative pronouns which have the high vowel /ī/ and relative pronouns which have the low vowel /ā/, where relative pronouns with /ā/ indicate distality and relative pronouns with /ī/ indicate proximity. Thus, while the distal/proximal distinction may not be categorical at present, the results of the tasks performed by native speakers strongly imply that the dialect had this distinction at some point.

1.0. Introduction

Relative pronouns are grammatical words which relate an element in a subordinate relative clause to a noun in the main clause of a sentence (Ryding 2005, 322). In Arabic, relative pronouns can reflect information about an antecedent, such as gender, number, and animacy. One piece of information that relative pronouns have not been said to denote is the location of the antecedent relative to the speaker or listener.

This paper aims to investigate the suggestion that Faifi Arabic relative pronouns are used to indicate distality or proximity, similar to how demonstratives in the dialect reflect this information. The paper first situates Faifi Arabic relative pronouns by providing a brief overview of relative pronouns in Modern Written Arabic and some Arabic dialects (§§2.0–3.0). Faifi Arabic relative pronouns are introduced in §4.0. §5.0 presents a description and discussion of the various tasks that were performed by Central Faifi Arabic speakers. The potential effect of the phonological makeup of words is discussed in §6.0. And, finally, §7.0 summarises and concludes the paper.

2.0. Relative Pronouns in Modern Written Arabic

Modern Written Arabic has fourteen relative pronouns. These relative pronouns are classified as *muxtaṣṣa* 'specific' and *ʿāmmah* 'common or generic' (Mughazy 2009). There are twelve specific relative pronouns which are characterised by having morphologically represented agreement features that reflect the head noun. They distinguish number (singular, dual, and plural), gender, referent character, and the nominative and obliguqe (genitive/accusative) case (Mughazy 2009), although case is distinguished only in the dual (Table 1).

Table 1: Specific Relative Pronouns in Modern Written Arabic (H= human; NH= non-human)

	Feminine	Neutral	Masculine
Singular	*allatī* (H & NH)	—	*allaḏī* (H & NH)
Dual Nominative	*allatāni* (H & NH)	—	*allaḏāni* (H & NH)
Dual Oblique	*allatayni* (H & NH)	—	*allaḏayni* (H & NH)
Plural	*allātī* *allawātī* *allāʾī* (H & NH)	*alʾulā* *alʾulāʾi* (H & NH)	*allaḏīna* (H)

The remaining two relative pronouns, *man* and *mā*, are in the category referred to as common relative pronouns. These are typically not feature-specific, since they do not distinguish number, gender, or case (Mughazy 2009, 61).

3.0. Relative Pronouns in Modern Arabic Dialects

In most Arabic dialects, the Modern Written Arabic relative pronouns are condensed to the relative pronoun *illi*, which is characterised mainly by the geminated /l/ and has several variants with the voiced interdental fricative, as in *alladi* and *allidi* (Johnstone 1967; Holes 1983; Watson 1993). Some Arabic dialects, predominantly the sedentary dialects spoken in Northern Mesopotamia and Anatolia, have been reported to have relative pronouns with an ungeminated /l/ (Retsö 2003, 265). All of these variants are case-, number-, and gender-neutral (Vicente 2009). While this relative pronoun typically replaces all other relative pronouns, some dialects have it in addition to other relative pronouns. One particular case can be found in Abha Arabic, spoken in the city of Abha in southwestern Saudi Arabia, as described in Behnstedt (2016, 74–75). This dialect has been reported to have the three relative pronouns *ḏā*, *tā*, and *illi*. Although used rarely, the first two are used for singular antecedents and distinguish the masculine and feminine genders, respectively, while the *illi* relative pronoun is used specifically for plural antecedents.[2]

While the *illī* relative pronoun is perhaps the most common in Arabic dialects, it is not present in all documented varieties. This is especially the case in dialects spoken in the southern parts of the Arabian Peninsula. Several studies have reported other relative pronouns, such as *bu* in Oman; the gender- and number-

---

[2] Al-Azraqi (1998, 277) mentions only *illi* and *ḏā* as relative pronouns in Abha Arabic. Considering that *ḏā* and *tā* are rare to begin with, this may be an indicator that the dialect is undergoing, or perhaps has undergone, a complete shift to the more common *illī* relative pronoun.

neutral *aḏī* in north-western Yemen, Ṣanʿā, Aslaʿ, Gurrān, Jabal aš-Širg, Qaryat Maʿdan Ḥīḏār, and Jabal Ḥubayš; the gender- and number-neutral *ḏī* in the dialects spoken in north-western and central Yemen in the regions of Ḍafār, al-Bayḍāʾ, Radā, Yāfiʿ, and Datīnah; and the gender-specific and number-neutral *ḏā* and *tā* in al-Ḥagw in southwestern Saudi Arabia (Rabin 1951, 204; Retsö 2003, 265; Behnstedt 2016, 74). A dialect that has a more intricate system of relative pronouns is the Arabic dialect of Rijal Almaʿ, spoken in the southwest of Saudi Arabia.

As detailed in Asiri (2008), the Arabic dialect of Rijal Almaʿ has four relative pronouns that must agree with the antecedent in terms of number and gender and are used only when the head noun is definite. These relative pronouns are *ḏa*, used with a singular masculine antecedent; *ta*, used with a singular feminine antecedent; *wula*, used with a human plural antecedent; and *ma*, used with a non-human plural antecedent. No relative pronoun in this dialect inflects for case or duality.

Table 2: Relative Pronouns in Rijal Almaʿ

	Masculine	Feminine
Singular	*ḏa* (H & NH)	*ta* (H & NH)
Plural	*wula* (H) / *ma* (NH)	*wula* (H) / *ma* (NH)

Examples (1)–(7) below demonstrate how these relative pronouns are used in Rijal Almaʿ (examples from Asiri 2008, 72–73):

(1) antah rayta m=walad ḏa šarad
    you.MS saw the=boy REL.MS ran_away
    'Have you seen the boy who ran away?'

(2) gābalt im=brat ta lisa yasmaʿ
    I_met the=girl REL.FS couldn't hear
    'I met the girl who couldn't hear.'

(3) sāfara   m=rajil   ḍa   šarayt   sayyāratūh
    travelled   the=man   REL.MS   I_bought   his_car
    'The man, whose car I bought, travelled.'

(4) waštari   m=bayt   ḍa   yabīʿ   jārna
    I'll_buy   the=house REL.MS   is_selling our_neighbour
    'I'll buy the house that our neighbour is selling.'

(5) antu   raytu   m=šajarat   ta   gaṭaʿaw
    you.PL   saw   the=tree   REL.FS   they_cut
    'Have you seen the tree that they cut?'

(6) gābalt   im=ʿuwāl   wula   saragu   m=maḥall
    I_met   the=boys   REL.PL(H)   stole   the=shop
    'I met the boys who stole from the shop.'

(7) im=bagar   ma   bāʿ (~ bāʿaha)
    the=cows   REL.PL(NH) he_sold
    'The cows that he sold.'

An interesting phenomenon is that anaphoric pronouns are typically absent in relative clauses when they are coreferential with the head—compare the verbs in the examples in (1) and (2) above. However, anaphoric pronouns must be expressed in possessive pronouns, as in the example in (3).

This phenomenon in the Rijal Almaʿ dialect may relate to the Accessibility Hierarchy (Keenan and Comrie 1977).

4.0. Relative Pronouns in Faifi Arabic

In the same general region of the Arabian Peninsula is another dialect that has a different set of relative pronouns. This dialect is Faifi Arabic, spoken in the Faifa Mountains near the southwestern border of Saudi Arabia (Figure 1).

Figure 1: Map of the Faifa Mountains in Saudi Arabia (Google Maps 2023)

As detailed in Alfaifi (2016, 250), Faifi Arabic has three pairs of postnominal relative pronouns, which are overt when the head noun is definite. When the head noun is indefinite, the relative pronoun is omitted. The three pairs are *ḏī* and *ḏā*, which are used with a masculine singular head noun; *tī* and *tā*, which are used with a singular feminine head noun; and *awḏī* and *awḏā*, which are used with feminine and masculine plural head nouns.[3]

All six relative pronouns (Table 3) can appear with animate or inanimate nouns. As with relative pronouns in Rijal Almaʿ, relative pronouns in Faifi Arabic do not inflect for duality or case.

---

[3] Alfaifi and Behnstedt (2010, 60) recognise only *ḏī*, Behnstedt (2016, 74–75) recognises only *ḏā*, *tā*, and *awḏā*, and Alfaife (2018, 117) recognises only *ḏī*, *tī*, and *awḏī*. Considering that Faifi Arabic has been shown to comprise several subdialects (Alfaifi 2022), these works may have been describing different varieties.

Table 3: Relative Pronouns in Faifi Arabic

	Masculine	Feminine
Singular	ḏī/ḏā (H & NH)	tī/tā (H & NH)
Plural	awḏī/awḏā (H & NH)	awḏī/awḏā (H & NH)

As the examples below show, relative pronouns in Faifi Arabic are overt only when the head noun is definite (8).

(8) lagīt   m=źawwāl   ḏī   xarbānin
    I_found   the=mobile_phone REL   broken
    'I found the mobile phone that is broken.'

(9) *lagīt   źawwālin   ḏī   xarbānin
    I_found   a_mobile_phone   REL   broken
    'I found a cell phone that is broken.'

(10) ḏī   źawwada   ḏī   yistāhil   jāyza
     REL   made   this   deserves   award
     'Whoever made this deserves an award.'

(11) m=bint   tī   gāman
     the=girl REL   stood_up
     'The girl who stood up.'

(12) m=walad   ḏī   gāma
     the=boy   REL   stood_up
     'The boy who stood up.'

As mentioned in Alfaifi (2016, 251), the Faifi Arabic relative pronouns ḏī, tī, and awḏī are homophonous to the proximal demonstratives ḏī 'this (M)', tī 'this (F)', and awḏī 'these', respectively, as shown in the following examples in Table (4).

Table 4: Homophony Between Relative Pronouns and Demonstratives

mwalad	ḏī	mwalad	ḏī	gāma
the=boy	this	the=boy	who	stood_up
'this boy'		'the boy who stood up'		
mbint	tī	mbint	tī	gāman
the=girl	this	the=girl	who	stood_up
'this girl'		'the girl who stood up'		
mawlād	awḏī	mawlād	awḏī	gāmū
the=boys	these	the=boys	who	stood_up
'these boys'		'the boys who stood up'		
mbanāt	awḏī	mbanāt	awḏī	gimna
the=girls	these	the=girls	who	stood_up
'these girls'		'the girls who stood up'		

In certain contexts, this homophony can potentially cause ambiguity, as shown in the pairs in Table 5. Ambiguity in this case is resolved by a very brief pause following the demonstrative, but mainly through intonation, where the demonstratives ḏī, tī, and awḏī tend to be comparatively higher in intonation than relative pronouns.[4]

---

[4] Relevant to the discussion is the fact that demonstratives in Faifi Arabic distinguish proximity to the speaker (ḏī/ḏayya, tī/tayya, awḏi/awḏayya), distality from the speaker (ḏaylī, taylī, awḏaylī), and distality from the speaker and proximity to the listener (ḏāla, tāla, awḏāla). For both demonstratives and relative pronouns, singular forms are characterised by initial /ḏ/ for the masculine gender and /t/ for the feminine gender. For plurals, /aw/ generally indicates gender-neutral demonstratives and relative pronouns. See Alfaifi (2016, 162–214) for a thorough discussion of the Faifi Arabic demonstratives.

Table 5: Potential Ambiguity as a Result of Homophony

mwalad	ḏī	gāma	mwalad	ḏī	gāma
the=boy	this	stood_up	the=boy	who	stood_up
'this boy stood up'			'the boy who stood up'		
mbint	tī	gāman	mbint	tī	gāman
the=girl	this	stood_up	the=girl	who	stood_up
'this girl stood up'			'the girl who stood up'		
mmawlāḏ	awḏī	gāmū	mmawlāḏ	awḏī	gāmū
the=boys	these	stood_up	the=boys	who	stood_up
'these boys stood up'			'the boys who stood up'		
mbanāt	awḏī	gimna	mbanāt	awḏī	gimna
the=girls	these	stood_up	the=girls	who	stood_up
'these girls stood up'			'the girls who stood up'		

5.0. Distal and Proximal Relative Pronouns in Central Faifi Arabic

As mentioned previously, Faifi Arabic has three pairs of relative pronouns: *ḏī* and *ḏā*, *tī* and *tā*, and *awḏī* and *awḏā*. The previous literature on the Faifi subdialects suggests that each pair is in free variation in the dialect and that the difference is only phonological (Alfaifi 2016, 250). This section presents details about an experiment that aimed to investigate the possibility that relative pronouns in the central dialect of Faifi Arabic, a dialect which appears to have all six relative pronouns, distinguish distality and proximity when the adverbs of place *hni* 'here', *ḥawla* 'there', and *ṭamma* 'there' are present in the same phrase.[5]

---

[5] As detailed in Alfaifi (2016, 299–303), the adverbs of place *ṭamma* and *ḥawla*, both meaning 'there', differ in that the latter is used to denote a visible location far from the speaker and close to the listener, while the former refers to an invisible location far from both the speaker and listener.

5.1. Methodology

This subsection describes the method used in this study, including the sampling of respondents, a description of the instrument, the types of tasks the subjects were asked to perform, and the purpose of each task.

5.1.1. Respondents

A total of fifteen Faifi Arabic speakers participated in this study. Speakers either currently live in the central region of the Faifa Mountains (n=9) or reside in other regions in Saudi Arabia, but originally descend from subtribes in the same region (n=6). All speakers reported that they use Faifi Arabic on a daily basis. Ten of the fifteen speakers were male and five were female. The participants' ages ranged from 19 to 68 (mean = 39.3). Data were collected in two phases with identical instruments and tasks. Eight subjects were recruited in the first phase and seven in the second.

5.1.2. Instrument

For the purpose of this experiment, a list of 44 phrases with and without adverbs of place and relative pronouns were used. These phrases were divided into five groups, with each group of phrases serving as stimuli for a specific task. The first group consisted of twelve phrases that had a definite head noun and a relative pronoun, but no adverb of place. The second group had eight phrases that contained a definite head noun, a verb, and an adverb of place, with the relative pronoun omitted. The third group consisted of eight phrases with a definite noun, a relative pronoun, and a verb, but without an adverb of place. The fourth group consisted of eight phrases that contained a definite head noun, a relative pronoun, and a verb, but the adverb of place was omitted. The last group of phrases consisted of phrases that had definite head nouns, relative pronouns, verbs, and adverbs of place. All stimuli were typed in Arabic to reflect the Faifi pronunciation of words. Modern Written Arabic glosses accompanied each stimulus in case subjects had any difficulty reading the Faifi Arabic pronunciation.

5.1.3. Tasks

The fifteen subjects were asked to complete a series of three forced-choice tasks, one meaning-differentiation task, and one grammaticality-judgment task. In the first forced-choice task, the speakers were asked to insert adverbs of place (*hnī* 'here', *ḥawla* 'there', or *ṭamma* 'there') at the end of each incomplete relative clause. In the second forced-choice task, the speakers were provided with relative clauses with the adverbs *ḥawla* and *hnī*, but with no relative pronoun and were asked to insert a relative pronoun given the context. In the third forced-choice task, the same speakers were presented with verbal clauses containing the six relative pronouns and were asked to determine whether they detected a difference in meaning. In the fourth task, the speakers were presented with the same verbal clauses and were asked to insert an appropriate relative pronoun. In the fourth task, the speakers were asked to judge the grammaticality of each clause.

All tasks were performed in the same succession for each speaker, starting with Task 1 followed by Task 2, Task 3, Task 4, and finally Task 5. In all forced-choice tasks, speakers were instructed to select only one option. In each task for each subject, the order of the presented choices (i.e., relative pronoun or adverb of place) was randomised. The results of these tasks are presented and discussed in the next section.

5.2. Results

In this section, the results are presented in the order the tasks were performed by the participants.

5.2.1. Task 1

In this task, the speakers were provided with twelve incomplete relative clauses. The participants were asked to add one adverb of place at the end of the clause from three possible adverbs: *ḥawla* 'there' *ṭamma* 'there', or *hnī* 'here'. The purpose of this task was to see which adverb of place (distal and proximal) was matched with which relative pronoun.

Table 6: Task 1 Results

Relative Clause	ḥawla / ṭamma 'there'	hnī 'here'
mwalad ḏā... 'The boy who is...'	15	0
mwalad ḏī... 'The boy who is...'	2	13
mbint tā... 'The girl who is...'	15	0
mbint tī... 'The girl who is...'	0	15
mwaladayn awḏā... 'The two boys who are...'	15	0
mwaladayn awḏī... 'The two boys who are...'	2	13
mbintayn awḏā...	11	4

Relative Clause	ḥawla / tamma 'there'	hnī 'here'
'The two girls who are...' mbintayn awḏī...	0	15
'The two girls who are...' mawalād awḏā...	15	0
'The boys who are...' mawalād awḏī...	5	10
'The boys who are...' mbanāt awḏā...	15	0
'The girls who are...' mbanāt awḏī... 'The girls who are...'	3	12

As Table 6 shows, for most relative clauses, the speakers matched the relative pronouns ḏā, tā, and awḏā (/ā/-relative pronouns) with the adverbs ḥawla (or tamma) 'there' (/ā/-adverbs of place), and matched ḏī, tī, and awḏī with the adverb hnī. The table shows the number of responses for each relative clause.

5.2.2. Task 2

In this task, the speakers were provided with eight incomplete relative clauses with a definite head noun and one of the adverbs ḥawla or hnī.

Table 7: Task 2 Results

Relative Clause	ḏī, tī, awḏī 'who (MS, FS, PL)'	ḏā, tā, awḏā 'who (MS, FS, PL)'
mwalad... ḥarraźa ḥawla 'The boy... talked there.'	0	15
mwalad... ḥarraźa hnī 'The boy... talked here.'	10	5
mbint... ḥarraźan ḥawla 'The girl... talked there.'	3	12
mbint... ḥarraźan hnī 'The girl... talked here.'	11	4
mawalād... ḥarraźū ḥawla 'The boys... talked there.'	0	15

Relative Clause	ḏī, tī, awḏī 'who (MS, FS, PL)'	ḏā, tā, awḏā 'who (MS, FS, PL)'
mawalād… harraẓū hnī 'The boys… talked here.'	12	3
mbanāt… harraẓna ḥawla 'The girls… talked there.'	0	15
mbanāt… harraẓna hnī 'The girls… talked here.'	13	2

The subjects were asked to insert an appropriate relative pronoun from a list that included all six relative pronouns. Unlike the first task, this task aimed to see which relative pronoun was chosen with the provided adverb of place. The results of this task are summarised in the table above.

As shown in the table above, the majority of speakers matched the relative pronouns ḏī, tī, or awḏī with the adverb hnī; and matched the relative pronouns ḏā, tā, and awḏā with the adverb ḥawla. However, this seems to be the case only with relative clauses that end with a place adverb; cf. the results of Task 3 next.

5.2.3. Task 3

In Task 3, speakers were presented with eight relative clauses in four pairs without adverbs of place at the end. The purpose of this task was to see whether the subjects detected any inherent difference between the relative pronouns when an adverb of place is not present in the clause.

The results from this task (Table 8) show that with relative clauses that do not end with an adverb of place, most speakers did not differentiate between the six relative pronouns when they were asked if they could detect a difference in meaning between the clauses in each pair.

The three participants who indicated a difference in meaning noted that the relative pronouns in these phrases implied how far in the past the action took place.

Table 8: Task 3 Results

Relative Clause	Different Meaning	Same Meaning
mwalad ḏā harraźa 'the boy who talked' mwalad ḏī harraźa 'the boy who talked'	3	12
mbint tā harraźan 'the girl who talked' mbint tī harraźan 'the girl who talked'	3	12
mawalād awḏā harraźū 'the boys who talked' mawalād awḏī harraźū 'the boys who talked'	3	12
mbanāt awḏā harraźna 'the girls who talked' mbanāt awḏī harraźna 'the girls who talked'	3	12

Since all phrases in this task are in the past tense, the relative pronouns with the vowel /ī/ implied that the verb *harraźa, harraźan,* or *harraźū* took place more recently in the past than the same verbs preceded with relative pronouns with the vowel /ā/.

However, as shown in the results of Task 4, when the participants were asked to insert one of the three adverbs of place (*ḥawla, ṭamma,* or *hnī*) after the verbs in Table 8, the responses were very similar to those obtained in Task 1.

5.2.4. Task 4

In Task 4, subjects were provided with the same list of clauses in Task 3 and were asked to attach one of the three adverbs of place (*ḥawla, ṭamma* 'there', or *hnī* 'here') at the end of the clause. Compared to Task 1, which also asked subjects to insert an adverb of place, this task aimed mainly to compare the responses in Task 3 with the responses in this task when the subjects were presented with identical clauses to those in Task 3, immediately after determining whether these clauses are different in meaning or not.

Table 9: Task 4 Results

Relative Clause	ḥawla / ṭamma 'there'	hnī 'here'
mwalad ḏā harraźa... 'The boy who talked...'	15	0
mwalad ḏī harraźa... 'The boy who talked...'	2	13
mbint tā harraźan... 'The girl who talked...'	15	0
mbint tī harraźan... 'The girl who talked...'	2	13
mmawalād awḏā harraźū... 'The boys who talked...'	12	3
mmawalād awḏī harraźū... 'The boys who talked...'	1	14
mbanāt awḏā harraźna... 'The girls who talked...'	13	2
mbanāt awḏī harraźna... 'The girls who talked...'	1	14

As shown in Table 9, in most responses, the participants chose the one of the two adverbs ḥawla or ṭamma 'there' in the relative clauses containing the relative pronouns ḏā, tā, and awḏā, and chose the adverb of place hnī 'here' in relative clauses with the relative pronouns ḏī, tī, and awḏī.

5.2.5. Task 5

In the last task, the participants were asked to judge the grammaticality of eight phrases, where the relative pronouns ḏā, tā, and awḏā were matched with the adverb hnī; and the relative pronouns ḏī, tī, and awḏī were matched with the adverb ḥawla.

Table 10: Task 5 Results

Relative Clause	Grammatical	Ungrammatical
mwalad ḏā harraźa hnī 'the boy who talked here'	15	0
mwalad ḏī harraźa ḥawla 'the boy who talked there'	15	0
mbint tā harraźan hnī 'the girl who talked here'	15	0
mbint tī harraźan ḥawla 'the girl wo talked there'	15	0
mmawalād awḏā harraźū hnī 'the boys who talked here'	15	0
mmawalād awḏī harraźū ḥawla 'the boys who talked there'	15	0
mbanāt awḏā harraźna hnī 'the girls who talked here'	15	0
mbanāt awḏī harraźna ḥawla 'the girls who talked there'	15	0

The matching of the relative pronouns containing /ā/ with adverbs of place containing the vowel /ī/ and vice versa is the opposite of the matching determined by the majority of speakers in Tasks 1, 2, and 4. The purpose of this task was to see whether pairing these relative pronouns and adverbs affected the grammaticality of these clauses.

While some native speakers noted that these sentences sounded slightly unnatural or did not have a natural flow, all speakers deemed the relative clauses in Table 10 grammatical. The unnatural element in these relative clauses was perhaps caused by the matching of /ī/-final relative pronouns with /a/-final adverbs of place and /ā/-final relative pronouns with the /i/-final adverb of place.

6.0. Potential Effect of Phonology

Overall, and based on the results discussed above, it appears that the choice of /ī/-final or /ā/-final relative pronouns is not always random and appears to extend beyond the gender-number distinction found in Modern Written Arabic, at least when solely considering the results of these tasks. This is especially clear when the relative clause is followed by one of the three adverbs of place in Faifi Arabic: *ḥawla* 'there', *ṭamma* 'there', and *hnī* 'here'.

Another point to make regarding these tasks is that it is possible that there was a phonological effect that cued the speakers to pair these relative pronouns and adverbs in a similar fashion, almost unanimously. These pairings may have been affected by the phonological components of the words in each phrase, specifically the vowels. This is supported by the results of the matching tasks of the relative clauses *mwalad ḏī...* and *mbintayn awḏā...* in Table 6; and *mwalad... harraźa hnī*, and *mbint... harraźan hnī* in Table 7. Additionally, in Table 9, when both the verb and the relative pronoun have the low vowels [ā] or [a], all respondents chose either *ḥawla* or *ṭamma* as the most suitable adverb of place.

On the other hand, an alternative explanation is that the vowel quality in relative pronouns and adverbs of place may have significance in relation to the proximity of the objects or entities being referred to, where the presence of the high front vowels /ī/ and /i/ reflects proximity.

In Faifi Arabic, demonstratives such as *ḏī*, *tī*, and *awḏī* all containing the high front vowels /ī/ and /i/, are used to express proximity to the speaker. Conversely, the demonstratives *ḏaylī*, *taylī*, *awḏaylī*, *ḏāla*, *tāla*, and *awḏāla*, which contain low vowels, are employed to denote distality from the speaker. This pattern of vowel usage in the demonstratives may reflect their spatial relationship with the speaker.

The same pattern can also be observed in the Arabic dialect of Rijal Almaʿ (Asiri 2009, 163). In this dialect, the proximal demonstratives consistently feature the high front vowels /i/ and /ī/ and are represented by terms like *ḏiyh*, *tijh*, *wulīh*, and *mahnīh*. Conversely, the distal demonstratives are characterised by the presence of low vowels: *ḏahnah*, *tahnah*, *wulahnah*, *wulāx*, and *mahnah*.

This consistent correlation between the presence or absence of the vowels /i/ and /ī/ and the proximal or distal nature of the demonstratives in both Faifi Arabic and the Arabic dialect of Rijal Almaʿ lends support to the idea that vowel quality plays a role in expressing proximity and distality. It suggests that the use of high front vowels may be a phonetic feature used across dialects to indicate proximity, while the use of low vowels indicates distality from the speaker.

7.0. Summary and Conclusion

This paper has compared relative pronouns in Central Faifi Arabic to relative pronouns in other Arabic varieties. Many of the facts about relative pronouns in Faifi Arabic had been previously discussed in detail in Alfaifi (2016) and briefly in Alfaife (2018). The main contribution of this paper, however, is to show, through a series of tasks performed by Central Faifi Arabic speakers, that relative pronouns in the subdialect can be divided into two groups: distal relative pronouns and proximal relative pronouns. This grouping is present only when an adverb of place is present. In other words, adverbs of place in the dialect draw out a possible historical distinction between relative pronouns which have the high vowel /ī/ and relative pronouns which have the low vowel /ā/. However, when the relative pronouns with /ī/ and adverbs of place with /a/ were matched, the speakers did not report the phrases to be ungrammatical, which indicated that this grouping of relative pronouns as distal and proximal is not categorical at present, but perhaps indicates that the dialect had this distinction at some point.

Future research will aim to collect audio recordings of Faifi Arabic speakers, especially speakers of the varieties with both /ī/-final and /a/-final relative pronouns. The recordings will be collected in a natural setting without probing stimuli. Future research will also investigate the observations raised by some of the participants that relative pronouns interact with verbs by carrying meaning about the temporal distality or proximity of the verb.

References

Al-Azraqi, Munira A. 1998. 'Aspects of the Syntax of the Dialect of Abha (South West Saudi Arabia)'. PhD dissertation, Durham University.

Alfaife, Saleem M. 2018. 'A Grammar of Faifi'. MA thesis, California State University, Long Beach.

Alfaifi, Abdullah. 2022. 'Aspects of the Phonology of a Faifi Arabic Dialect'. PhD dissertation, Indiana University.

Alfaifi, Abdullah A., and Peter Behnstedt. 2010. 'First Notes on the Dialect of Ğabal Fayfāʾ (Jazan Province/Saudi Arabia)'. *Zeitschrift für Arabische Linguistik* 52: 53–67.

Alfaifi, Ali H. 2016. 'Aspects of the Morphosyntax of the Faifa Dialect of Saudi Arabic: A Descriptive Study'. PhD dissertation, Ulster University.

Asiri, Yahya. 2008. 'Relative Clauses in the Dialect of Rijal Alma (South-West Saudi Arabia)'. *Proceedings of the Seminar for Arabian Studies* 38: 71–74.

———. 2009. 'Aspects of the Phonology and Morphology of Rijal Almaʿ Dialect: South-West Saudi Arabia'. PhD dissertation, University of Salford.

Behnstedt, Peter. 2016. *Dialect Atlas of North Yemen and Adjacent Areas*. Leiden: Brill.

Google Maps. n.d. Map of Southwestern Saudi Arabia and Northwestern Yemen. https://goo.gl/maps/bNVBWcu8ab8rRTWN6

Hassan, Abbas. 1975. *Al-Naḥw al-Wafī*. Vol. 1. Cairo: Dar Al-Maʾaarif.

Holes, Clive. 1983. 'Bahraini Dialects: Sectarian Differences and the Sedentary/Nomadic Split'. *Zeitschrift für Arabische Linguistik* 10: 7–38.

Johnstone, Thomas M. 1967. *Eastern Arabian Dialect Studies*. Oxford: Oxford University Press.

Keenan, Edward L., and Bernard Comrie. 1977. 'Noun Phrase Accessibility and Universal Grammar'. *Linguistic Inquiry* 8/1: 63–99.

Mughazy, Mustafa. 2009. 'Relative Clause'. In *Encyclopedia of Arabic Language and Linguistics*, edited by Kees Versteegh, Mushira Eid, Alaa Elgibali, Manfred Woidich, and Andrzej Zaborski, IV: 60–70. Leiden: Brill.

Rabin, Chaim. 1951. *Ancient West-Arabian: A Study of the Dialects of the Western Highlands of Arabia in the Sixth and Seventh Centuries A.D.* London: Taylor's Foreign Press.

Retsö, Jan. 2003. 'Relative-Clause Marking in Arabic Dialects: A Preliminary Survey'. In *Approaches to Arabic Dialects*, edited by Martine Haak, Rudolf de Jong, and Kees Versteegh, 263–73. Studies in Semitic Languages and Linguistics 38. Leiden: Brill.

Ryding, Karin C. 2005. *A Reference Grammar of Modern Standard Arabic*. Cambridge: Cambridge University Press.

Vicente, Ángeles. 2009. 'Relative Pronoun (Arabic Dialects)'. In *Encyclopedia of Arabic Language and Linguistics* IV, edited by Kees Versteegh, Mushira Eid, Alaa Elgibali, Manfred Woidich, and Andrzej Zaborski, 70–72. Leiden: Brill.

Watson, Janet C. E. 1993. *A Syntax of Sanʿani Arabic*. Wiesbaden: Harrassowitz.

VERBAL NOUN FORMATION IN MEHRI

Anton Kungl

1.0. Introduction

Most Semitic languages show a specific category of deverbal nouns, usually referred to as 'Verbal Nouns' (henceforth VN).[1] Whereas the precise semantic and morphosyntactic properties of VNs diverge across languages, for the purpose of this study the minimal definition of VNs in Mehri will be taken from Morris (1981, 251): "[VNs being]... gerunds or nouns describing the action of the verb, they have no plural forms" (Morris 1981, 251).

---

[1] Ar. – Arabic (Classical Arabic/Modern Standard Arabic), EM – Eastern Mehri, IG – Idle Glottis (consonant), *JL* – *Jibbali Lexicon* (Johnstone 1981), J/S – Jibbali/Sheḥri, *ML* – *Mehri Lexicon* (Johnstone 1987), MSAL – Modern South Arabian (Languages), PS – Proto-Semitic, PMSAL – Proto Modern South Arabian, Soq. – Soqotri, VN – verbal noun, WM – Western Mehri.

The terms 'Eastern Mehri' and 'Western Mehri' are used here as shorthand for the varieties described in Johnstone (1987)/Morris (1981) and Jahn (1902) respectively. As is well known, the dialectal distinctions of Mehri do not correspond to an exact East–West divide, nor to the modern-day borders between Yemen and Oman, however, since a precise account of the different varieties of Mehri and their geographical and sociological (tribal/urban) contexts has not been provided as of yet, these—descriptively defective—terms are used in the present study.

The exact meaning of VNs is dependent on the semantics of the corresponding root, and not all verbal roots necessarily have corresponding VNs, at least not in accordance with the definition given above. Also, an overlap between VNs and other nominal forms, sharing the same root with a given verbal form, is to be expected, particularly in the G-stems.

In this study, a descriptive overview of VN formation in Mehri will be given, together with an investigation of certain pertinent phonological and morphological features. Previous descriptions of Mehri, with the exception of the aforementioned thesis by Morris (1981), make no or only passing mention of VNs. Looking to other Semitic languages, one would expect derived-stem VNs to display more regular patterns, while G-stem VNs would show quite divergent patterns.

As will be shown in this paper, this situation is also broadly so in Mehri, and most likely in all MSAL. However, the parameters of VN formation in derived stems, as well as some prominent VN patterns for G-stem verbs, are quite distinct from patterns in other Semitic languages. §2.0 will provide a concise discussion of different VN patterns across stems, with particular focus on various pertinent phonological and morphological features. In §3.0, a resumé of the most prominent VN patterns and their surface realisations discussed in §2.0 will be given, followed by a summary discussion of a number of questions raised in §2.0 with consideration of the broader Semitic context.

The previously published data for this study come from Johnstone's (1987) *Mehri Lexicon* and Jahn's (1902) glossary, as well as the discussion by Morris (1981). Whereas in the *Mehri*

Lexicon (henceforth *ML*), VNs appear quite underrepresented, and for most verbs no VNs are indicated,[2] in Jahn's (1902) glossary, almost every verb is listed with a corresponding VN "*Infinitiv*." However, many common VN patterns appear in non-corresponding stems, which suggests the need for caution regarding the feasibility of some of the items provided.[3] Also, as will be shown, the previously published data quite often appear to be contradictory, both within a single publication and between different publications. Thus, for the sake of expanding and correcting previous data, further data were collected by the author in a fieldwork session in Salalah in February and March of 2022. The varieties of all speakers recorded appear to be examples of Eastern Mehri (henceforth EM); unfortunately, no speakers of Western Mehri (henceforth WM) could be consulted by the author. During this session, VNs in J/S were also collected, which were previously barely attested at all.

In terms of methodology, after giving a summary overview of VN surface patterns attested for each type in §2.0, pertinent features will be investigated, on the basis of, inter alia, previously described phonological features of Mehri, such as the IG-effect (Bendjaballah and Ségéral 2014), the effects of guttural and glottalic consonants (Rubin 2018; etc.), the vowel-spread of sonorants to their left (Dufour 2017; Rubin 2018), the status of vowels (Bendjaballah and Ségéral 2017; Rubin 2018), etc.

---

[2] Yet, significantly more VNs are present in ML than in JL.

[3] Although this does not seem to be uncommon—in the data collected by the author, informants would also sometimes give non-corresponding derived-stem VNs.

2.0. Verbal Nouns in Mehri

2.1. G-Stem VNs

For G-Stem VNs, the following surface patterns are attested in ML:

Table 1: G-stem VN patterns in ML

Surface Pattern	Attestations
CəyCəC	83
CaCC	10
CəCC	5
CəCayC	9
CēCəC	4
CōCəC	5
+ Others (lexicalised)	

As evident, by far the most productive pattern of VN formation appears to be the pattern *CəyCəC*. Most other patterns seem interspersed and most likely lexicalised. In terms of the distribution between Ga- and Gb-stems, Ga-stem VNs are much more frequently attested, otherwise no significant difference can be found, with a few salient exceptions (see §2.1.2).

Table 2: Ga- and Gb-stem VN patterns in ML.

Pattern	Ga	Gb
CəyCəC	həlūb (VN haylǝb)	rīdǝf (VN raydǝf)
CaCC	nəkūf (VN nakf)	śīrəġ (VN śarġ)
CəCC	dəkk (VN dəkk < dək >)[4]	
CəCayC	rəḥāś (VN rəḥayś)	wīzək (VN wəzayk)
CēCəC	ləhūh (VN lēhi)	wīṣəl (VN wēṣəl)
CōCəC	fərūd (VN fōrəd)	—

---

[4] All attestations of the VN pattern CəCC in ML show biradicals CəCC > CəCC.

One thus observes from Table 2 that by and large no VN pattern seems to be reserved for one particular G-stem (Ga or Gb), although the pattern *CəCayC* is problematic in this regard, as will be shown below.

In the following section the patterns *CayCəC* (§2.1.1), *CəCayC* (§2.1.2), *CvCC* (§2.1.3), and *C̄vCəC* (§2.1.4) will be discussed, followed by a brief overview of some of the other (lexicalised) patterns attested (§2.1.5).

2.1.1. *CayCəC*

Of all G-stem VNs, the pattern *CayCəC* is by far the most well attested. As mentioned above, the pattern *CayCəC* is attested for both Ga- and Gb-stems. In fact, a number of examples can be found of Ga- and Gb-stem verbs derived from the same root which appear to take both *CayCəC* and *CīCəC* as their VN pattern:

(1) *CayCəC*-type VNs Ga-Gb in ML

 ṭəbūr (Ga) / ṭibər (Gb) – ṭaybər (VN)

 ḥəsūd (Ga) / ḥaysəd (Gb) – ḥaysəd (VN)[5]

In Johnstone's data, based on EM, this pattern generally surfaces as *CayCəC*, whereas in Jahn's data this pattern usually surfaces as *CīCəC*, with diphthongisation only appearing when the first radical is a guttural or glottalic consonant, e.g., lītaġ 'to kill' versus ġaylek̲ 'to look for, search' (Jahn 1902).

There are a few exceptions in Jahn's data, where a diphthong appears with R1 = [−Gutt., −Glott.] and, concomitantly,

---

[5] The nominal form ḥaysəd in ML is glossed as a generic noun 'envy', however, it is almost certainly a VN formation.

where no diphthong appears with R1 = [+Gutt., +Glott.]. The indicative value of these examples remains unclear. In any case, the possibility of these forms being erroneous (due to over-elicitation?) remains, particularly when viewed against the overall number of attestations of VNs in general, and *CayCəC/CīCəC* in particular.

(2) *CayCəC* / R1 = [−Gutt., −Glott.]: *kéynes, kaytb, śaymer, śayreṭ, kéysī, téylī, déyḥar, téylef*

   CīCəC / R1 = [+Gutt., +Glott.]: *xīnek, ṣīber, ṣīdek, ḳīṣem*

Regarding the question of the nature of the diphthong/monophthong in the first syllable, the surface presence of such a diphthong in a stressed syllable in EM would suggest an underlying glide /y/. Also, in EM distinct noun patterns *CīCəC* and *CayCəC* are attested outside of VNs (see also Dufour 2016, 371–72). However, the question remains whether an underlying glide can be assumed for the whole of Mehri, e.g., also for the western varieties in Jahn (1902). Thus, in the following section the following factors will be considered to evaluate the underlying nature of the stressed monophthong/diphthong of the VN patterns *CayCəC* and *CīCəC*: IG-effect between R2 and R3 (§2.1.1.1.); the presence of gutturals in R2 (§2.1.1.2.); cognates from other MSAL (§2.1.1.3.).

2.1.1.1. IG-Effect between R2 and R3

The first argument concerns the application of the IG-effect between R2 and R3.[6] If the initial syllable was entirely vocalic, one would expect shortening of the stressed vowel, since no $C\bar{v}CəC$-type nouns with R2 + R3 = [+IG] are attested.

A significant difference between the data provided by Johnstone and Jahn lies in the application of the IG-effect in the forms in question. The forms collected in ML do not show any traces of IG, and hence they surface as $CayCəC$:

(3) *faytəḥ, raykət, bayḥət, dayhəf, mayḥəś*

By contrast, amongst the forms in Jahn's glossary, almost no surface forms $C\bar{\imath}CəC$ with R2 + R3 = [+IG] appear.[7] However, amongst the surface pattern $CəCC$ (<$CeCC$>/<$CiCC$>) one finds a number of forms R2 + R3 = [+IG]. Hence it would appear that $CayCəC/C\bar{\imath}CəC$ regularly displays the IG-effect between R2 and R3, and therefore, the stressed surface vowel between R1 and R2 is shortened.

(4) *ʿeks* (*ʿks* Ga), *liḥs* (*lḥs* Gb), *misḥ* (*msḥ* Ga), *nifh* (*nfh* Ga) *nefś* (*nfś* Ga), *niḥt* (*nḥt* Gb), *nikś* (*nkś* Ga), *nisf* (*nsf* Ga), *nitf* (*ntf* Ga), *nitx* (*ntx* Ga)

In the data collected by the author, surface forms $CayCəC$ with R2 + R3 = [+IG] were attested, thus corresponding to the situation in ML:

---

[6] I.e., the elision of an unstressed vowel between voiceless, non-glottalic consonants (see Bendjaballah and Ségéral 2014).

[7] With the exception of *lišet*.

(5) layḥəs – lḥays (lḥās)
    naykəf – nakf (nkūf)
    bayḥəṭ – baḥṭ (bəḥāṭ)
    āykəs – aks (ākūs)

Furthermore, amongst the attestations of *CəCC* only two examples of R2 + R3 = [+IG] could be found: *nəkś* (*nkūś*) and *məsḥ* (*məsḥ*). Some attestations of *CaCC* with R2 + R3 = [+IG] could be found (e.g., *nakf*, *faḥs*, *maḥś*, *natf*, *aks*, *natx*, etc.), however, in at least some of the aforementioned examples, no reason seems apparent why the vowel in the stressed syllable should be considered to be a phonetic variant of /ə/,[8] hence—at least most of—these forms cannot be explained as underlying *CayCəC*, since the shortened stressed vowel should be /ə/ in these cases and not /a/.

Therefore, it appears that in EM the IG-effect does not apply to *CayCəC*. Whereas the question remains open why apparently in some varieties of Mehri the initial diphthong is (not) shortened, the fact that it is not shortened in EM highlights the distinctness of this pattern from *C̄VCəC*-type nouns.

2.1.1.2. The Presence of Gutturals in R2

The next aspect is connected to the surface similarity between Jahn's *CīCəC* and the 3MS perfective form of Gb-stem verbs (also *CīCəC* in Mehri). If this surface similarity is to be understood as underlying identity, one would expect a similar surface outcome with R2 = [+Gutt.] roots, i.e., a lack of patterns *CayCəC/CīCəC*

---

[8] This would be expected when adjacent to a guttural, which is not the case in *nakf*, *natf*, *natx*, etc.

with R2 as a guttural and a number of corresponding surface forms of the type *CəCēC* or *CəCāC*. Yet, both Johnstone's and Jahn's data show a good number of VNs with R2 = [+Gutt.]:

(6) *CayCəC* / R2 = [+Gutt.] in ML
    bayhər, bayḥəṭ, dayhəf, dayxəl, ḏayhəb, mayḥək, mayḥəś, rayḥəl, rayxəṣ, zayhəd

(7) *CīCəC* / R2 = [+Gutt.] in Jahn (1902)
    ṣayġab, ṣayhar (ṭayhar), déyḥar, ṣayhel, ṭeyhan, zayġaf, bīġaś, līheg, sīḥaṭ, bīhel, dīheb (ḏīheb), dīher, dīḥak, līheg, līḥak, nīhek, rīhez, rīḥek, sīher, sīḥek, tīhel, wīhed, wīhem

Note also that among the rare VN pattern *CəCēC*, only two attestations of G-stem *CəCēC* with a guttural as R2 were found in ML (*ṣəḥāk* and *ṭəʾēn*), and none in Jahn (1902) (see §2.1.5). Thus, one observes that in terms of the behaviour of gutturals as R2, both Johnstone's and Jahn's data pattern in opposition to verbal forms Gb *CīCəC*, the latter presumably only showing an underlying vowel between R1 and R2.

An important note of consideration is that amongst the VNs elicited by the author, *CayCəC*-type VNs of II-Gutt. roots were almost completely lacking,[9] and usually surface as *CəCayC*. The question of the relationship between *CayCəC* and *CəCayC* will be discussed in §2.1.2.

---

[9] With the exception of *layḥas* and *bayḥəṭ*, both of which were also elicited alternatively as *CəCayC* (*lḥays, bəḥayṭ*).

2.1.1.3. Cognates from other MSAL

Cognates from other MSAL would seem to support the interpretation of an underlying glide. Whereas intra-MSAL vowel correspondences are an intricate subject, with no one-to-one alignments, a few pertinent trends can be noted. Thus, /i/ in Mehri often corresponds to either /i/ or /e/ in J/S and Soq. Examples for the latter correspondence can be found in the 3MS perfective forms of the Gb-stem (Mehri *CīCəC* – J/S *CéCəC* – Soq. *CéCəC*) or in the G-stem passive participle (Mehri *məCCīC* – J/S *məCCéC* – Soq. *méCCeC*).

In places where an underlying /y/ is to be expected in Mehri, due to the non-conditioned surface diphthong, the reflex in J/S and (when applicable) Soq. appears to be /i/, as witnessed in the frequent MS adjective pattern *CəCayC* and its J/S reflex *CəCīC*.

Regarding potential cognates to VN *CayCəC/CīCəC* in JL, the possible cognate form *CéCəC* is attested in JL. Johnstone mentioned only one potential item of this pattern, namely the item he transcribed as *hédər*. Amongst all J/S informants the author consulted, this item was consistently produced as *ḥídər*. Hence, apparently Johnstone's form is erroneous both in terms of the nature of R1 and the vowel between R1 and R2. Other examples of the same pattern show /i/ between R1 and R2 and not /e/, and there are enough VNs attested without a neighbouring nasal consonant or /r/ to ascertain that this is not due to vowel raising (see Rubin 2014, 40):

(8) VN pattern CíC(ə)C in J/S (author's data)

ḥíḏər (Ga ḥɔḏɔ́r),ríkəb (Gb rékəb), ṣílb (Ga ṣɔlɔ́b), hídəm (Ga hɔdúm), ʿíks (Ga ʿɔkɔ́s), díhf (dɛhɛ́f), fírd (Ga firɔ́d), díḥar (daḥár), nikf (Ga nkɔf), bíxəṣ (baxáṣ), bírk (berɔ́k), líṣəḳ (léṣḳ), díġəl (daġál), ġílk (ġɔlɔ́k), ṭíʿan (ṭaʿán), ríǧaʿ (réǧaʿ)

Note in these forms the application of the IG-effect between R2 and R3, as well as the lack of a surface vowel between R2 and R3 in forms where R2 is a sonorant (more specifically, a liquid). With regard to the former aspect, the behaviour of *CíCəC* in J/S resembles the putative behaviour of *CīCəC*-type VNs in Jahn (1902). It should be noted that this does not necessarily imply that *CíCəC*-type VNs in J/S have a synchronically underlying glide. The sound-correspondences, however, do point towards cognacy with forms which on the Mehri end would typically have an underlying glide. In the case of Soq., the cognate pattern appears to be *CíCiC* (Kogan and Bulakh 2019, 302).[10] Hence we also observe /i/ as the first vowel.

Thus, the vowel correspondence between /vy/ (ML) and /i/ (Mehri) (Jahn 1902), /i/ (J/S) and /i/ (Soq.), implies an underlying glide in Mehri, as witnessed in the aforementioned singular adjectival pattern *CəCayC*.

2.1.1.4. Summary on *CayCəC / CīCəC*

For EM, when taking into account that the first syllable shows a surface diphthong, that no IG-effect is observed between R2 and R3 (§2.1.1.1), that no simple-vowel shift is observed when R2 is a guttural consonant (§2.1.1.2. in Johnstone's and Jahn's data,

---

[10] Examples ṣífin and ḥíṣiḳ in Kogan, Naumkin et al. (2018).

for the author's data see §2.1.2.), and that sound-correspondences exist between Mehri and other MSAL—indicating the non-vocalic nature of the first syllable in Mehri (§2.1.1.3)—one arrives at the conclusion that the initial syllable of *CayCəC* shows an underlying glide /y/.

For the western varieties described by Jahn (1902), the situation appears somewhat more problematic. While the sound-correspondences mentioned in §2.1.1.3 apply, as well as the lack of shift with gutturals as R2 (§2.1.1.2), (almost) no forms with R2 + R3 = [+IG] could be found (§2.1.1.1). However, even with this being the case, this does not necessarily constitute a counter-argument against the notion of an underlying glide in WM, since the shortening of non-glottalised/gutturalised diphthongs in a stressed and phonologically closed syllable is attested otherwise.[11] To explain the distinction between EM *CayCəC* and WM *CīCəC* a more promising explanation could perhaps be found in different dialectal realisations of underlying /y/, rather than by assuming distinct underlying patterns.[12]

---

[11] E.g., *bayt* > *abə́tk* (Rubin 2018, 56). As mentioned, it remains an open question why exactly this effect does not seem to apply in the case of EM *CayCəC* / R2 + R3 = [+IG]. Any connection with a possible historical long vowel between R2 and R3? (see §3.0 and Dufour 2016, 376–78).

[12] Potentially due to a distinction in the underlying vowel of stressed underlying *vy/vw* sequences – /ə/ in WM, /a/ in EM? Therefore /əy/ > /ī/ in the western data as opposed to /ay/ > /ay/ in EM? This solution might also pattern well with non-secondary diphthongs in EM and their monophthong counterparts in WM in a more general sense.

2.1.2. CəCayC / CəCyūC (and CayCəC)

VNs of the patterns *CəCayC* and *CəCyūC* deserve separate discussion due to their peculiar distribution. Unlike other G-stem VN patterns, these two patterns appear to be restricted almost entirely to R2 = [+Gutt.] verbs, as well as to a few Gb-stem verbs R2 = [−Gutt.].[13]

(9) *CəCayC* with R2 = [+Gutt.] verbs in ML

dəhayr, dəhayk, dəhayk̠, ṭəhayl, śəhayd, śəxayl, ṭəʕaym

(10) *CəCayC* with R2 = [−Gutt.] Gb verbs in ML

fəḏayr, wəzayk

(11) *CəCyūC* with R2 = [+Gutt.] verbs in Jahn (1902)

deheyūb, daḥayūk̠, ṭaḥayūl, zaġayūf, taʔayūn (tʕn), ġayūr (gʕr), etc.

(12) *CəCyūC* with R2 = [−Gutt.] Gb verbs in Jahn (1902) rakiūb, ṣabyūṭ

Moreover, the VN patterns *CəCayC* and *CəCyūC* appear to be in complementary distribution (see dəḥayk – daḥayūk̠, ṭəhayl – ṭaḥayūl), in ML one does not find any attestations of *CəCyūC* as a

---

[13] In Morris (1981, 255), the pattern *CəCayC* is described as a prominent VN pattern for *CəCēC*-type verbs, that is G-stem verbs with R2 = [+Gutt.], although there is at least one attestation of *CəCayC* in a verb R2 = [−Gutt.] in Morris's data (fiḏər > fəḏayr, Morris 1981, 254, also to be found in ML). No attestations of *CəCyūC* as a VN pattern are to be found in Morris's study. By contrast, Watson (2012, 26) notes that "...a more common verbal noun pattern for the simple verb [referring to VN fʕūl] is faʕyūl." Also, Bittner (1909, 22–23) describes *CəCyūC* as a particular VN (infinitive) pattern, mostly attested for roots II-Gutt., which he connects with *CiCāC.

VN pattern, while in Jahn's glossary one does not find any attestations of $CəCayC$ ($CəC\bar{\imath}C$)[14] as a VN pattern.

As has been shown §2.1.1, according to the published data, the presence of a guttural as R2 cannot be taken to be a sufficient indication for the occurrence of $CəCayC/CəCy\bar{u}C$ alone, since $CayCəC$-type VNs with R2 = [+Gutt.] are attested. Also, as one has seen above, the patterns $CəCayC$ and $CəCy\bar{u}C$ do not appear to be exclusively reserved for roots R2 = [+Gutt.]. Hence, if the patterns $CəCayC$ and $CəCy\bar{u}C$ do indeed constitute distinct common VN pattern(s), it has to be assumed, that this pattern would be distinct from $CayCəC/C\bar{\imath}CəC$.

In terms of the internal structure of roots showing the patterns $CəCayC$ and $CəCy\bar{u}C$, no salient features which might explain the two patterns as being conditioned variants of each other (or of $CayCəC/C\bar{\imath}CəC$) could be found, aside from the aforementioned overrepresentation of R2 = [+Gutt.]. Thus, R1 and R3 of all forms in question are shown in the tables below.

Table 3: Positional Analysis R1 and R3 of $CəCayC/CəCy\bar{u}C$ / R2 = [+Gutt.] and $CayCəC/C\bar{\imath}CəC$ / R2 = [+Gutt.] in ML and Jahn (1902)

Combinations R1-R3 *1ə2ay3* (ML)		Combinations R1-R3 *1ə2(ə)yū3* (Jahn 1902)	
d-r	ś-d	d-k	ṭ-l (ṭ-l)
d-k	ś-l	d-b (ḏ-b)	z-f
d-ḳ	ṭ-m	l-m	ś-t
ṭ-l	w-k	r-l	b-r
f-r		r-b	ṭ-n
		r-ṣ	z-k
		g-r	

[14] There is one example of a VN of the pattern $CəC\bar{\imath}C$ in Jahn (1902), kəṣīd, which is unlikely to be a cognate, since it is a probable loan from Arabic.

Combinations R1-R3 1ay2ə3 (ML), R2 = Gutt.		Combinations R1-R3 1ay/ī2ə3 (Jahn 1902)	
b-r	m-ḳ	b-l	s-ḳ
b-ṭ	m-ś	b-ṣ	s-ṭ
d-f	r-l	d-b	ṣ-l
d-l	r-ṣ	d-r	t-l
ḏ-b		d-ḳ	ṭ-n
		l-g	w-d
		l-ḳ	w-m
		n-ḳ	z-f
		r-z	z-r
		r-ḳ	ś-b
		s-r	ś-r

Hence, one finds a diverse configuration of possible groupings of neighbouring consonants in VN patterns *CəCayC/CəCyūC* / R2 = [+Gutt.] and also an overlap with groupings of neighbouring consonants in VN patterns *CayCəC/CīCəC* / R2 = [+Gutt.], indicating that the distinction between *CəCayC* and *CəCyūC* cannot be immediately traced to factors pertaining to the neighbouring consonants (other than R2). In the absence of any other discernible factors, it would thus have to be assumed that the two patterns do indeed represent two synchronically distinct VN patterns between the different dialects of Mehri, and both similarly distinct from *CayCəC/CīCəC*. Note that both patterns are well attested otherwise: *CəCayC* is otherwise attested as the most prominent adjective pattern, while *CəCyūC* (and *CəCyōC*)[15] is attested as a plural/collective noun pattern in all dialects of Mehri.

In the data collected by the author, there is another distinct patterning of *CəCayC* and *CayCəC*. Whereas in ML, II-Gutt. roots seamlessly take *CayCəC* and *CəCayC*, almost all G-stem II-Gutt.

---

[15] *CəCyōC* appears to be the EM cognate of WM *CəCyūC* (in non-VN items)? Note the curious relation of EM /o/ – WM /u/.

items collected by the author took the latter pattern. The only exceptions are *layḥəs*, which was also collected as *lḥays*, and *bayḥəṭ*, which was also collected as *bəḥayṭ* and *baḥṭ*. *CəCayC* type VNs with a guttural consonant as R2 include those which are given as *CayCəC* in ML.

Table 4: *CayCəC* / R2 = [+Gutt.] in ML and their reflexes in the author's data

ML	Author's Data
bayḥər	bəhayr
bayḥəṭ	abḥayṭ (baḥṭ, bayḥəṭ)
dayḥəf	dəhayf (mdəhfēt)
dayxəl	- (dəxōlət)
ḏayḥəb	ḏəhayb (ḏəhīb in Morris 1981)
mayḥəq	- (maḥq)
mayḥəś	mḥayś (maḥś)
rayḥəl	rḥayl
rayxəṣ	- (raxṣ)
zayḥəd	- (zahd)

Therefore, on the basis of the author's data it almost appears as if *CayCəC* and *CəCayC* are conditioned variants of each other, based on the presence of a guttural consonant as R2. When no guttural is present, the pattern surfaces as *CayCəC*, whereas a guttural R2 seems to trigger a shift to *CəCayC*. Also, in the author's data some additional items *CəCayC* that do not show a guttural as R2 could be found:

(13) VN *CəCayC* / R2 = [−Gutt.] (author's data)
   ūṣayk – laṣk (līṣək)
   nśayz – nśawz (nīśəz)
   ṭəbayr – ṭōbər – ṭaybər (ṭībər)
   awkayb – waykəb (ūkūb)
   awṣayl – ūṣawl – wayṣəl (wīṣəl)

nfayś – mənfēś (nfūś)

anaydəf – ndayf – nadf (ndūf)

ūzayk (wīzək)

fədayr (fīdər)[16]

Note that amongst these forms R1 is mostly either a /w/ glide or a /l/ or /n/ sonorant. Variant forms could be found for most of the items above, some of which include *CayCəC*-type VNs. Also, *CayCəC* is attested otherwise with R1 as a /w/ glide or /l/ or /n/ sonorant. Hence it might very well be that the nature of R1 is of no particular relevance for the surfacing of a given item as *CayCəC* or *CəCayC*.

(14) Other attestations of *CayCəC* / R1 = [/w/, /l/, /n/] (author's data)

layḥəs (lḥās)

laybəd – waybəd – labd (ūbūd)

nayka (nūka)

naykəf – nakf – nkfūt (nkūf)

In J/S, most examples of II-gutt. roots do not take a form resembling *CəCayC*. However, a few examples of prima-facie cognates can be found:

(15) VN *C(ə)CíC* in J/S (author's data)

ṭəhí(h)l (ṭaḥál) viz. *ṭəhayl (ṭəḥāl)*

ṣ(ˤ)aykk (ṣaˤák) viz. *ṣ(ˤ)ayk̲ – ṣ(ˤ)awk̲ (ṣāk̲)*

śəḥík (śəḥák) viz. *śəḥāk – śəḥkēt (ləḥāk)*

fḥís – faḥs (fḥás) viz. *fḥays – faḥs (fḥās)*

---

[16] See Johnstone (1987); Morris (1981, 254). In the data recorded by the author, the VN to this item was given as *fədrēt* by all informants.

kšíś (*kéšš*) viz. *kəśś* (*kəśś*)

lfíf (*lɛff*) viz. *lɛff* – *mǝlɛff* (*lǝff*)

mḥík̠ (*maḥák̠*) viz. *maḥk̠* (*mḥāk̠*)

nfíś (*nfoś*) viz. *nfayś* – *mǝnfēś* (*nfūś*)

msíḥ (*mésḥ* also VN *mísḥ*) viz. *mǝsḥ* (*mǝsḥ*)

Note that among these examples, those forms that do not show a guttural as R2 either have a sonorant /n/ or /m/ as R1, or—unlike Mehri—have a biradical root. The latter feature might be a peculiarity of J/S, although further research on J/S would be needed to establish this.

Concerning *CíCǝC*, the putative cognate of Mehri *CayCǝC*, some attestations of *CíCǝC* with R2 as a guttural could be found:

(16) VN *CíCǝC* in J/S / R2 = [+Gutt.] (author's data)

dɛhéf – *díhf*

daḥár – *díḥar*

daġál – *díġǝl*

ṭaʿán – *ṭíʿan*

ǧaʿár – *ǧíʿar*

k̠aḥár – *k̠íḥar*

The J/S data collected by the author hence show both *CíCǝC* and *CǝCíC* being attested as VN patterns for G-stem VNs of roots with a guttural as R2, hence resembling the picture from ML and Jahn (1902).

To conclude, while the data in previously published sources show conspicuous parallels between the VN pattern *CǝCayC* in EM and the VN pattern *CǝCyūC* in WM, there is no reason to assume that *CǝCayC* and *CǝCyūC* are in any ways conditioned variants of each other. This, in turn, suggests genuine dialectal differences within Mehri in terms of the usage of VN patterns. On the basis of the author's data, the impression emerges that *CəCayC/CəCyūC* and *CayCəC* are mutually exclusive VN patterns, with *CəCayC* appearing with roots where R2 is a guttural consonant. However, in the published data, as well as in J/S, *CayCəC*-type VNs with R2 = [+Gutt.] are well attested, and also *CəCayC*-type VNs with R2 = [−Gutt.] are attested, hence underlining the distinctness of these patterns. Taking all of this together, no cogent argument emerges to assume allophony between *CayCəC* and *CəCayC/CəCyūC*, and considering the lack of said arguments, one might assume that they represent synchronically distinct VN patterns as well. Nevertheless, there remains the unsatisfying situation, where one notices significant overlap between a given (set of) noun pattern(s), namely *CəCayC/CəCyūC* and phonological (mainly II-Gutt. roots) and morphological (mainly Gb-stem) features associated to it. Perhaps an answer to this puzzle is to be found when considering this issue from a diachronic perspective, which will be left for further research.

2.1.3. CvCC

The patterns *CaCC* and *CəCC* are less frequently attested as VNs, however, still relatively prominent VN patterns, particularly for G-stems.

In ML, two of the *CaCC* VNs show *CayCəC* as a variant VN, *fark – fayrək* and *ḥark – ḥayrək*. This agrees with the overall impression of the data collected by the author, where speakers would frequently oscillate between *CayCəC* and *CaCC* as G-stem VN patterns. In the data provided by Johnstone, no sonorants were found as R3 in *CvCC*-type VNs, as expected. In the author's data, a few such examples could be found, which might very well represent over-generalisations on the part of the speaker (all items *CvCC* / R3 = [+Son.] come from the same speaker), considering the general near-absence of sonorants as R3 in *CvCC*-type nouns. Note that for all of these VNs other patterns were also given, and that two of the three attestations were given as T2-stem VNs.

(17) VNs *CaCC* / R3 = [+Son.] (author's data)
 fahm – fthəmūt (fthūm)
 fagr – fəgōrət (fəgūr)
 wakl – tūkəlēt – ūtkəlūt – ūtkəlēt (ūtkūl)

In Johnstone's data three items of the pattern *CaCC* show IG consonants as R2 + R3, namely *nakf*, *ṭahs*, and *hasf*.[17] It is a priori possible that these forms represent underlying *CēCəC* or *CōCəC*. However, this cannot be ascertained, and in a more general sense, these examples would still not change the overall picture that *CvCC*-type VNs are more frequently attested than *CV̄CəC*-type VNs.

As for the pattern *CəCC*, as mentioned above (§2.1), examples in ML are drawn from biradical roots, where the VN would be identical with the 3MS perfective. This corresponds to a more general feature of *CəCC* in ML, where most attestations of this pattern across all (nominal) forms are to be drawn from biradicals or transparent Arabisms. The reasons for this odd configuration are beyond the scope of this paper. However, when

---

[17] The latter is listed as the VN for a D/L verb.

considering that this situation is attested for the noun pattern *CəCC* beyond VNs, it is to be assumed that the answer to this question also lies beyond the domain of VNs.

In the author's data two attestations of *CəCC* of triradical roots could be found, the aforementioned *nəkś* and *məsḥ*, with the other attestations of *CəCC* being similarly restricted to biradicals. In at least two examples of biradical roots, the corresponding VN did not appear identical to the 3MS perfective, hence *lɛff – məlɛff* (*ləff*) and *śedd – mśedd* (*śədd*).

2.1.4. *CV̄CəC*

Amongst patterns of the type *CV̄CəC*, *CēCəC*, and *CōCəC* are attested, which are also, in a more general sense, the most frequently attested noun patterns of the type *CV̄CəC*. Most of the examples given in ML show other patterns in the material collected by the author; hence, it is questionable whether the items given in ML actually represent VNs of the type *CV̄CəC* or rather simple nouns of the same root.

(18) *fēḳəś, wēṣəl, lēhi, āḏər, fōrəd, tōnəg, hōwi, ḥōśi, bōni* (H-stem),
    wəṣayl, fayrəd, ḥaywi (author's data)

A few other items of the patterns *CōCəC* and *CēCəC* were collected by the author:

(19) *lōtəġ* (*ūtūġ*)
    ṭōbər – ṭəbayr – ṭaybər (*ṭībər/ṭəbūr*)
    śēni – məśənay (*śīni*)

2.1.5. Other Patterns

The following types of patterns were only quite sparsely attested as VN patterns in ML. Hence, they likely represent examples of lexicalised VNs. The following list is not a complete set; various other yet smaller VN patterns are attested.

2.1.5.1. Prefix m-

A few VNs taking a prefix m- could be found. These forms can take the FS suffix(es) and various stressed vowel qualities and stress positions.

Table 5: G-stem VNs with a prefixed m- (author's data)

Pattern	Attestations
məCáCC	msayr (səyūr)
məCɛCC	məlɛff (ləff), mśɛdd (śədd)
məCCaC	məśənay (śīni)
máCCəC	mádḥək (dəḥāḵ)
məCCəCēt	mdəhfēt (dəhayf)
məCCē	mətwē (təwōh)
məCCēC	mənfēś (nfūś)
məCCūC – məCCawC	mərḳawd (rḳawd)

2.1.5.2. Suffix -Vn

Whereas in J/S a suffix -Vn appears to be more prominently attested, in Mehri this suffix is quite sparsely attested. Nevertheless some attestations can be found, e.g., ṭəhəkayn (ML), ġəśśīn, ḥalmīn, ġafirōn, geḥeydōn, etc. (Jahn 1902). Jahn's glossary shows a somewhat larger number of forms with a suffix -Vn, with both -īn and -ōn being attested. The examples above do not appear to show any particular phonological features which might explain the appearance of the -Vn suffix. They thus should probably be considered lexicalised.

2.1.5.3. Reduplication

In ML and in the author's elicitation efforts, only a single item of (partial) reduplication could be found, namely *kəbkēb* (Ga *wkb*). In Jahn (1902) one also finds the forms *śakaṣēḳ* and *zemzēm*, both I-*w*. Also, in other MSAL more examples of partially reduplicated I-*w* VNs can be found, which might imply the presence of more of such VNs in Mehri, hence J/S *gəhgə́ḥ* (JL), *zəkzə́k* (author's data).

2.1.5.4. CəCv̄C

Patterns of the type *CəCv̄C* are sparsely attested. ML shows *ṣəḥāk*, *śədēd*, *ṭəʔēn* and *ādōm* (the latter being the VN of a H-stem verb). In addition, the form *hīḳōy* is attested for the irregular (T-stem) verb *təkk*, which should probably be understood as *CīCōC*. In Jahn (1902) more examples are to be found. However, most examples are attested for derived stems, and hence questionable in terms of their convergence with the initial definition of VNs. For G-stem verbs, the following items are attested in Jahn (1902), all but three of which show *CəCēC* (and its conditioned variant *CəCāC*, also attested for apparently non-integrated Arabisms):

(20) ḥabēr (ḥbr Gb)
mirēṣ́ (mrṣ́ Gb)
ṭarēf (ṭrf Ga?)
sedēd (sdd Ga)
zetēt (ṣetēt?) (ztt/ṣtt? Ga)
śədēd (śdd Ga)
ftāḥ (fth Ga)
nśāḳ (nśḳ Ga)
ṭayām (ṭˤm Gb)
amāl (ˤml Gb)

Only two G-stem VNs of the pattern *CəCōC* are attested, namely *ṣabōḥ* and *gizōz*, and one (presumably Arabic) pattern *CəCīC* *ḳaṣīd*.

2.1.5.5. Simple Base with Suffix -v̄t

Some G-stem VNs show a stressed suffix -v̄t, hence, ML *rābūt* (rˤb) or *təmərēt*. These patterns are less frequently attested for G-stem VNs, and most attestations of *CəCCūt/CCəCūt* are H-stem VNs (see §2.3).

2.1.5.6. Distinct Root

In one example, the VN of a G-stem verb is formed from a distinct root, namely *šəwkūf – šənēt*. This is most likely a feature inherited from PS, as argued by Kogan and Militarev (2000, 336—noting that the verbal usage of this root in other Semitic languages might be a secondary development).

2.1.5.7. Arabisms

Furthermore, a number of items in the data collected by the author take various VN patterns which seem to be formed in analogy to their Arabic counterpart, most prominently *CəCawC* (Ar. *CuCūC*) and *CəCōCət* (Ar. *CvCāCa*):

(21) *ktūb – ktōbət* (Ar. *kitāba*)
 śhēd – śhōdət (Ar. *šahāda*)
 rkūb – rkawb (Ar. *rukūb*)
 wīṣəl – ūṣawl (Ar. *wuṣūl*)

2.2. D/L-Stem VNs

In the D/L stem, almost all VNs appear as *təCCáyC* (ML) or as *təCCīC* in Jahn's data. However, in a few cases forms appear which take a prefix t- and usually a stressed suffix.

Table 6: Irregular D/L Stem VNs in ML

Pattern	Attestations
tāCəCēt	*tābəlēt* (I-ʕ)
təCCəCēt	*təwkəlēt*
təCCāt	*tərbāt* (III-ʕ)
təCōCōt	*təwōṣōt* (III-y)
təCCē	*tərgē* (III-ʕ) (< *təCCayC*?)

In the data collected by the author, similar forms to the ones in ML appeared.

Table 7: Irregular D/L Stem VNs in author's data/ML

Pattern	Attestations
tāCəCēt	*tābəlēt* (ML), *tābəlēt / tābáwlət* (author's data)
təCCəCēt	*təwkəlēt* (ML), *tūkayl / tūkəlēt* (author's data)
təCōCōt	*təwōṣōt* (ML), *tūṣōt* (author's data)

The VNs in question show a 'weak' consonant either as R1 (/ʕ/, /w/) or as R3 (/y/, /l/). Other *təCCayC*-type VNs can also be found for roots containing 'weak' consonants as R1 (*tālaym, tāṭaym, tākayb* [all I-ʕ]), but not as R3. This might indicate that the appearance of a suffix (and the seemingly lack of a diphthong between R2 and R3) is conditioned by the nature of R3. However, more data are needed to clarify the matter.

Since a cognate pattern does not seem to be attested in Soq. as an equally productive VN pattern,[18] and the long vowel /ī/ is represented by a surface diphthong in EM, it seems that *təCCayC* might be a loan from Arabic. According to Kogan and Bulakh (2019, 302), the D/L-stem VN in Soq. is of the shape *CɛCíCo*, which implies a cognate form with a suffix *-ūt* or *-ōt* in Mehri, which is not attested for the D/L-stem. Regarding the forms with suffixes in Mehri, these do not seem to be the simple outcome of *təCCayC* and a suffix *-v̄t*, since in other forms with an underlying stressed glide, stress does not usually shift when a suffix is added, i.e., the FS adjective pattern *CəCayCət* (MS *CəCayC*). Hence, these forms appear to be distinct (verbal) noun patterns. Note that, with the potential exception of animal nouns of the type *təCCēC*, no other patterns with an initial /t/ which is not part of the root are attested amongst Mehri nouns (at least in ML), which might indicate that this initial /t/ is connected in some way or another to the initial /t/ in *təCCayC* (and Arabic and presumably PS *taC-CīC*).

2.3. H-Stem VNs

VNs of H-stem verbs are attested in the following surface forms: *həCCəCv̄t, həCəCCv̄t*, and *C(ə)C(ə)Cv̄t*. The latter form is the

---

[18] Although nouns of the type *tvCCiC* do exist, some of which might be classified as VNs.

regular reflex of a root with R1 = [+IG]. Namely, the /hə-/ prefix does not surface, as is the case with finite verbal forms (see Rubin 2018, 131–32). As for the distribution between *həCCəCv̄t* and *həCəCCv̄t*, this is clearly explainable via the presence of a sonorant as R2 or a glottalic consonant as R1.

Table 8: Surface *həCCəCūt* versus *həCəCCūt* in ML

həCCəCūt	*həCəCCūt*
hənġəmūt	həkəfdūt
hənḳəbūt	həmərtūt
hənsəmūt	hənəwfūt
hərdəfūt	həṣərdūt
həwgərūt	həməwkūt (II-*l*)
həwgəśūt	
həwrədūt	
həzbərūt	

(22) H-Stem VNs without a surface h- prefix in ML

kəbərūt, xəṣbūt, xəwfūt, təhmīt (!), kəbbūt, hḳəṭawt, fəlḥawt, fərḳawt, fḳawt

One observes in the examples from ML given above that the presence of a sonorant as R2 or, in at least one case (*həḳəfdūt*), of a guttural consonant as R1 occasions vowel insertion between R1 and R2, whereas the lack of said features yields the outcome *həCCəCūt* (e.g., *həzbərūt*). Therefore, it appears that the standard form of the base of H-stem VNs is *həCCəC_*, with the presence of a sonorant as R2 triggering vowel insertion to its left and vowel elision to its right. The data collected by the author confirm this situation.

Table 9: *həCəCCūt / həCCəCūt* (author's data)

həCCəCūt	həCəCCūt
həghədūt	həkˀəfdūt
həghəbūt	həmərtūt
	həmərṣawt
	həṣərdūt

The vowel quality of the suffix appears consistently as *-ūt* and its conditioned variant *-awt* in both Morris (1981) and the data collected by the author. In ML, the problem of distinguishing *-ūt* and *-ōt* applies (see §2.7), whereas in Jahn (1902), despite the larger number of forms *-ōt* attested, a number of forms showing *-ūt* (or *-awt*) could be found as well.

Table 10: *-ūt* and *-awt* H-Stem VNs in Jahn (1902)

Pattern	Attestations
həlƏ23ūt	hamertūt (*mrt* H)
həl(ə)2awt	hadaḥawt (*dḥw* H)
həlƏ2ūt	hegerūt (*gry* H), haġaśūt (*ġśy* H), haḳowūt (*ḳwy* H), hamelūt (*ml*ˀ H)
həlƏ3ūt	haġaṭūt (*ġwṭ* H)
həl2ūt	henhūt (*nhy* H), h(a)uzūt (*wzˤ* H)
hū2ūt	hūfūt (*wfy* H)

Almost all of these examples (with the exception of *hamertūt*) are III-*w* or III-*y*, with one item II-*w* (*haġaṭūt*), and thus might mirror the situation in EM, where nominal *-ōt* is attested with a number of *tertiae infirmae* roots (usually III-ˤ), but is quite rare otherwise.

2.4. T-Stem VNs

For T-stem VNs, previously published sources give contradictory accounts. Consider the attestations of T-stem VNs in ML and Jahn (1902):

Table 11: Surface T-stem VN patterns in ML

	T1	T2
CətəCCV̄t	8	3
əCtəCCV̄t	4	6
CtəCCV̄t	0	0
CətCəCV̄t	0	0

Table 12: (Selection of) Surface T-stem VN patterns in Jahn (1902)

	T1	T2
CətəCCV̄t	4	5
əCtəCCV̄t	0	0
CtəCCV̄t	6	9
CətCəCV̄t	1	3

One is thus confronted with at least four surface varieties of T-stem VNs: *CətəCCV̄t*, *CtəCCV̄t*, *əCtəCCV̄t*, and *CətCəCV̄t*, all of which are spread across both the T1- and T2-stems,[19] begging the following questions:

(a) Is the initial vowel in the pattern *əCtəCCV̄t* in ML underlying or epenthetic?

(b) Is the presence or lack of a vowel between R1 and the *t*-infix a result of phonological processes (i.e., IG-effect and sonorant as R1)?

(c) Are the vowels between the infix and R2 and between R2 and R3 underlying (considering the distinct distribution between finite T-stem verbal forms T1/T2)?

When reviewing the evidence in ML against the backdrop of these questions, an incoherent picture emerges.

Concerning the question of the initial vowel (a)—in Johnstone's data most surface *əCtəCCV̄t* forms show a sonorant or IG

---

[19] A few additional surface configurations can be found in Jahn (1902), all of which seem explainable via IG/Sonorant effects, see below.

consonant as R1 (e.g., əḥtərfūt, əntəġsūt, əwtəlmūt, ərtəḳyūt, əḥtəfḳawt, əftərtōt, ərtəfōt, ərtəwōt). However, not all do, e.g., əġtyəṭawt (T1), əġtəwṭōt (T2). In these two counterexamples, a glide and /l/ are attested as R2. However, it does not seem immediately clear why this should influence the behaviour of R1 (at least in the case of the T1 verb). If one wants to accept these items as valid, one might imagine that the initial surface vowel actually represents the initial underlying vowel of finite T2-stem perfective verbs. However, if this was the case, it would seem completely unexplainable why this vowel would surface with some T1 and T2 stem verbs and not with others, namely with those of the surface pattern $CətəCC\bar{v}t$ (lətəwḳawt, etc., see below), where one would expect to see a pattern $əCtəCC\bar{v}t$ regardless of the nature of the initial consonant.

Concerning the question of a vowel between R1 and the t-infix (b)—if there was an initial underlying vowel, one might aprioristically assume that no vowel would surface between R1 and the t- infix. However, this is not always the case. Drawing upon phonological factors, one might assume, that the presence of a vowel is conditioned by the nature of R1—if R1 is an IG consonant or a sonorant, no surface vowel is to be expected; otherwise, one might expect a surface vowel to be present. However, in ML there are examples where this does not seem to apply, for no evident reason: śətəwḳawt – T1, not (ə)śtəwḳawt or (ə)śtūḳawt; mətənyūt – T2, not (ə)mtənyūt; and mətəwyūt – T1, not (ə)mtəwyūt or (ə)mtūyūt.

Concerning the rest of the base (c)—one notes that in Jahn's data at least, the IG-effect and the effect of sonorants do seem to apply, hence the *CətCəCv̄t* pattern in items such as *gitfiōt*, *wutxerōt*, *wutkelōt*, and *atwurōt*, with all but *atwurōt* showing an IG consonant as R2. The underlying status of a vowel (or lack thereof) between the infix and R2 is, of course, not prejudiced by the presence of a surface vowel.

Hence, if one takes Johnstone's sparse data seriously, no coherent picture on the formation of T-stem VNs emerges, with both *CətəCCv̄t* and *əCtəCCv̄t* being attested for both T1- and T2-stems, and with no coherent application of phonological factors to the initial sequences of the noun. Jahn's data seem to suggest—despite inconsistencies[20]—that no underlying initial vowel exists and that the surface differences of T-stem VNs might be due to well-known phonological effects, hence suggesting a default T-stem VN pattern *Cət(ə)C(ə)Cv̄t*.

To clarify the picture these and further items of T1- and T2-stems were checked by the author:

---

[20] Non-application of IG: *ḥaterfōt*, *ḥatemiyōt* (both T1), *ḥateṯtōt* (T2); lack of vowel after R1 in *ṣterfōt* (T1).

Table 13: T1- and T2-stem VNs (author's data)

Pattern	Attestations
CətəCəCūt	ḳətənəmūt (T1)
CətəCCūt	gətənbūt (T1, T2),[21] ġətərbūt (T2), ḳətūbūt (T1, II-l), ūtəlmūt (T2)[22]
əCtCəCūt	əntfəzūt (T1), əntəġsūt (T2), (ə)rtəkəyūt (T1), ərtfōt (T1)[23]
CətCəCūt	ūtxərūt/wətxərūt (T2), mətwəyūt (T1), gətfəyūt (T1), ūtkəlūt (T2)[24]
CtəCCūt	ftərtūt (T1), ftərkūt (T1), ftərḳawt (T1), ḥtərfūt (T1), ktūṭūt (T1, II-l)
CtCCūt	fthsūt (T1), ḥtfḳawt (T1, T2), ftshawt (T1)

Concerning the appearance of an initial vowel (a)—the presence or lack of an initial vowel seems to be simply the result of the presence or lack of an IG consonant or sonorant as R1. Hence, any initial vowel should probably be considered epenthetic (or a definite article), rather than a cognate of the initial vowel of finite T2 perfect forms. Concerning the initial sequence $Cət$ or Ct (b)—this seems to be also exclusively governed by the presence of an IG consonant or sonorant as R1. Hence, in the aforementioned examples no vowel surfaces between R1 and /t/, and in the case of R1 = [+Son.], an initial (epenthetic) vowel surfaces.

Also, the IG-effect was observed between the t- infix and R2, as in Jahn (1902), e.g., gətfəyūt, ūtkəlūt, etc. Hence, it seems that the aforementioned rules do in fact apply, and that the small number of contradictory examples given in ML contain a number of errors.

---

[21] It is also attested with an initial vowel, as in əgtənbūt, which was described as the definite article by informants.

[22] The form ūtəlmēt is also given for this verb. This an ūtkəlēt are the only example of T-stem VNs with a suffix -ēt, perhaps implying that these are errors.

[23] R3 = /ˤ/, hence -ōt (to be observed in other nominal patterns).

[24] See above, fn. 23.

Concerning the rest of internal structure of the base (c)—it should be noted that the assimilation of R2 to the *t*-infix of T1 stems, known from finite T1 perfect-forms, is not observed in T1 (and in T2) VNs. One hence finds the pattern *CətəCCv̄t* in these cases, e.g., *kətəllūt* (*káttəl*), *ntəbbūt* (*náttəb*). This indicates the presence of an underlying vowel between the infix and R2.

Furthermore, if one accepts the notion that no underlying initial vowel is present, it would seem reasonable to assume that an underlying vowel must be present between R1 and the *t*- infix. Hence, one might assume that the initial sequence of T-stem VNs is underlyingly *Cət_*, although this is not empirically proven. As for the question of an underlying vowel between R2 and R3, this question is hard to prove on the basis of the Mehri data. J/S VNs would, however, suggest the presence of an underlying vowel, since /b/ and /m/ are dissolved as R3:

(23) *əġtɔ́rɔ́t* (T2 *aġtéréb*), *əbtulūt* (T2 *əbtélím*)

Hence, the underlying pattern of the base of T-stem VNs can be assumed to be either *CətəCCv̄t* or—in the light of J/S, perhaps more likely—*CətəCəCv̄t*. Note the presence of an initial vowel in the aforementioned two J/S T2-stem VNs, the non-epenthetic status of which is underlined by the shift /w/ > /b/ in *əbtulūt*.

Concerning the vowel quality of the stressed suffix, no significant differences between T1- and T2-stems could be observed, with both surfacing as -*ūt* in Morris (1981) and in the data collected by the author. In more western varieties of Mehri, again, -*ūt* is less prominent than -*ōt*, although two attestations of a suffix -*ūt* could be found in Jahn (1902), e.g., *ftekedūt* and *stiḥawt* (both T2).

2.5. Š-Stem VNs

In the case of the Š-stems, both *šəCCəCīt* and *šəCəCCīt* are attested. Similar to the H-stem, the distribution of *šəCCəCīt* and *šəCəCCīt* seems to be conditioned by the presence of a sonorant as R2 or a glottalic consonant as R1, and not by the stem of the corresponding finite verbal form (Š1/Š2). The majority of attestations from ML show *šəCCəCīt*, and the two examples of *šəCəCCīt* (*šəhəwbūt* and *šənəwṣawt*) show /w/ as R2. However, the examples of *šəCəCCīt* given by Jahn show a sonorant as R2.

Table 14: *šəCCəCīt* and *šəCəCCīt* in ML and Jahn (1902)

Stem	Pattern	Attestations
Š1	*šəCCəCūt*	*šəwgaśūt, šəwkəfūt, šəxbərūt, šəwzūt, šəśyəkawt, šəġbərōt, šəġfərōt, šənḥərōt, šāsərōt*
Š2	*šəCCəCīt*	*šəwhəkāt, šədxəlēt, šəbśərēt, šərgəlēt, šəxṭərūt*
Š1	*šəCəCCūt*	*šəhəwbūt* (+ *šxargōt, šaḳarṣōt* [Jahn 1902])
Š2	*šəCəCCīt*	*šənəwṣawt* (+ *šḳarbōt* [Jahn 1902])

In ML one item is listed with a long vowel between R1 and R2, namely *šəxārəgūt* for the corresponding Š2 verb *šxērəg*. While this form might very well be an error, since it stands alone in the previously published sources, and neither this nor other Š2-stem items were produced with a long vowel in this position by the author's informants, it should be noted that 'secondary' stress would fall on exactly this position in the corresponding J/S forms (i.e., Š2 *šədɔ́xɔlɔ́t*), showing (at least) phonetic lengthening of the vowel between R1 and R2.

In terms of the vocalism of the suffix, Jahn (1902) and Morris (1981) only record -ōt/-ūt and -ūt, respectively. In ML, however, one finds -ūt for Š1 and -ēt for Š2, with a few exceptions of -ūt for Š1. This image is mirrored in the data collected by the author, where some informants would use -*ūt* and others -*ēt* for Š2-stem VNs.

2.6. Quadriliteral, Quinqueliteral, Reduplicated VNs

Morphologically more complex forms, such as quadriliterals, 'quinqueliterals', reduplicated forms, etc., broadly pattern in a similar fashion to the derived-stem VNs, insofar as they also generally take a stressed suffix. Attestations from both previous sources and from the author's data are not particularly numerous and examples are given in Table 15 (overleaf).

For simple quadriliterals of the type *aCáCCəC*, one finds the suffix -*ēt* and (with the potential exception of Johnstone's *əmərḥəbēt?*) no trace of an initial vowel, though Jahn (1902) attests three exceptions ending in -*ōt*: *karbelōt*, *maseblōt*, and *xarbəśōt*.

Table 15: Quadriliteral, 'quinqueliteral', and reduplicated VNs in previous sources and author's data

	Johnstone (1987)	Jahn (1902)	Morris (1981)	Author's data
4rad	bərḳāt (IV-ˤ)	karbelōt markaḥāt	dərbəśēt	kərbəlēt
	əmərḥəbēt	marḥabēt maseblōt	kərbəlēt	
		xarbeśōt	kərbəṭāt, tərḏəmēt	
			xərbəśēt	
n-	ənḥəṭməlūt	naḥayrrōt	ḳayta	ḳəfərrāt
	ənḳəlādūt		kərbəṭāt	ngərdəśēt
			tərtərēt	nšərxfēt
			xərbəśēt	əḳəfərrawt
			xəṣxəṣāt	(ənḳəfərrawt?)
			ənḥəṭməlūt	ngərdəśūt
			ənḥəṭbəlūt	
š-	—	—	—	šədərbəśēt
redup.	dəgdəgēt dəmdəmēt	kalkalōt	dəgdəgēt	dəmdəmēt
		ḳalḳalōt	dəbdəbēt	
		ḥuwaḥáwt	ḳaśḳəṣāt	
5rad/R	āfērráwt śxəwəllūt	kiriddōt	zəhəwllēt	āfərrāt
		metxoulīl	ṣəġayrrāt	ḥəwərrāt/ḥawr
				mśxūlīl

For patterns with a prefixed n-, the suffix appears as -ūt/-ōt when the prefix is preserved. There are, however, attestations where the prefix does not appear, and in these cases the suffix surfaces as -ēt, as to be seen in Morris (1981) and in the author's data.

In the case of a quadriliteral root prefixed by a š- prefix, the single example collected by the author shows the suffix -ēt (šədərbəšēt).

Reduplicated forms without an additional morpheme show the suffix -ōt (-ūt) in Jahn (1902) and -ēt in all other sources.

'Quinqueliterals' take either the suffix -ēt or -ūt (-ōt in Jahn 1902). The distinction in the vowel quality of the suffix does not seem to exactly match Rubin's distinction of Qw- and Qy-stem verbs (Rubin 2018, 160–61), insofar as one finds Qw-type VNs with -ūt (śxəwəllūt [Johnstone 1987]) and -ēt (zəḥəwllēt [Morris 1981]). More data from more speakers would be needed to investigate these forms in further detail.

2.7. Vowel Quality of the Suffix(es) of Derived-Stem VNs

As one has seen, various vowel qualities are attested for the suffixes of those derived-stem VNs with stressed suffixes. In Jahn's data the most frequently attested suffix is -ōt, although some attestations of -ūt can be found as well, mainly with III-*infirmae* roots. In Morris's data, all derived-stem suffixes show the suffix -ūt. In ML, the transcription of the suffix varies, and is given as -ōt before ⟨ġ⟩ and -ūt after ⟨ġ⟩, with some exceptions. In the case of ML, a significant divergence is found in the Š2-stem suffixes, which show -ēt and -ūt. In the author's data, the derived-stem suffixes also surface as -ūt, with the exception of the Š2-stem, where some speakers would use -ēt, and others would use -ūt. Hence, most derived-stem VNs appear on the surface identical to their corresponding 3FS perfective forms, as shown in the table below.

Table 16: Vocalism of derived-stem VN suffixes and the 3FS perfective

	3FS perfective	ML	Jahn (1902)	Morris (1981)	Author's data
D/L	-ēt	(-ēt, 1 -ōt)	(-ōt)	(-ēt)	(-ēt, 1 -ōt)
H	-ūt	-ūt/-ōt	-ōt (-ūt)	-ūt	-ūt
T1	-ōt	-ūt/-ōt	-ōt	-ūt	-ūt
T2	-ūt	-ūt/-ōt	-ōt (-ūt)	-ūt	-ūt
Š1	-ūt	-ūt/-ōt	-ōt (-ūt)	-ūt	-ūt
Š2	-ēt	-ēt; -ūt	-ōt (-ūt)	-ūt	-ēt; -ūt

As can be seen, the only derived-stem VN where the vocalism of the stressed suffix is not identical with that of the corresponding 3FS perfective form is the case of the T1-stem, and the (speaker-based?) variation in the Š2-stem, whereas in all other derived stems (disregarding the obvious example of the D/L-stem), the vocalism of the VN and the corresponding 3FS perfective form seems to be identical. When considering exclusively the factor of vowel quality, one might infer that the distinction of the T1-stem might be due to the collapse of T1- and T2-stem VNs, with the common T-stem VN being based on the T2-stem VN, hence explaining the non-correspondence of T1-stem VNs and their 3FS perfective forms in terms of suffix vocalism. However, as has been shown, this assumption fails to account for the apparent lack of the underlying initial vowel of T-stem VNs. Whereas more data might be needed to explore this question in greater detail, on the basis of the data gathered by the author, it seems that at least the T-stem VNs are formally distinct from their corresponding 3FS perfective forms, which might imply formal distinctness of the other derived-stem VNs as well.

3.0. Summary and Outlook

A summary of the most prominent G-stem VNs and derived stem VNs is given in the table below.

Table 17: Overview of the most prominent Mehri VN patterns

	Stem	Notes
CayCəC	Ga+Gb	Surface CīCəC in Jahn (1902)
CəCayC	Gb, II-Gutt.	Only EM in Johnstone (1987), Morris (1981), and author's data
CəCyūC	Gb, II-Gutt.	Only WM in Jahn (1902) and Sima (2009)
CaCC	Ga+Gb	Mainly triradical
CəCC		Mainly biradical
CV̄CəC	Ga+Gb	CōCəC and CēCəC
Others	Ga+Gb	Many, lexicalised
təCCayC	D/L	Surface təCCīC in Jahn (1902); some təCCəCēt/ təCCōt attested for D/L
həCCəCūt	H	-ūt in EM, -ōt in WM; həCCəCūt / R2 = [+Son.] or R1 = [+Glott.]
šəCCəCūt	Š1, Š2	-ūt in EM, -ōt in WM; šəCəCCūt / R2 = [+Son.] (+Glide?); -ūt/-ōt attested for Š2 in WM and at least amongst some speakers of EM
šəCCəCēt	Š2	Amongst some speakers of EM; šəCəCCēt / R2 = [+Son.] (+Glide?).
CətəC(ə)Cūt	T1+T2	-ūt in EM, -ōt in WM; other surface forms əCtəCCūt, CtəCCūt, CətCəCūt, CtCCūt, etc.
CəCCəCēt	IVrad. redupl.	-ōt also attested in Jahn (1902)
ənCəCCəCūt	NQ	Forms are also attested without initial n-, in these cases suffix -ēt
šəCəCCəCēt	ŠQ	šədərbəšēt

One has thus seen that amongst G-stem VNs the most prominent and apparently productive VN pattern is CayCəC (EM). This pattern is used for both Ga- and Gb-stem verbs and appears to be distinct from nominal *CiCəC* due to the presence of an underlying glide. In other dialects of Mehri, this pattern appears to surface as *CīCəC*, and at least partly shows behaviour of a form with an underlying glide, with further research into the dialectology of Mehri being needed to ascertain the distinct behaviour of glides in Mehri. Cognates from other MSAL are also known for this pattern, which seem to strengthen the notion of an underlying glide, as well as the presence of this type of VN formation—with Dufour (2016), possibly historical **CaCīC* as a VN pattern in PMSAL. The VN patterns *CəCayC* and *CəCyūC* mostly show a guttural consonant as R2, and almost appear to be in complementary distribution with *CayCəC*, at least amongst the speakers consulted by the author. However, no conditioning factors between *CayCəC* and *CəCayC/CəCyūC* could be found for the corpus as a whole. Hence it seems most reasonable to consider these patterns as distinct for the moment.

Other G-stem VN patterns seem largely unpredictable and hence lexicalised, with a slight tendency towards *CvCC*-type patterns. In terms of the distribution between Ga- and Gb-stems, the only VN patterns which show distinct distribution (II-Gutt. and Gb) are *CəCayC* and *CəCyūC*.

For derived stems and quadri/quinqueliteral roots (with the exception of the D/L stem), the VN patterns in Mehri show similarities with the corresponding 3FS perfective forms. While a solution for the determination of the distribution of vocalism akin to the one proposed by Bendjaballah and Rubin (2020) might seem appealing, particularly when assuming the merger of T1- and T2-stem VNs into a VN pattern based upon the T2-stem (see §2.4), the T-stem VNs also show the clearest formal distinctness from their corresponding 3FS perfective forms, implying underlying distinctness of at least the T-stem VN from its corresponding (T1 and T2) 3FS perfective forms, in spite of surface similarities. In broad terms, other MSAL show similar ways of derived-stem VN formation, insofar as the derived-stem affix surfaces and a stressed suffix -v́(t) is added.[25] Note, in particular, that the suffix vocalism of derived stem J/S cognates corresponds to the situation in Mehri insofar as that the stressed suffix vowel is identical in quality (/ɔ/ in J/S) to that of the 3FS perfective.

As has been mentioned, Dufour (2016, 376–78) has suggested historical *CaCīC as the origin of the G-stem VN pattern CayCəC. Another suggestion comes from Bittner (1909), who suggested original *CiCC. However, Bittner's proposal seems outdated, based on the different framework used. A VN pattern CaCīC (and patterns derived from it) is also found in other Semitic languages of the Arabian peninsula (at least in Classical Arabic), and more productively in Ethiosemitic (e.g., Gəʿəz CaCiC < *CaCīC), with Mehri (and MSAL) CayCəC falling apparently into a broader southern Semitic (in an areal sense) trend of *CaCīC as a G-stem VN pattern.

In the case of the derived-stem VNs, a salient point to mention for a comparative perspective lies in the fact that these forms show both the derived-stem affix and a stressed suffix -v́t. The underlying structure remains unclear for most derived-stem VNs.

---

[25] E.g., J/S tfkír (D/L), ǧitenfɔ́t/ktɔlṭɔ́t (T1), ftɔkɔrɔ́t (T2), šɔǧfɔ́rɔ́t (Š1), šəlɔ́hɔḳɔ́t (Š2), nǧɔrdɔśɔ́t/kafarrɔ́t (NQ), etc. (own data). For Soq. cognates see Kogan and Bulakh (2019).

However, the case of the T-stem VN urges caution against the assumption that the surface similarities of derived stem VNs and their 3FS perfective counterparts are to be understood as formal identity. In any case, regular and fully productive derived-stem VN formation by simple suffixation of a stressed suffix *-vt* onto what appears to be the base of the derived stem—although quite possible, with an internal configuration of underlying vowels distinct from the corresponding 3FS perfective—appears to be a particular MSAL feature.

Hence, VN formation in Mehri adheres to the common Semitic notion of a plethora of VN patterns for the G-stem(s) with more regular patterns for the derived stems. Some of the patterns attested show parallels with other relatively productive VN patterns in most Semitic languages, whether through borrowing (D/L *təCCayC?*) or retention (*CvCC?*), and the most productive G-stem VN pattern *CayCəC* appears to show parallels to forms particular to Arabic and Ethiosemitic (as VNs). Finally, as alluded to previously, putative cognates for the Mehri VN patterns discussed here are to be found in other MSAL as well, thus alluding to a basically similar repertoire of VN formation in PMSAL (and hence potentially providing an interesting set of PMSAL innovations), although more research is needed, particularly on the other MSAL, to further advance this question.

References

Bendjaballah, Sabrina, and Philippe Ségéral. 2014. 'The Phonology of "Idle Glottis" Consonants in the Mehri of Oman

(Modern South Arabian)'. *Journal of Semitic Studies* 49/1: 161–204.

———. 2017. 'The Vocalic System of the Mehri of Oman: Stress, Length and Syllabic Structure'. *Brill's Journal of Afroasiatic Languages and Linguistics* 9: 160–90.

Bendjaballah, Sabrina, and Aaron Rubin. 2020. 'The 3fs Perfect in Omani Mehri'. *Journal of Semitic Studies* 65/2: 511–29.

Bittner, Maximilian. 1909. *Studien zur Laut- und Formenlehre der Mehri-Sprache in Südarabien. I. Zum Nomen im engeren Sinne.* Vienna: Hölder.

Dufour, Julien. 2016. 'Recherches sur le verbe sudarabique moderne'. Habitation, École Pratique des Hautes Études.

———. 2017. 'Nouns and Adjectives of the Shape $C_1\acute{V}C_2(\partial)C_3(\text{-})$ in Jibbali (Śħri) and Mehri'. *Brill's Journal of Afroasiatic Languages and Linguistics* 9: 191–217.

Jahn, Alfred. 1902. *Die Mehri-Sprache in Südarabien* III. Vienna: Hölder.

Johnstone, Thomas Muir. 1981. *Jibbali Lexicon.* Oxford: Oxford University Press.

———. 1987. *Mehri Lexicon and English-Mehri Word-List.* London: Routledge.

Kogan, Leonid. 2015. *Genealogical Classification of Semitic: The Lexical Isoglosses.* Berlin: De Gruyter.

Kogan, Leonid, and Alexander Militarev. 2000. *Semitic Etymological Dictionary. Volume I: Anatomy of Man and Animals.* Münster: Ugarit-Verlag.

Kogan, Leonid, and Maria Bulakh. 2019. 'Soqotri'. In *The Semitic Languages. Second Edition*, edited by John Huehnergard and Naʿama Pat-El, 280–320. London: Routledge.

Kogan, Leonid, and Vitaly Naumkin (eds). 2018. *Corpus of Soqotri Oral Literature* II. Leiden: Brill.

Morris, Miranda. 1981. 'The Phonology and Morphology of the Mahri Noun'. PhD dissertation, SOAS.

Rubin, Aaron. 2014. *The Jibbali (Shaḥri) Language of Oman: Grammar and Texts*. Leiden: Brill.

———. 2018. *Omani Mehri: A New Grammar with Texts*. Leiden: Brill.

Sima, Alexander. 2009. *Mehri-Texte aus der Jemenitischen Šarqiyah*. Wiesbaden: Harrassowitz.

Watson, Janet. 2012. *The Structure of Mehri*. Wiesbaden: Harrassowitz.

TECHNOLOGICAL SUPPORT FOR ENDANGERED/MINORITY LANGUAGES: CREATING CROSS-PLATFORM KEYBOARD LAYOUTS FOR MODERN SOUTH ARABIAN LANGUAGES[*]

Hongwei Zhang

1.0. Introduction

The rapid development of computer and internet technology has made digital space an indispensable part of modern life. With respect to the importance of technological support to minority languages, this paper presents the author's personal experience with creating cross-platform keyboard layouts for Modern South Arabian Languages. While affirming the positive role of new technology and social media for language preservation, Jany (2018, 74) points out the need to introduce literacy for oral languages and the practical issue for languages with orthographies that are

---

[*] I would like to thank Janet Watson and Fabio Gasparini for coordinating a special session to allow me to present on the project. My gratitude also goes to Nathaniel Wong, who edited my paper and helped with alpha-tests of keyboard. All remaining errors are mine. This paper was supported by grants 22PJC098, 2022114016, and 23BYY097.

not easily represented using standard keyboards. Thus, it is hoped that the products of this project will help promote the online presence of the Modern South Arabian Languages to contribute to their revitalisation.

2.0. The Internet and Endangered/Minority Languages

The internet has led to the emergence of new varieties of "internet language" (Crystal 2006). Strictly speaking, though, this process has much more to do with thriving languages that are fortunate enough to occupy a large portion of the digital space and dominate internet users' daily communications. Cunliffe (2007) correctly points out that the internet has brought about a variety of new possibilities for language use which could become opportunities for the revitalisation of minority languages, but it is crucial first to promote their online presence.

While technological advancement has enabled more creative ways for linguists to document endangered/minority languages, such as collaboration with trained native speakers (Villa 2002), insufficient technological support (for typing and font display, etc.) still leaves members from those language communities with very limited digital space online. This is true for minority languages with special traditional writing systems, such as the Plains Cree syllabary (Santos and Harrigan 2020), and the situation is even more difficult for those without an established writing system, such as the Modern South Arabian Languages. As a precious branch of the Semitic language family that has survived to the present day, these minority languages—some facing endangerment—lack official recognition. Moreover, they have had no conventional writing system until very recently, when field linguists proposed the Arabic-based orthographies (Watson et al. n.d.; Naumkin and Kogan 2015).

It should be admitted that technical difficulties need not necessarily constitute an insurmountable barrier for users of modern technology. In fact, there have been vivid examples observed over the years when the dominant coding standard was ASCII. ASCII stands for 'American Standard Code for Information Interchange' which is, of course, based on the English alphabet. At that time, for users whose native languages employ a script different from English, be it Cyrillic, Arabic, or even Latin with diacritics, using the computer meant they had to make compromises to type their languages using the limited number of ASCII symbols, see Figure 1.

Figure 1: ASCII's 'Standard Code' set (American National Standards Institute, Inc. 1977, 8)

b_4	b_3	b_2	b_1	COLUMN ROW	0	1	2	3	4	5	6	7
0	0	0	0	0	NUL	DLE	SP	0	@	P	`	p
0	0	0	1	1	SOH	DC1	!	1	A	Q	a	q
0	0	1	0	2	STX	DC2	"	2	B	R	b	r
0	0	1	1	3	ETX	DC3	#	3	C	S	c	s
0	1	0	0	4	EOT	DC4	$	4	D	T	d	t
0	1	0	1	5	ENQ	NAK	%	5	E	U	e	u
0	1	1	0	6	ACK	SYN	&	6	F	V	f	v
0	1	1	1	7	BEL	ETB	'	7	G	W	g	w
1	0	0	0	8	BS	CAN	(	8	H	X	h	x
1	0	0	1	9	HT	EM	)	9	I	Y	i	y
1	0	1	0	10	LF	SUB	*	:	J	Z	j	z
1	0	1	1	11	VT	ESC	+	;	K	[	k	{
1	1	0	0	12	FF	FS	,	<	L	\	l		
1	1	0	1	13	CR	GS	-	=	M	]	m	}
1	1	1	0	14	SO	RS	.	>	N	^	n	~
1	1	1	1	15	SI	US	/	?	O	_	o	DEL

Therefore, the chatting symbols created by users in the Arab world to type (colloquial) Arabic naturally consist of a subset of the ASCII characters. These symbols, known as 'Arabizi' (Yaghan 2008) or, somewhat less commonly, as 'Arabish' or 'Franco-arabe' (Allam 2014), employ not only the 26 *letters* on the English keyboard, but also a few of the *numbers*. In the age of ASCII, Arabizi thrived and became the best solution for the Arabs to engage in Computer-Mediated Communication, "communication that takes place between human beings via the instrumentality of computers" (Herring 1996, 1). When mobile text messages became a popular means of contact after the 1980s, mobile users in the Arab world carried on using Arabizi's unofficial transcription symbols to type text messages on their mobile phones, due to the lack of proper support for Arabic letters.[1] It should be noted that Arabizi remains far from standardised (Table 1) and the spelling conventions vary from one country to another.[2]

---

[1] In 2010, Android users had to 'root' their phones—which voids the warranty—to install the patch 'Arabic libraries' written by Ayman al-Sanad in order to obtain the correct display of Arabic on their phones. This was because, even though Android 2.2 added the ability to display Arabic, the letters were rendered disconnected and backwards.

[2] Yaghan (2008, 42) highlights that the differences depend "on the local dialect," but it should also be noted that the dominant European languages also play a role. This is most evident in the representation of Arabic /ʃ/ ⟨ش⟩: in countries where there was French colonial influence, e.g., Algeria (Benmoussat 2011), the Arabizi would employ the digraph ⟨ch⟩ as in the French orthography, whereas elsewhere with English colonial influence, e.g., in Kuwait (Akbar, Taqi, and Sadiq 2020), the Arabizi would employ the digraph ⟨sh⟩. The representations of the

Table 1: Various possibilities for Arabizi spellings[3]

ء	2	س	s	ل	l
ب	b	ش	sh, ch, $, sy, 4	م	m
ت	t	ص	9, S, s	ن	n
ث	th, t',[4] s, 4	ض	9', D, d, z	ه	h
ج	j, g	ط	6, T, t	و	w, u, o, oo, ou
ح	7, h	ظ	6', D, dh, d, z, d', D'	ي	y, i, e, ee
خ	7', 5, kh	ع	3	ا	aa, a
د	d	غ	3', gh	ةَ	a, e
ذ	d', th, z, 4	ف	f	ةِ	e, i
ر	r	ق	q, 2, g, k, 8	ةُ	o, u
ز	z	ك	k		

Curiously though, after Unicode replaced ASCII to become the coding standard, Arabizi has retained its popularity among Arabic speakers even to the present day, when Arabic keyboards are

emphatics and gutturals are more fluid, ranging from various numeric symbols to capitalisation. As also noted by Yaghan (2008, 42), the representation of vowels can be optional.

[3] The Arabizi symbols are collected from the different sources on Arabizi listed in the reference. Capitalisation typos are ignored, e.g., ⟨م⟩ rendered by ⟨M⟩ instead of ⟨m⟩.

[4] The apostrophe ⟨'⟩ (Unicode U+0027) is *the* apostrophe symbol in ASCII (binary code value 010 0111). In practice, however, it constantly shows up as the single quotation mark ⟨'⟩ or ⟨'⟩ (Abu Elhija 2014, 208), likely due to the smart quote conversion setting in word processors: Jeníková (2019, 111) lists systematic preposed *single quotes* with numerals, e.g., ⟨'9⟩ for ⟨ض⟩, ⟨'6⟩ for ⟨ظ⟩, but the source (Bianchi 2012), adapted from Palfreyman and Al Khalil (2003), reports a system with preposed *apostrophes*. The same illustration becomes left single quotes in Biachi (2015). Al Hajjaj's (2021) unique report might be typos in the manuscript (*pace*): ⟨'3⟩ for ⟨غ⟩, but illustrated by ⟨mosha3'eb⟩ for ⟨مشاغب⟩; ⟨6'⟩ for ⟨ظ⟩, but illustrated by ⟨6'areef⟩ for ⟨ظريف⟩, etc.

readily available on every digital device. Recently there has been a surge of literature on Arabizi, not only in terms of its sociolinguistic implications,[5] but also regarding its processing in computational linguistics,[6] as quite an amount of Neo-Arabic materials composed in Arabizi has become an important source of data for corpus research.

The Arabic story, at first sight, appears to be a successful case in favour of an indifferent let-it-be solution among speakers to deal on their own with technical difficulties. However, it would *not* work if the language in question were a marginalised minority language and especially if it were already facing

---

[5] Apart from general sociolinguistic surveys (Bahrainwala 2011; Benmoussat 2011; Allehaiby 2013; Al-Shaer 2016; Abu-Liel, Eviatar, and Nir 2019; Abu-Liel, Ibrahim, and Eviatar 2021), there is also research on the use and implications of Arabizi in different countries (Keong, Hameed, and Abdulbaqi 2015; Sullivan 2017; Alghamdi 2018; Alghamdi and Petraki 2018; Akbar 2019; Alsulami 2019; Akbar, Taqi, and Sadiq 2020), on users' gender differences (Bardaweel and Rababah 2022), on attitudes to Arabizi among second language learners (Farrag 2012), on Arabizi from the perspective of code-mixing (Kenali et al. 2016), etc.

[6] A number of studies deal with computational solutions to convert Arabizi texts into normative Arabic for further analysis (Al-Badrashiny et al. 2014; Bies et al. 2014; Guellil et al. 2017; Masmoudi et al. 2019; Klouche and Benslimane 2020; Shazal, Usman, and Habash 2020). Many others conduct sentiment analysis of the Arabizi texts (Duwairi et al. 2016; Guellil et al. 2018; Chader et al. 2019; Tobaili et al. 2019; Baert et al. 2020; Guellil et al. 2020; Tobaili 2020; Guellil et al. 2021). Others work on the detection of Arabizi online to analyse its use (Tobaili 2016) and machine translation solutions for Arabizi texts (van der Wees, Bisazza, and Monz 2016; Guellil, Azouaou, and Abbas 2017).

endangerment: Arabizi emerged precisely due to speaker willingness to *use* Arabic despite the technical difficulties, whereas those languages in need for revitalisation—i.e., those facing not just technical difficulties, but real-life existential challenges—lack speakers characterised by such willingness and/or ability.[7]

3.0. Creating Cross-Platform Keyboard Layouts for Modern South Arabian Languages

Long before the current Unicode Standard, Version 15.0 (The Unicode Consortium 2022), and by no later than Version 4.0.1 (Aliprand et al. 2003, 473), all the special characters involved in the proposed Arabic-based orthographies for the Modern South Arabian Languages were incorporated into the Unicode Standard. The Arabic-based orthography designed by Watson et al. (n.d.) targeted Śḥerēt[8]—the language with the largest consonantal inventory among the Modern South Arabian Languages—to allow for the other languages to utilise a subset of these orthographical symbols. The rationales for the letter shapes include both quasi-

---

[7] See Al-Ghanim and Watson (2020: 11):

> Speaker numbers are 12 (Bathari), ~1,000 (Harsusi, Hobyot), ~30,000 (Shehret), 60,000 (Soq.), ~200,000 (Mehri). The precise number of speakers is, however, impossible to ascertain: there are no census figures relating to MSAL speakers specifically, and many members of the language communities no longer speak the languages fluently or at all. Since the 1970s, the spread of Arabic has meant that the MSAL have increasingly fallen into disuse.

[8] See Bellem and Watson's (2017, 622) note discussing this more appropriate designation than 'Jibbali'.

established workaround practices in the community (e.g., ⟨پ⟩ for ś as an upside-down ⟨ث⟩, which was already used by the speakers in SMS messaging) and Semitic cognancy (e.g., ⟨ض⟩ for ṣ́, since it is cognate with Arabic ḍ ⟨ض⟩). Naumkin and Kogan (2015, 11–12) did not adopt every aspect of the aforementioned system for their Soqoṭri orthography, but there are only two additional letters outside the set of letters for Śḥerēt. See Table 2 for the key letters of the Arabic-based orthographies:[9]

---

[9] There are, in fact, other Arabic-based orthographies. One was claimed to have been proposed by *almahrah.net*, a website which is unfortunately no longer accessible and whose captures on the Internet Archive Way Back Machine do not seem to contain content on any orthography proposal. The other was proposed by the 'Mehri Language Center for Studies and Research', available in the Android keyboard app released by the centre and online at https://saeedalqumairi.wordpress.com/2019/10/13/-خاص-خطاب باللغتين-المهرية-والعربية-ال/. The latter is said to be far less preferred among speakers than the one designed by Watson et al. (n.d.). Therefore, I have not included the additional consonantal letters in that system. I have, however, included some letters to make it possible to type the vowels in that system, but that was mainly due to other considerations (see §3.2).

Table 2: Most commonly used additional letters needed for the Arabic-based orthographies of Modern South Arabian Languages

Translit-eration	Letter	Unicode code point value	Notes
ḍ	ظ	U+0638	Included in Arabic keyboards
ž	چ	U+0686	
s̄	پ	U+067E	Naumkin and Kogan (2015) propose ⟨ݭ⟩
ṣ	ض	U+0636	Included in Arabic keyboards
š̄[10]	ش	U+0634	Included in Arabic keyboards; used for s̄ in Śḥerēt but for š in the other sister languages
ṣ̌	ڞ	U+069E	
ẓ	ڌ	U+068C	Only for Śḥerēt
š̌	ڜ	U+069C	Only for Śḥerēt
~	ۨ	U+06E8	
ḷ	ڸ	U+06B8	Naumkin and Kogan (2015) propose it for the allophonic [ɫ] of l in Soqoṭri

The corresponding input methods did not become available until a Mehri layout was added to Google's Gboard app. However, at present, the Mehri layout remains available for Gboard only on Android devices and it has not yet been added to the iOS Gboard app. Prior to this project, there did not seem to have been any computer keyboards available either.

To fill in the gap, I decided to create *system keyboards* for both Windows and MacOS platforms and an iPhone keyboard working via the iOS app Keyman. The process and the relevant

---

[10] See Bellem and Watson (2017) for a discussion on the research history and the features of this phoneme in Śḥerēt based on analyses of the acoustic and visual data from phonetic experiments.

software are detailed in this section to illustrate how convenient it has become even for members in the minority/endangered language communities to claim their own digital space.

3.1. Designing System Keyboards for the Modern South Arabian Languages

The keyboard layouts are designed based on the 'Arabic 101' layout, which is one of the three existing keyboard layouts for Arabic in Windows. It also serves as the basis for the 'Arabic – PC' keyboard layout in MacOS. The arrangement of the keys goes back to the first Arabic typewriter keyboard designed by Selim S. Haddad. While Nemeth (2017, 75) is certainly correct that "no specific claims to any implementation or particular machine can be found" in the description for his patent (Haddad 1899) and there is no illustration for a keyboard design, his invention of the typewriter is indeed reported in both *The New York Times* (1904) and *Typewriter Topics* (1915), the latter containing an image of the "patented Arabic keyboard" (Figure 2).

Figure 2: *Typewriter Topics* 29/2 (1915): 24

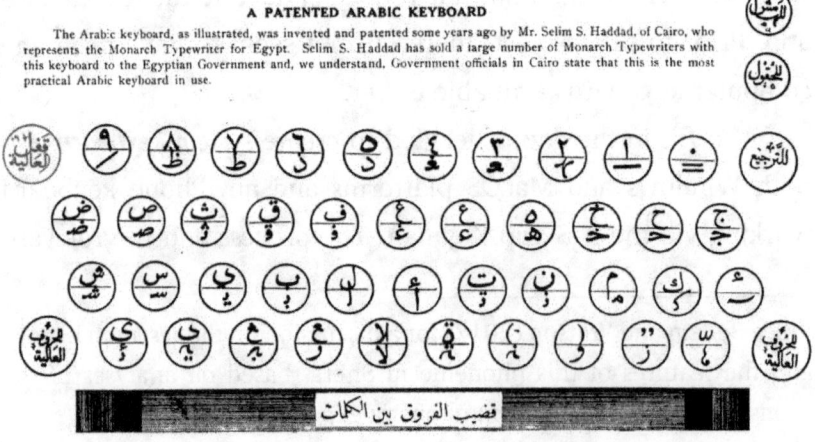

Technological Support for Endangered/Minority Languages   251

The conventional status of this typewriter layout has been passed down via the typewriter realm in later patents, such as Figure 3 (Khalil 1960) until the computer layouts today—'Arabic 101' (Figure 4), 'Arabic 102' (Figure 5), 'Arabic 102 AZERTY' (Figure 6), and the default MacOS 'Arabic' keyboard (Figure 7):

Figure 3: Khalil's (1960) keyboard layout

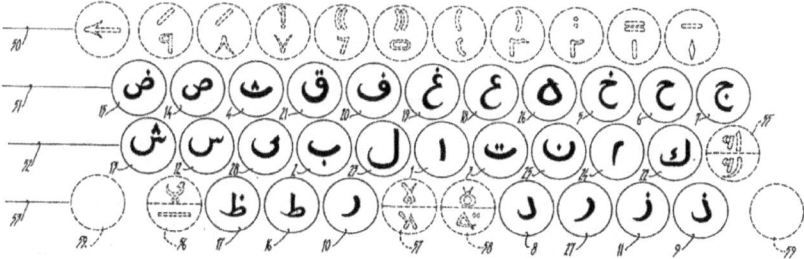

Figure 4: 'Arabic 101' keyboard layout

!	!	@	#	$	%	^	&	*	(	)	_	+	
ذ	1	2	3	4	5	6	7	8	9	0	-	=	BS
Tab	ض	ص	ث	ق	ف	غ	ع	ه	خ	ح	ج	د	\
CL	ش	س	ي	ب	ل	ا	ت	ن	م	ك	ط	Enter	
Shift	ئ	ء	ؤ	ر	لا	ى	ة	و	ز	ظ	Shift		
Ctrl		Alt						Alt			Ctrl		

Figure 5: 'Arabic 102' keyboard layout

>	!	@	#	$	%	^	&	*	(	)	_	+	
<	1	2	3	4	5	6	7	8	9	0	-	=	BS
Tab	ض	ص	ث	ق	ف	غ	ع	ه	خ	ح	ج	د	ذ
CL	ش	س	ي	ب	ل	ا	ت	ن	م	ك	ط	Enter	
Shift	ئ	ء	ؤ	ر	لا	ى	ة	و	ز	ظ	Shift		
Ctrl		Alt						Alt			Ctrl		

Figure 6: 'Arabic 102' AZERTY keyboard layout

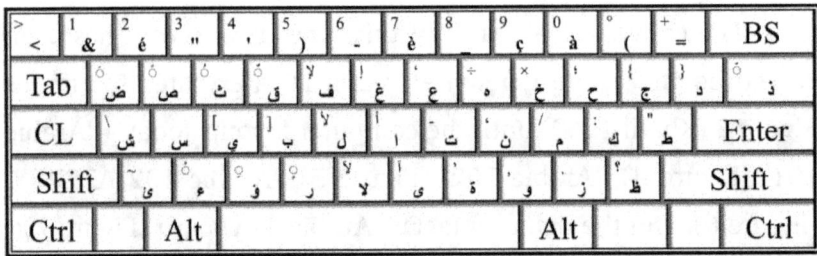

Figure 7: The default 'Arabic' keyboard layout on MacOS

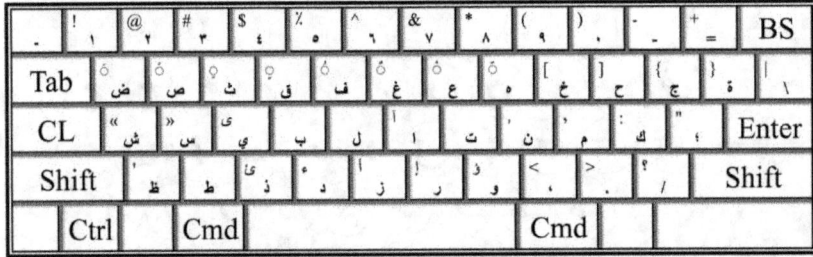

Of course, there are also various QWERTY-based[11] Arabic keyboard layouts (Aknuranda, Syawli, and Setiawan 2020), one of which is readily available in MacOS. Another better known QWERTY-based Arabic keyboard might be the Arabic layout of Google Input Tools.[12] However, it is evident that the core layout

---

[11] QWERTY refers to the first six keys on the default English keyboard, which also signifies the arrangement of the keys as opposed to, e.g., AZERTY. The QWERTY-based Arabic keyboards map the Arabic letters onto the Latin alphabet based on certain similarities in pronunciation, e.g., ⟨ب⟩ would be located on the key for ⟨b⟩ in the standard QWERTY Latin keyboard, i.e., the fifth in the third row of keys. Not all key assignments are equally intuitive and different keyboard layout designers can make very different decisions on those letters that cannot be easily compared to the 26 English letters.

[12] Google used to offer standalone installation files for different language versions of Google Keyboard prior to the release of Gboard. Nowadays, Google Input Tools is offered as a feature of Google Services. Users of

of the mostly commonly available keyboards essentially follows that of the conventional typewriter designs (especially in the top two rows of keys). Unless they have obtained a computer without an Arabic keyboard or somehow got accustomed to the QWERTY or AZERTY *Latin* keyboards first,[13] computer users in the Arab world are more likely to be familiar with the basic Arabic layout above. As noted by Santos and Harrigan (2020, 95), "there is a high cost in introducing an unfamiliar typing system and asking people to adapt to it."

Google Translate can access it easily when the virtual keyboard is turned on. Several virtual keyboards support 'transliteration' (https://www.google.com/inputtools/services/features/transliteration.html), which essentially involves the mapping of non-Latin scripts (including Arabic) onto the QWERTY layout.

[13] In fact, this is the case in Aknuranda, Syawli, and Setiawan's (2020) study, in which they attempt to test the usability of QWERTY-based Arabic keyboard layouts in comparison to the 'Arabic 101' keyboard layout. However, the target users were Indonesian speaking, i.e., they were already familiar with both the QWERTY Latin keyboard layout and the Latin script employed in the official orthography of their native language. Here, however, we assume that the target computer users in the Arab world are not completely unfamiliar with the traditional Arabic keyboard layout(s) which are generally preinstalled on computers with a Windows operating system.

3.2 Creating System Keyboards for the Modern South Arabian Languages

The letters outside of the 'Arabic 101' layout were added via two custom keyboard creator software: MKLC[14] (Microsoft Keyboard Layout Creator) for the Windows system keyboard and Ukelele[15] (by SIL International) for the MacOS system keyboard. Both are free and easy to use, with very intuitive interfaces.

Figure 8: Working interface of MKLC with 'Arabic 101' modified

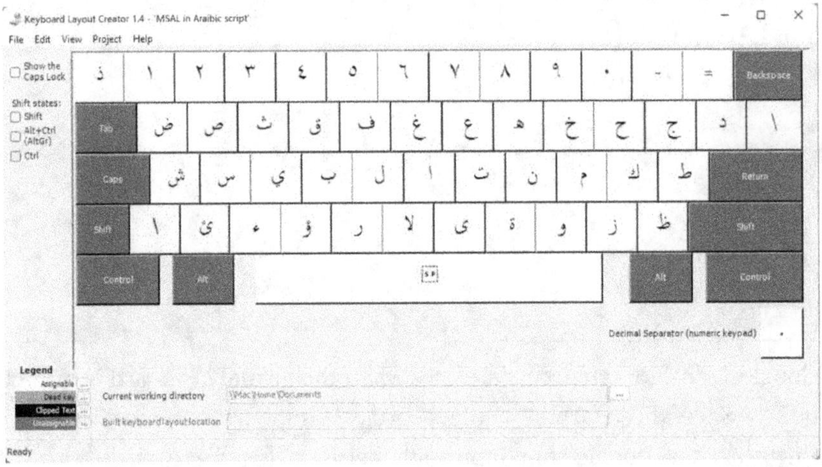

Utilising the software, one can create a custom keyboard from scratch, but there is also the option to load an existing system keyboard and modify it. In the present project, loading the existing 'Arabic 101' is apparently the most convenient way. To define the key values, one can either paste a Unicode character or type the proper Unicode code point values (each Unicode code

---

[14] Available free of charge at https://www.microsoft.com/en-us/download/details.aspx?id=102134.

[15] Available free of charge at https://software.sil.org/ukelele/#downloads.

point is expressed via "U+" followed by the hexadecimal representation of the code point). The latter option is easier in MKLC than in Ukelele, because the Unicode code points can be used directly.

Ukelele, on the other hand, demands the XML code format if the output value of a key is not pasted/typed directly. One, therefore, has to bracket the hexadecimal representation in the Unicode code point with "&#x" and ";"—e.g., in order to define a key with the output of ⟨ض⟩, whose Unicode code point is U+069E, one has to type "ڞ" in Ukelele.

Figure 9: Working interface of Ukelele with "Arabic – PC" modified

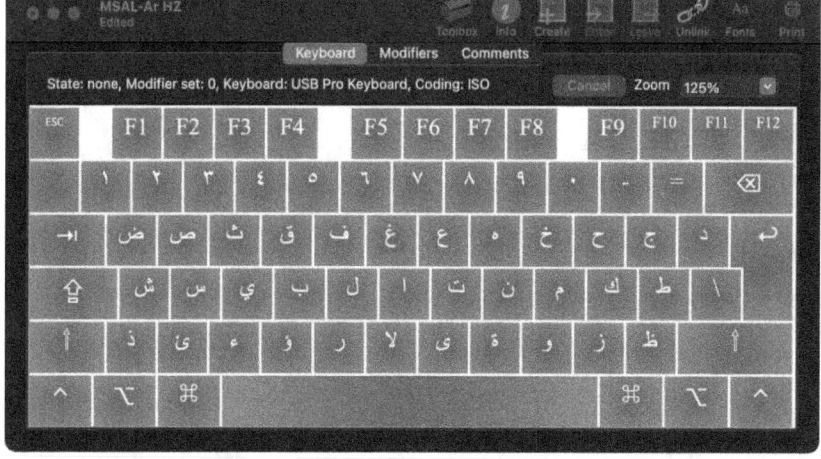

As illustrated above, the 'Arabic 101' layout is only slightly modified: the default numeric keys are changed to the 'Eastern Arabic' numerals, a useful feature of the default MacOS 'Arabic' keyboard layout, which the 'Arabic 101' layout lacks. The (Western) Arabic numerals are made available together with the additional letters, all placed in the additional 'shift-state'—key assignments to enable different outputs while holding the Shift key, as well as

Ctrl and Alt on Windows keyboards, Control and Option on MacOS keyboards).

There are only two shift-states in the original 'Arabic 101' layout, the shift-state dedicated chiefly to diacritics. I have decided to add the additional key assignments to the Alt+Ctrl state on Windows and the Option state on MacOS. This makes it possible for users to hold only one additional key—Right Alt on Windows and Option on MacOS, preferably with the right thumb—when additional letters/diacritics are needed. The Alt+Ctrl state for the Windows keyboard is shown in Figure 10; the Option state for the MacOS keyboard is basically the same.

Figure 10: The Alt+Ctrl state for the Windows keyboard

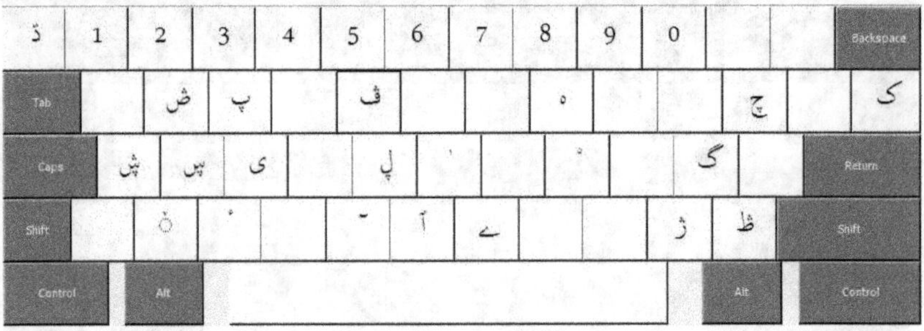

All the additional letters needed for Modern South Arabian Languages in the orthography designed by Watson et al. (n.d.) are located on the key for the 'related' Arabic letters, e.g., ⟨ڎ⟩ was based on the workaround practice in the community using Arabic ⟨ذ⟩It is, therefore, located on the key for ⟨ذ⟩ in the additional shift-state.

As illustrated in Figure 10, I have added some more letters and diacritics. Some of them are for the purpose of enabling users to type potentially relevant sounds in the local Neo-Arabic varieties, if other orthographies (such as Persian) left their marks on their non-official Arabic orthography. Others are actually useful for Arabic. Personally, I have always found it frustrating not to be able to type the dagger *alif* ⟨ó⟩ (U+0670), the *maddah* ⟨ỗ⟩ (U+0653), and the *alif al-waṣl* ⟨ỉ⟩ (U+0671) when using the Windows 'Arabic 101', but I found them available in MacOS's 'Arabic – PC'. So I added them, too. Finally, considering the fact that users typing predominantly in Arabic may also need typing in English letters (usernames, etc.), I added the standard QWERTY keys, lowercase in the Ctrl state for the Windows keyboard and the Command state for the MacOS keyboard, uppercase in the Ctrl+Shift state for the Windows keyboard and the Command+Shift state for the MacOS keyboard.

3.3. The iOS keyboard on Keyman for the Modern South Arabian Languages

Users of iOS devices were in the past restricted to built-in iOS keyboards that included only a small set of languages. Even now, relying on the official system updates is not at all ideal for minority/endangered languages. One can mention the fact that, e.g., the keyboard(s) for Uzbek—the official language of a sovereign state—became available only very recently, in iOS 13 (released in 2019).

Since Apple first allowed them in iOS 8 (released in 2014), third-party keyboard apps have gradually become among the common apps that one can easily obtain from the App Store these days. A number of third-party apps supporting multiple languages/scripts have also been released as host apps and provide addons for those languages/scripts. The Gboard app mentioned above is one such example. However, it is Keyman that has offered a convenient way for users to tailor mobile keyboard layouts themselves—by means of the Keyman Developer software (by SIL International).[16]

Like MKLC and Ukelele, Keyman Developer is characterised by a straightforward design and a very user-friendly interface. Once a project is initiated, the software allows one to create keyboard layouts loadable to Keyman apps on various operating systems, a process not too different from that in MKLC and Ukelele (Figure 11).

Figure 11: Creating keyboard layouts in Keyman Developer

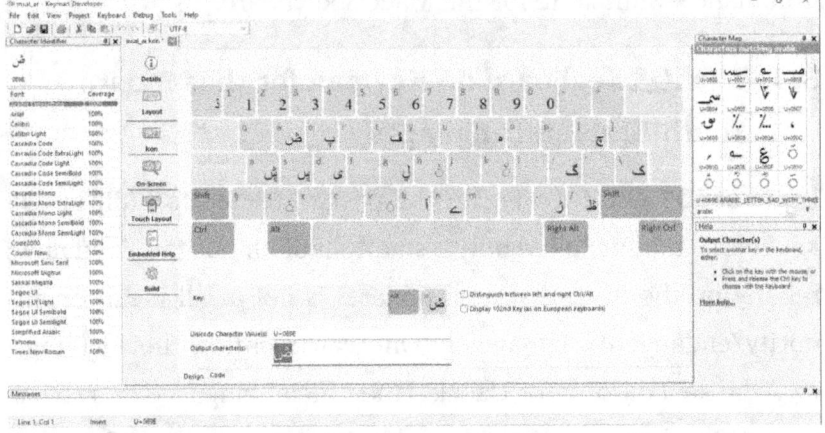

More importantly, it also provides the option to create a 'Touch Layout' either from 'Template' or via 'Import from On Screen'. The interface allows for both amateur users and coding experts to manipulate the details of the mobile keyboard, the former via the 'Design' tab and the latter via the 'Code' tab (Figure 12).

---

[16] Available free of charge at https://keyman.com/developer/download.php.

Figure 12: Making the 'Touch Layout' in Keyman Developer

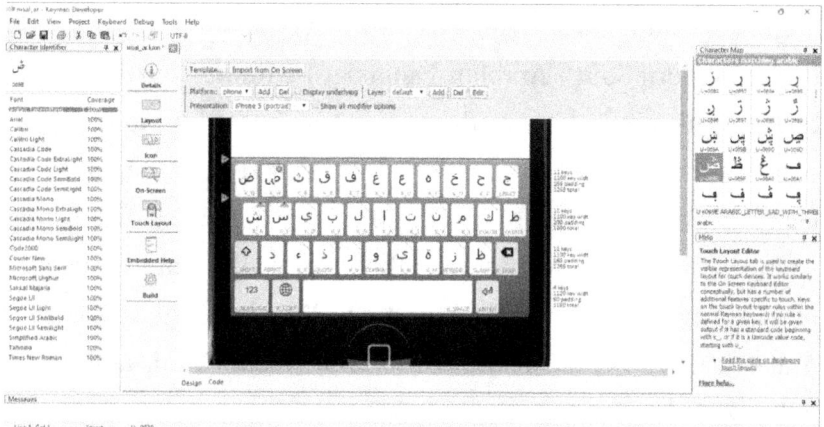

As can be seen in Figure 12, the software also offers the option to switch between different platforms for the Touch Layout, i.e., either 'phone', as in Figure 12, or 'tablet'. For the present project, I have concentrated on the phone platform and included the additional letters as I did for the computer system keyboards, except for the standard QWERTY Latin keys to reduce the complexity of the layout for mobile users.

At this point, the only shortcomings of the Keyman iOS keyboard in this project are that it is not yet equipped with a dictionary[17] for predictions and, if one uses it to type Arabic, it also lacks the prediction and autocorrection features in the original iOS Arabic keyboard. However, in their present forms, these keyboards for Modern South Arabian Languages (for Windows,

---

[17] It should be noted—as it was also kindly pointed out by one of this article's anonymous reviewers—that this *is* indeed a possible feature in Keyman Developer via its Lexical Models: if the keyboard package is equipped with the proper wordlist file, whether pre-existing in digital format or composed by the developer, the keyboard will be able to provide limited predictive text functionality.

MacOS, and iOS) can serve as the only keyboard needed for bilingual or trilingual speakers, as they can type both in Arabic and in the Modern South Arabian Languages without switching keyboards. This could be significant because, according to some research surveys, one of the reasons for Arabizi's continued popularity is the fact that bilingual Arabic and English users find Arabizi convenient, as it allows them to type in both languages with a single keyboard (Farrag 2012, 25; Alghamdi 2018, 160; Akbar 2019, 314; Alsulami 2019, 265; Akbar, Taqi, and Sadiq 2020, 206; Haghegh 2021, 165–66).

3.4 Some Potential Issues

Anyone attempting to customise system keyboards using Ukelele should be aware that initiating a project via modifying a loaded system keyboard sometimes fails,[18] which was what happened in this project when the 'Arabic – PC' keyboard was loaded. Therefore, it may be preferable to build a new layout from scratch in Ukelele.

Regarding system keyboards, sometimes newly installed keyboards might not be fully functional immediately in every software application. This is particularly relevant to the Microsoft Office components. One would need to reboot the system in this case. Since the key combinations are defined again for the specific layouts, they generally do not trigger conflicts with the

---

[18] The reason remains unclear to me; there seems to be some problems with the Ukelele application, perhaps specific to the version I worked on, since I do recall previously succeeding in initiating projects via loading system keyboards.

'access keys' in Microsoft Office, but in the rare instances when such conflicts do arise, it is advisable to turn off the 'access keys', most of which are infrequently used by common users.

4.0. Conclusion

In this paper, I have described the keyboard project I conducted for the Arabic-based orthographies proposed for the Modern South Arabian Languages. This project was situated in the broader context of highlighting the importance of information technology and online space for endangered/minority languages. The products of this project are two system keyboards (one for Windows, the other for MacOS) and one iOS keyboard on the host app Keyman.[19] All of them have been created with the basic goal of enabling speakers/researchers to type both in Arabic and in Modern South Arabian Languages with ease. For the computer keyboards, further consideration has been given to occasional

---

[19] The two computer keyboards have been publicly available on my ResearchGate page since I presented on the keyboards at the 'Language and Nature in South Arabia' workshop and I have also recently updated the installation files. One can easily find them via a Google search for an exact match of the name "MSAL-Ar" or for an exact match of "Modern South Arabian" plus "keyboard" without quotation marks. The iOS Keyman app had some issues with the layout I created, so I had been in communication with Keyman Developer's technical support members while participating in their alpha releases to test the performance of my keyboard layout. With the latest version, the issue was resolved and I have been privately distributing the installation package for speaker and researcher testing. The keyboard layout file will eventually be submitted to Keyman's online database for easier access among iPhone users.

need for the Latin alphabet. These thoughts were further motivated by the wish that the factor of convenience could in some way encourage speakers of Modern South Arabian Languages to use their language(s) more in the digital era. Ariyani et al.'s (2022) study indicates that the Android dictionary app for the Lampung language (Province of Lampung, Indonesia; Austronesian: Malayo-Polynesian) has successfully contributed to its maintenance and preservation. With the hope for similarly positive effects, this project is one response to the practical need for tools to promote the beneficial roles of new technology and social media in reversing language loss (Jany 2018).

Since "[a]ll people, even the illiterate or semiliterate, are empowered to become part of the information society more readily if they are able to use their own languages" (Pretorius and Bosch 2003, 57), it is hoped that the products of this project will help promote the online presence of the Modern South Arabian Languages. Crystal postulates that "[a]n endangered language will progress if its speakers can write their language down" (2000, 138) and that "[a]n endangered language will progress if its speakers can make use of electronic technology" (2000, 141). This project thus follows the orthography designers who have worked on the former consideration in an attempt to work on the latter consideration (Watson et al. n.d.; Naumkin and Kogan 2015) so as to ultimately contribute to the revitalisation of the Modern South Arabian Languages.

References

Abu Elhija, Dua'a. 2014. 'A New Writing System? Developing Orthographies for Writing Arabic Dialects in Electronic Media'. *Writing Systems Research* 6/2: 190–214.

Abu-Liel, Aula Khatteb, Zohar Eviatar, and Bracha Nir. 2019. 'Writing between Languages: The Case of Arabizi'. *Writing Systems Research* 11/2: 226–38.

Abu-Liel, Aula Khatteb, Raphiq Ibrahim, and Zohar Eviatar. 2021. 'Reading in Multiple Arabics: Effects of Diglossia and Orthography'. *Reading and Writing* 34: 2291–316.

Akbar, Rahima. 2019. 'Arabizi Among Kuwaiti Youths: Reshaping the Standard Arabic Orthography'. *International Journal of English Linguistics* 9/1: 301–23.

Akbar, Rahima, Hanan Taqi, and Taiba Sadiq. 2020. 'Arabizi in Kuwait: An Emerging Case of Digraphia'. *Language & Communication* 74: 204–16.

Aknuranda, Ismiarta, Almira Syawli, and Budi Darma Setiawan. 2020. 'Comparative Evaluation of Usability between QWERTY-Based Arabic and Non-QWERTY-Based Arabic Keyboard Layout: Empirical Evidence'. *Journal of Information Technology and Computer Science* 5/2: 177–93.

Al Hajjaj, Mae. 2021. 'The Creation of Arabish: How Young People Are Adapting Technology to Communicate in the Arab World'. In *IASL Conference Proceedings (Doha, Qatar): The Shifting Sands of School Librarianship*. https://doi.org/10.29173/iasl7790

Al-Badrashiny, Mohamed, Ramy Eskander, Nizar Habash, and Owen Rambow. 2014. 'Automatic Transliteration of Romanized Dialectal Arabic'. In *Proceedings of the Eighteenth*

Conference on Computational Natural Language Learning, edited by Roser Morante and Scott Wen-tau Yih, 30–38. Baltimore: Association for Computational Linguistics.

Alghamdi, Hamdah. 2018. 'Arabizi: An Exploration of the Use of the Contemporary Youth Netspeak on Social Networking Sites in Saudi Arabia'. PhD dissertation, University of Canberra.

Alghamdi, Hamdah, and Eleni Petraki. 2018. 'Arabizi in Saudi Arabia: A Deviant Form of Language or Simply a Form of Expression?'. *Social Sciences* 7/9: 155.

Al-Ghanim, Kaltham, and Janet C. E. Watson. 2020. 'Language and Nature in Southern and Eastern Arabia'. *European Journal of Social Sciences* 3/2: 10–18.

Aliprand, Joan, Julie Allen, Joe Becker, et al. (eds.) 2003. *The Unicode Standard, Version 4.0: The Unicode Consortium*. Boston: Addison-Wesley.

Allam, Réda Ali. 2014. '"Arabizi", "Arabish" ou "Francoarabe"! Les pratiques orthographiques des clavardeurs arabophones égyptiens sur Facebook: quelle langue!'. *Journal of Faculty of Arts, Zagazig University* 70. http://www.jarts.zu.edu.eg/index.php/jarts/article/view/175/65

Allehaiby, Wid H. 2013. 'Arabizi: An Analysis of the Romanization of the Arabic Script from a Sociolinguistic Perspective'. *Arab World English Journal* 4/3: 52–62.

Al-Shaer, Ibrahim M. R. 2016. 'Does Arabizi Constitute a Threat to Arabic?'. *Arab World English Journal* 7/3: 18–30.

Alsulami, Ashwaq. 2019. 'A Sociolinguistic Analysis of the Use of Arabizi in Social Media among Saudi Arabians'. *International Journal of English Linguistics* 9/6: 257–70.

American National Standards Institute, Inc. 1977. 'American National Standard Code for Information Interchange'. X3.4-1977. New York: American National Standards Institute. https://doi.org/10.6028/NBS.FIPS.1-2-1977

Ariyani, Farida, Gede Eka Putrawan, Afif Rahman Riyanda, et al. 2022. 'Technology and Minority Language: An Android-Based Dictionary Development for the Lampung language Maintenance in Indonesia'. *Tapuya: Latin American Science, Technology and Society* 5/1: 2015088.

Baert, Gaétan, Souhir Gahbiche, Guillaume Gadek, and Alexandre Pauchet. 2020. 'Arabizi Language Models for Sentiment Analysis'. In *Proceedings of the 28th International Conference on Computational Linguistics*, 592–603. Barcelona.

Bahrainwala, Lamiyah. 2011. 'You Say Hello, I Say Mar7aba: Exploring the Digi-Speak that Powered the Arab Revolution'. MA thesis, Michigan State University.

Bardaweel, Mahmoud Radwan, and Luqman M. Rababah. 2022. 'Gender Differences in Using Arabizi Among Jordanian Undergraduate Students: A Socio-Linguistic Study'. *Theory and Practice in Language Studies* 12/1: 86–95.

Bellem, Alex, and Janet C. E. Watson. 2017. 'South Arabian Sibilants and the Śḥerēt s̃~š Contrast'. In *To the Madbar and Back Again: Studies in the Languages, Archaeology, and Cultures of Arabia Dedicated to Michael C. A. Macdonald*, edited by Laïla Nehmé and Ahmad Al-Jallad, 622–44. Leiden and Boston: Brill.

Benmoussat, Smail. 2011. 'Use of Arabic in Computer-Mediated Communication'. *Revue maghrébine des langues* 7/1: 245–50.

Bianchi, Robert. 2012. '3arabizi-When Local Arabic Meets Global English'. *Acta Linguistica Asiatica* 2/1: 89–100.

———. 2015. '3arabizi, Greeklish, and SMSki: The Hybrid Making of Language in the Age of the Internet and Mobile Technology'. *Tasmeem* 1. http://dx.doi.org/10.5339/tasmeem.2015.1

Bies, Ann, Zhiyi Song, Mohamed Maamouri, et al. 2014. 'Transliteration of Arabizi into Arabic Orthography: Developing a Parallel Annotated Arabizi-Arabic Script SMS/Chat Corpus'. In *Proceedings of the EMNLP 2014 Workshop on Arabic Natural Language Processing (ANLP)*, 93–103. Doha.

Chader, Asma, Dihia Lanasri, Leila Hamdad, et al. 2019. 'Sentiment Analysis for Arabizi: Application to Algerian Dialect'. In *Proceedings of the 11th International Joint Conference on Knowledge Discovery, Knowledge Engineering and Knowledge Management*, 475–82. SCITEPRESS.

Crystal, David. 2000. *Language Death*. Cambridge and New York: Cambridge University Press.

———. 2006. *Language and the Internet*. 2nd edition. Cambridge: Cambridge University Press.

Cunliffe, Daniel. 2007. 'Minority Languages and the Internet: New Threats, New Opportunities'. In *Minority Language Media: Concepts, Critiques and Case Studies*, edited by Mike

Cormack and Niamh Hourigan, 133–50. Clevedon, Buffalo, and Toronto: Multilingual Matters Ltd.

Duwairi, Rehab M., Mosab Alfaqeh, Mohammad Wardat, and Areen Alrabadi. 2016. 'Sentiment Analysis for Arabizi Text'. In *2016 7th International Conference on Information and Communication Systems (ICICS), 5–7 April, 2016, Jordan University Of Science and Technology Irbid, Jordan*, 127–32. IEEE.

Farrag, Mona. 2012. 'Arabizi: A Writing Variety Worth Learning? An Exploratory Study of the Views of Foreign Learners of Arabic on Arabizi'. MA thesis, The American University in Cairo.

Guellil, Imane, Ahsan Adeel, Faical Azouaou, et al. 2021. 'A Semi-Supervised Approach for Sentiment Analysis of Arab (ic + izi) Messages: Application to the Algerian Dialect'. *SN Computer Science* 2/2: 1–18.

Guellil, Imane, Ahsan Adeel, Faical Azouaou, et al. 2018. 'Arabizi Sentiment Analysis Based on Transliteration and Automatic Corpus Annotation'. In *Proceedings of the 9th Workshop on Computational Approaches to Subjectivity, Sentiment and Social Media Analysis*, 335–41. Brussels: Association for Computational Linguistics.

Guellil, Imane, Faical Azouaou, and Mourad Abbas. 2017. 'Neural vs Statistical Translation of Algerian Arabic Dialect Written with Arabizi and Arabic Letter'. In *PACLIC 31: The 31st Pacific Asia Conference on Language, Information and Computation, November 16–18, 2017, University of the Philippines Cebu*. Cebu: University of the Philippines.

Guellil, Imane, Faiçal Azouaou, Mourad Abbas, and Sadat Fatiha. 2017. 'Arabizi Transliteration of Algerian Arabic Dialect into Modern Standard Arabic'. In *Social MT 2017: First Workshop on Social Media and User Generated Content Machine Translation*, Prague, Czech Republic.

Guellil, Imane, Faical Azouaou, Fodil Benali, et al. 2020. 'The Role of Transliteration in the Process of Arabizi Translation/Sentiment Analysis'. In *Recent Advances in NLP: The Case of Arabic Language*, edited by Mohamed Abd Elaziz, Mohammed A. A. Al-Qaness, Ahmed A. Ewees, and Abdelghani Dahou, 101–28. Cham, Switzerland: Springer.

Haddad, Selim S. 1899. 'Types for Type-Writers or Printing-Presses'. United States Patent Office 637109, filed October 13, 1899, and issued November 14, 1899. https://patents.google.com/patent/US637109A

Haghegh, Mariam. 2021. 'Arabizi across Three Different Generations of Arab Users Living Abroad: A Case Study'. *Arab World English Journal for Translation & Literary Studies* 5/2: 156–73.

Herring, Susan C. (ed.). 1996. *Computer-Mediated Communication: Linguistic, Social, and Cross-Cultural Perspectives*. Amsterdam and Philadelphia: John Benjamins Publishing.

Jany, Carmen. 2018. 'The Role of New Technology and Social Media in Reversing Language Loss'. *Speech, Language and Hearing* 21/2: 73–76.

Jeníková, Jitka. 2019. 'Arabīzī—arabština jedenadvacátého století?' *Svět literatury* 60/29: 109–14.

Kenali, Ashwaq Mohammad Salleh, Nik Mohd Rahimi Nik Yusoff, Hamadallah Mohammad Salleh Kenali, and Mohd Yusri Kamarudin. 2016. 'Code-Mixing Consumptions among Arab Students'. *Creative Education* 7: 931–40.

Keong, Yuen Chee, Othman Rahsid Hameed, and Imad Amer Abdulbaqi. 2015. 'The Use of Arabizi in English Texting by Arab Postgraduate Students at UKM'. *The English Literature Journal* 2/2: 281–88.

Khalil, Seyed. 1960. 'Typing Machines for Arabic Group Languages'. United States Patent Office 2940575, filed December 19, 1957, and issued June 14, 1960. https://patents.google.com/patent/US2940575A

Klouche, B., and S. M. Benslimane. 2020. 'Arabizi Chat Alphabet Transliteration to Algerian Dialect'. In *Artificial Intelligence in Renewable Energetic Systems*, edited by Mustapha Hatti, 790–97. Cham, Switzerland: Springer.

Masmoudi, Abir, Mariem Ellouze Khmekhem, Mourad Khrouf, and Lamia Hadrich Belguith. 2019. 'Transliteration of Arabizi into Arabic Script for Tunisian Dialect'. *ACM Transactions on Asian and Low-Resource Language Information Processing (TALLIP)* 19/2: 1–21.

Naumkin, Vitaly, and Leonid Kogan. 2015. *Corpus of Soqotri Oral Literature, Volume 1*. Leiden; Boston: Brill.

Nemeth, Titus. 2017. *Arabic Type-Making in the Machine Age: The Influence of Technology on the Form of Arabic Type, 1908–1993*. Leiden and Boston: Brill.

Palfreyman, David, and Muhamed Al Khalil. 2003. '"A Funky Language for Teenzz to Use": Representing Gulf

Arabic in Instant Messaging'. *Journal of Computer-Mediated Communication* 9/1. https://doi.org/10.1111/j.1083-6101.2003.tb00355.x

Pretorius, Laurette, and Sonja E. Bosch. 2003. 'Enabling Computer Interaction in the Indigenous Languages of South Africa: The Central Role of Computational Morphology'. *Interactions* 10/2: 56–63.

Santos, Eddie Antonio, and Atticus G. Harrigan. 2020. 'Design and Evaluation of a Smartphone Keyboard for Plains Cree Syllabics'. In *Proceedings of the 1st Joint Workshop on Spoken Language Technologies for Under-Resourced Languages (SLTU) and Collaboration and Computing for Under-Resourced Languages (CCURL)*, edited by Dorothee Beermann, Laurent Besacier, Sakriani Sakti, and Claudia Soria, 88–96. Paris: European Language Resources Association (ELRA).

Shazal, Ali, Aiza Usman, and Nizar Habash. 2020. 'A Unified Model for Arabizi Detection and Transliteration Using Sequence-to-Sequence Models'. In *Proceedings of the Fifth Arabic Natural Language Processing Workshop*, 167–77. Barcelona: Association for Computational Linguistics.

Sullivan, Natalie. 2017. 'Writing Arabizi: Orthographic Variation in Romanized Lebanese Arabic on Twitter'. Plan II Honours thesis, The University of Texas at Austin.

The New York Times. 1904. 'An Artist = Inventor From Mount Lebanon: Selim Haddad's New Alphabet and Typewriter Will Facilitate Study of Oriental Literature', August 21, 1904, Archives. https://www.nytimes.com/1904/08/21/archives/anartistinventor-from-mount-lebanon-selim-haddads-new-alphabet-and.html

The Unicode Consortium. 2022. *The Unicode Standard, Version 15.0 – Core Specification*. Mountain View, CA: The Unicode Consortium.

Tobaili, Taha. 2016. 'Arabizi Identification in Twitter Data'. In *Proceedings of the 54th Annual Meeting of the Association for Computational Linguistics: Student Research Workshop*, 51–57. Berlin: Association for Computational Linguistics.

———. 2020. 'Sentiment Analysis for the Low-Resourced Latinised Arabic "Arabizi"'. PhD dissertation, The Open University.

Tobaili, Taha, Miriam Fernandez, Harith Alani, et al. 2019. 'Senzi: A Sentiment Analysis Lexicon for the Latinised Arabic (Arabizi)'. In *International Conference Recent Advances In Natural Language Processing 2019 Natural Language Processing in a Deep Learning World: Proceedings*, 1204–12. Varna, Bulgaria: INCOMA Ltd.

Typewriter Topics: The International Business Equipment Magazine. 1915. 'A Patented Arabic Keyboard', January 1915.

Villa, Daniel J. 2002. 'Integrating Technology into Minority Language Preservation and Teaching Efforts: An inside Job'. *Language Learning & Technology* 6/2: 92–101.

Watson, Janet C. E., Miranda Morris, Alex Bellem, and Domenyk Eades. n.d. 'Orthographic Characters'. University of Leeds. http://ahc.leeds.ac.uk/download/downloads/id/166/orthographiccharacters.pdf

Wees, Marlies van der, Arianna Bisazza, and Christof Monz. 2016. 'A Simple but Effective Approach to Improve Arabizi-to-English Statistical Machine Translation'. In *Proceedings of the 2nd Workshop on Noisy User-Generated Text (WNUT)*, 43–50. Osaka: The COLING 2016 Organizing Committee.

Yaghan, Mohammad Ali. 2008. '"Arabizi": A Contemporary Style of Arabic Slang'. *Design Issues* 24/2: 39–52.

INDEX

adverbs of place, 173–74, 182, 183–91, 193
aqua-culture, 27
Arabic, 1–3, 5–7, 9–11, 13–21, 29, 31, 42–43, 49–54, 68, 75, 81, 84, 127 n. 31, 128 n. 33, 130 n. 38, 133 n. 42, 133 n. 43, 133 n. 45, 134 n. 46, 137–41, 145–47, 150–52, 156–58, 160–61, 165–66, 173–77, 184, 191–92, 197, 210 n. 14, 220–22, 237, 243–57, 259–61
    Arabic dialects, 151, 157, 173–74, 176
    Attuwair Arabic, 156, 158, 160–62, 164–66
    Classical Arabic, 12, 15, 141, 146, 155, 197, 236
    Faifi Arabic, 137–38, 173–74, 178–80, 181 n. 4, 182–84, 191–93
    Gulf Arabic, 5, 8, 10, 15–20
    Haʔili Arabic, 138–42, 145–46, 166
    Najdi Arabic, 5, 14 n. 5, 138–40, 147, 158, 161, 165–66
    Shihhi Arabic, 52
    southwestern Saudi Arabic, 137–38, 148, 166, 176–77
    Urban Hijazi Arabic, 138, 147
Aramaic, 1–6, 10, 18, 20

augmentative, 138–46, 166
beautification, 107
building materials, 107–8, 110, 113–19
coastal watching, 27
consonantal inventory, 110, 247
degemination, 139, 156–58, 160–66
Dhalkut, 109
Dhofar, 60, 78, 107–9, 111 n. 1, 113–19
digital space, 241–42, 250
diminutive, 10, 12–13, 18–19, 140–46
distality, 173–74, 181 n. 4, 182, 192–93
Documentation and Ethnolinguistic Analysis of Modern South Arabian (DEAMSA), 107–9
ecolinguistics, 47–48, 62, 87–88
endangered, 28–29, 31, 66, 241–42, 250, 257, 261–62
fishing, 16, 27–28, 44, 47, 49, 54–55, 57, 59–60, 62, 64–66, 69–76, 85, 87
flora, 14, 66, 86, 107, 110, 113
forced-choice tasks, 184–85
Gabgabt, 109
gender-number distinction, 191
goat husbandry, 28, 69, 79
grammaticality-judgment, 184

historical distinction, 174, 193
imperialism, 32–33, 36–37, 39, 44
Jibbali, 197, 247 n. 8
Jufa, 109
keyboard layout, 241, 247, 250–52, 253 n. 13, 254–55, 258, 261 n. 19
Keyman Developer, 258–59, 261 n. 19
Kumzari, 5, 12, 27–33, 40–41, 43, 46–65, 67–70, 72–88
language contact, 5, 17
linguistic situation, 2
livestock, 70, 108, 113, 115–16, 119, 120 n. 7, 126 n. 30, 127, 128, 130, 134
marine ecosystem, 27, 47
marine life, 44
medicine, 107, 116
Mehri, 59–60, 108, 113, 197–200, 202, 204, 206–8, 211, 214–15, 218–19, 222, 229, 234–37, 247 n. 7, 248, 249
minority languages, 241–42, 246, 261
MKLC, 254–55, 258
Modern South Arabian, 17, 52–54, 107–8, 110, 197, 198, 202, 206, 208, 219, 235–37, 241–42, 247, 249–50, 254, 256–57, 259–61, 261 n. 19, 262
morphology, 17–18, 51, 69, 137–38

Musandam, 10–11, 14–16, 21, 27–28, 32–33, 35, 37–38, 40–41, 45–46, 48, 51, 53, 56–57, 62–68, 70–72, 75–81, 84–86
navigation, 58, 60–61, 75, 86
Oman, 1, 4 n. 4, 5, 7–9, 11, 13, 15–16, 20, 28, 32–34, 38–40, 43–44, 46, 51, 53–57, 59, 64–66, 70–71, 75, 78, 80–83, 109, 176, 197 n. 1
onomastics, 1–2, 7, 16, 20–21
palm harvesting, 28
Persian, 1, 3–6, 11–12, 18, 20–21, 50–52, 55, 70 n. 11, 78–79, 256
Persian Gulf, 2, 32–39, 40 n. 3, 41–44, 46, 55–56, 63–66, 75
phonology, 50, 137–38, 156–57, 191
possessive, 139, 146–54, 156, 163, 166, 178
pre-aspirated sonorants, 110–13, 120 n. 7, 121 n. 9, 121 n. 12, 122 n. 14, 122 n. 17
proximity, 32, 173–74, 181 n. 4, 182, 191–93
relative pronoun, 173–93
revitalisation, 242, 247, 262
Sakaka City, 139, 158, 165–66
Semitic languages, 19, 197–98, 220, 236–37
Shammar, 140, 146
Sharjah, 1–2, 5–6, 10–11, 13, 16, 19–20, 36, 40

Shehret, 107–15, 247 n. 7, 249 n. 10
shelters, 84, 108, 113–16, 131, 133 n. 42
shrubs, 116–20
Tayy, 140, 145–46
technological support, 241–42
Tihama (Saudi), 137, 148, 156, 166
toponyms, 1–2, 4–5, 7, 9–10, 12–21
trees, 4, 9, 78–79, 81–83, 86, 112, 114–17, 119, 120 n. 7, 129, 130 n. 38, 132 n. 41, 144, 178
Ukelele, 254 n. 15, 255, 258, 260
Unicode, 245, 247, 249, 254–55
United Arab Emirates, 1–2, 28, 43, 46–47, 65
unofficial orthography, 257
verbal nouns, 15, 52, 197, 200, 209 n. 13
vowel quality, 109, 155, 191–92, 218, 224, 229, 232–33
weather, 58, 60–62, 69–70, 84, 133 n. 43, 160

About the Team

Anne Burberry and Benjamin Kantor were the managing editors for this book.

Aaron Hornkohl performed the copyediting of the book in Word. The fonts used in this volume are Charis SIL and Scheherazade New.

Cameron Craig created all of the editions — paperback, hardback, and PDF. Conversion was performed with open source software freely available on our GitHub page at https://github.com/OpenBookPublishers.

Jeevanjot Kaur Nagpal designed the cover of this book. The cover was produced in InDesign using Fontin and Calibri fonts.

Cambridge Semitic Languages and Cultures

General Editor Geoffrey Khan

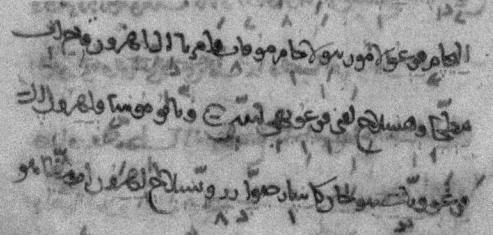
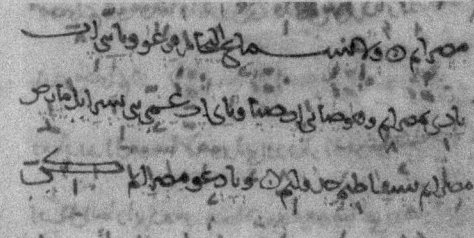

www.ingramcontent.com/pod-product-compliance
Lightning Source LLC
Chambersburg PA
CBHW050208240426
43671CB00013B/2260